THE ART OF BLACKSMITHING

THE ART OF
Blacksmithing

ALEX W. BEALER

Revised Edition

CASTLE BOOKS

Published in 1995 by

Castle Books ®

A division of Book Sales, Inc.
276 Fifth Ave., Suite 206
New York, NY 10001

Published by arrangement with and permission of
Mrs. Alex Bealer

Library of Congress Cataloging in Publication Data

Bealer, Alex W.
   The art of blacksmithing.
   Bibliography: p.   Includes index.
   1. Blacksmithing.   I. Title.
TT220.B35   1976   682   76-4546

ISBN-13: 978-0-7858-0395-9
ISBN-10: 0-7858-0395-5

Printed in the United States of America

THIS BOOK IS DEDICATED TO THE MEMORY OF

JAMES F. WHITLEY (1873–1962)

of the upper settlement of Vinings, Georgia, a firm friend and a living relic of the days when the hand-craftsman was the bedrock of civilization and industry. It was in his log shop that I was first introduced to the mysteries and pleasures of blacksmithing and related folk art.

CONTENTS

PREFACE
TO THE SECOND EDITION

There are a number of very good reasons for a revised edition of this book. Originally it was written as a history of what I and most people considered a lost art. Its purpose was to record the techniques of the blacksmith as historical lore before the last smith died and the imagination, ingenuity and mystique of smithing were lost to future generations.

After the book was published in 1969, however, I found, to my delight, that far more men and women were interested in using the techniques I had described than merely reading about them. For some reason, quite inexplicable, many, many people had become interested in blacksmithing without ever having seen a forge. A number of people, mostly young, who read my book out of curiosity, became interested in the art and several have since set up forges and are making a living by shaping iron with forge and anvil, hammer and tongs. One finds the number of professional smiths growing steadily in every part of the country, not just in restoration villages but as independent craftsmen who find a ready market for contemporary work.

These smiths and the even greater number of skilled amateurs in the art have demonstrated that blacksmithing is flourishing, after a brief limbo, rather than dying. History is still being made in the fascinating field of ironworking. Interestingly, while some of the younger smiths deal mostly with traditional items, reflections of an older day, several use their talents to create beautiful pieces of contemporary, very original design. This, too, is exciting art history which must be recorded, and is covered in my revisions.

Also, I have learned much about techniques in the years since this book was first published. The original book itself has acted as a catalyst between me and the hundreds of amateur and professional smiths I have met and corresponded with in the last six years. As a consequence I have learned a great deal more than I should ever have learned had I not written the book. Part of my revision includes some of this new knowledge, little nuggets of information developed over thousands of years, no doubt, which in some cases can save the beginning smith, and perhaps established professionals, untold hours of frustration. How to maintain a fire, for instance, was rather neglected in the first edition, yet no technique is more important than this in producing good wrought iron in minimum time.

Because of the publication of this book, I have been honored by invitations to conduct several blacksmith workshops at universities and craft schools in various parts of the country. Of course, often a teacher learns more than his pupils, which was certainly the case with me. And I greatly benefited from new and thrilling exposure to what was happening in the craft movement.

Additional revisions include more about working modern mild steel with modern equipment. Such knowledge, basically presented herein, is essential to the continuance of blacksmithing as a vigorous, growing art form.

Let me repeat, the art of blacksmithing is not dead or dying. It is hoped that this revised edition will help assure its future; indeed, its immortality.

INTRODUCTION

Blacksmithing is hardly a subject one expects to discuss at social gatherings. Those who are interested in the subject are very much interested indeed, and might talk for hours about all the myriad facets of the art without exhausting the subject. But while growing rapidly in numbers during the last quarter of the twentieth century, the true aficionados of forge and anvil are relatively small. Those who actually practice the art, as a profession or as a hobby, however, do number in the thousands. Yet, even this relatively small figure surprises the millions who have not yet been exposed to the art. The skill and knowledge needed to work hot iron is still obscure.

Of course, most people, especially those with rural backgrounds or those above forty years old, remember the state of blacksmithing as it was years ago, with a shop or its remains on every farm of any size and a general shop in every village and more shops in many of the industries in which men worked every day. Those shops have practically all disappeared. As a consequence, the past thirty generations of Americans look upon blacksmithing as a subject for nostalgia, a legend, a lost art which has lost its place in the modern world. They are right to some extent, for the type of blacksmithing produced by those long-closed shops is no longer needed. They have indeed been washed away by progress in America, though still fairly common in less developed nations of the world.

Yet, when one talks to young art students, particularly those in their twenties who have been exposed to crafts in university art schools, one finds an entirely different attitude. To these younger people, men and women, blacksmithing is an exciting discovery, a new art form, an important addition to the crafts. They have no memories of the ubiquity or essentiality of the blacksmith to an older, pre-electronic culture.

But once they are exposed to the magic of flame and red hot iron they eagerly seek more knowledge of blacksmithing history and technique. They develop and bring to the ancient and honorable art a fresh new attitude. They weld the old and the new equipment together and apply the results to modern society. These young people are keeping blacksmithing alive.

Certainly blacksmithing is a fascinating subject: logical yet mysterious; elementary in its importance to the development of civilization, yet highly sophisticated in its practice. To most, the blacksmith is epitomized by sheer brute strength, but such an epitome misses the mark widely. Brains, imagination, the power of visualization are far more important than brawn to the smith. The secret of success in the trade is really intellect, and this must have been true of its beginnings.

Such a hypothesis is not just the product of narrow personal enthusiasm. There is much historical evidence to support it. The creative genes of remote blacksmiths have possibly had their good and bad effects on modern history and the mass-production-oriented society of our time.

For instance, Sir Winston Churchill was descended from blacksmiths on both the American and the British sides of his family. Also, the founder of the militant Krupp armament industry in Bismarckian Germany started his adult life as a blacksmith before he applied his native intelligence and organizational ability to founding the world's most powerful industrial cartel.

Richard Sears, founder of Sears, Roebuck and Company, was the son of a blacksmith. The father has been somewhat overshadowed by the merchandising brilliance of the son, but the blacksmith father had the distinction of making the first surgical scalpels for the Mayo Clinic in his hometown of Rochester, Minnesota.

President Dwight D. Eisenhower was the descendent of ironworkers, as is obvious from his name. His great-great-grandfather, while not a smith—he did not *smite* iron with a hammer—was an ironchiseler, his life devoted to sculpting the products of the forge. The name means "ironhewer."

Thomas Jefferson had a nail manufactory, now excavated and partially restored at Monticello, in which two of his slaves turned out handmade nails to satisfy the building demands of a new country. George Washington, it is reported, took great interest in the working of his smithy at Mount Vernon, no doubt directing his plantation smith in shaping plows and other agricultural implements. John C. Calhoun is said to have known as much about the techniques of the blacksmith and wheelwright as most masters in the trade.

Other great men in history have shown equal interest in the mysteries of forming iron into elaborate shapes. Richard the Lion-Hearted, redoubtable warrior that he was, is said to have spent a great deal of time working in his armorer's smithy, learning and advising. Maximilian the Great was responsible for much of the extremely artistic, yet wholly effective, armor of his period. The "Wise King" has been depicted in contemporary accounts of his reign working in the armorer's shop alongside his favorite artisan, the armorer Sensenhofer, supervising and directing the work of the master workman and his corps of journeymen; Charles V, a later

Emperor of the Holy Roman Empire, personally worked on the guns used by his armies. The hapless Louis XVI, before he went to the guillotine, revealed his share of royal iron-worker's creative genes through his interest and his skill in actually designing and making gunlocks and doorlocks, a specialty of the smith's. Louis had his own personal shop at Versailles.

The twentieth century, too, has produced its great smiths. Chief among these, perhaps, is the late Samuel Yellin of Philadelphia, who came from Poland as an illiterate teen-ager and rose to be acclaimed the most valuable citizen of his adopted city. The Children's Gates of the National Cathedral in Washington reflect his genius as an artist in iron. On the same level are three German artists, all only recently deceased. Fritz Ulrich, of Aachen, who died in 1975, was a superb craftsman and an outstanding teacher. His artistry was surpassed only by his depth of character. Fritz Kuhn and Julius Schramm, of Berlin, were leaders in the development of modern design in wrought iron. The late Julius Speer of the same city was another. And such young contemporary smiths as Ivan Bailey, Dimitri Gerarkaris, Peter Happny, Steven Rosenberg, Eric Moebius and others show great promise in upholding the highest standards of their exciting art.

Research for the material in this book has not been easy. Much of the information contained herein is an accumulation over a thirty-year period of what seemed to be useless information. It all started when, as a neophyte gun collector, I met Mr. James F. Whitley of Vinings, Georgia. Mr. Whitley was a blacksmith and the son of a blacksmith, and a few opportunities to watch him at his old wood-and-stone forge, blown with old-fashioned bellows, lit a fire of yearning within me for more information. Jim was a true relic of pioneer days, an individualist, and a fine craftsman in wood as well as iron. He made his own shingles for the log cabin in which he was born and in which he lived most of his life. He built his own blacksmith shop of squared pine logs, and he made furniture and fiddles as well as the special tools needed for these jobs. Behind the blacksmith shop was the traditional scrap pile, inherited from his father and maintained by Jim, which included all manner of metal from Model-T-Ford parts to sections of flat iron railroad rail (the kind that was spiked to wooden rails), which his father had collected around 1850 when the nearby railroad was modernized with solid I rails. Despite his fourth-grade education, Jim was highly intelligent, well-read, imaginative, inquisitive, and articulate. He had learned much of the lore of blacksmithing from his father and his uncle when he was growing up in the 1880s and 1890s, and he passed on much of this ancient lore to me.

My interest in the subject was so piqued that as a sixteen-year-old boy I did primitive forging in the basement of my city home, using the coal furnace as an awkward forge and a lump of iron as an anvil. As in any craft, the rudimentary experience I gained stimulated more questions.

It was not until I was a fully grown man with a family, however, that I adopted blacksmithing as a weekend avocation. Engaged in making a model Civil War cannon, I soon found that I simply could not form many of the parts properly without a forge. Accordingly I built a very small forge of a size suitable to making miniature cannon parts. Using it and an anvil found in a junkyard, my knowledge of smithing and my curiosity of its techniques grew. As my interest in the subject expanded I found a little literature on the subject, chiefly an out-of-print, poorly written book, *Spon's Mechanics Own Book*, which has a chapter on industrial forging that describes blacksmithing techniques and illustrates many of the tools needed in a well-equipped blacksmith shop of the late nineteenth century. By the time the model cannon was finished I had developed the insatiable curiosity that seems to affect most of those, professional or avocational, who are exposed to the adventures of ironworking. Eventually I built a larger forge, equipped with old-fashioned wood-and-leather bellows, and I began collecting blacksmith tools in earnest. Smithing has turned into a most satisfying hobby, and the increasing interest developed by actually smiting hot iron and learning the mysteries of welding led to a more formal research on the subject than that of my younger years, and, eventually, to this book.

There is little available written authority on blacksmithing for the literally thousands of people of all ages and walks of life who wish to learn the art as a hobby or for professional purposes. In the last twenty-five years there have appeared, to my knowledge, only the three short but excellent books on the subject published by the Council on Small Industries in Rural Areas in England, this book, and two books by the sculptor, Alexander G. Weygers, published in 1973 and 1974. Also, the U.S. Department of Commerce offers an interesting archaeological study of Russian iron making and ironworking in the Middle Ages.

Although a good deal of my research was accomplished by reading the basic texts that are found in libraries, my best research turned out to be the forge itself—the only place to really learn the art.

My most interesting initial research, then, was through interviews and consultations with retired and active blacksmiths. Through the help of journalist Celestine Sibley, who writes a syndicated column, I was able to locate about a dozen retired smiths, most of them in the Southeast, some of them still available for desultory work in their communities. Time did not allow talking to all of them. Much was learned, however, from the few I was able to visit.

Among these helpful informants were Mr. Ernest York of Gay, Georgia, who kept his shop open more out of sentiment and the need for a place to go than out of necessity. Mr. York has now retired but has not lost his interest. The late Mr. Herbert Mitchum of Durand, Georgia, was the only smith I found with experience in using charcoal in his forge, and his knowledge of how to use this ancient fuel was helpful in reconstructing historical techniques. Mr. E. W. Horne of Atlanta, Georgia, the son and grandson of blacksmiths, whose own son has a master's degree in metallurgy, is a full-time smith with boundless knowledge of the properties of various steels. While considering himself a specialist in tool dressing, Mr. Horne learned much of general smithing from his father and grandfather and made this knowledge available to me.

Fortunately I had the opportunity to visit the Rev. Jim Hood two times before he died. Reverend Hood, a Baptist minister, lived in the Choestoe Creek Community in the Georgia mountains near Blairsville. A teacher as well as a preacher, he had as a boy taught himself to weld steel and iron on a forge that burnt chunks of green chestnut wood instead of coal or charcoal. After becoming a master smith, he taught blacksmithing and the Bible for years at Young Harris College, Young Harris, Georgia, a very fine small college for mountain youths. Later he built himself a most marvelous machine shop run by waterpower. He also built all the equipment, including the waterwheel, a metal lathe, a band saw, a brick forge, a drill press, and all the other machines found in a well-equipped shop. Just seeing him and his shop was a revelation and a minor education.

Of all my informants since Jim Whitley died in 1962, the most helpful has been Sump Brown. Fortunately Sump lives only about ten miles from my suburban Atlanta home, and he is available on weekends. Not only have I learned much from working on his forge, but he comes to my shop to teach me there. Sump suggested changes that made my own forge and bellows more efficient. He demonstrated many techniques and advised on others. Between us we have wrought iron gun cradles, Colonial toasting forks, tomahawks of iron with

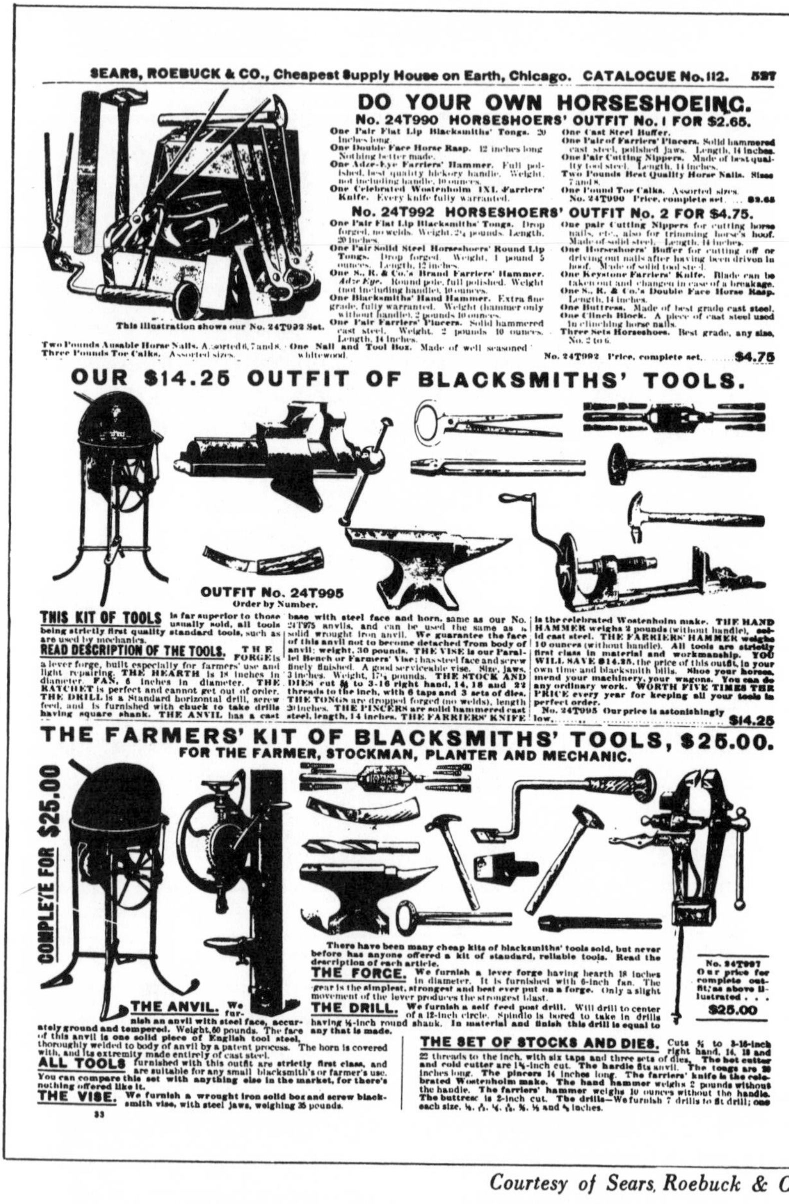

SEARS, ROEBUCK & CO., Cheapest Supply House on Earth, Chicago. CATALOGUE No. 112. 527

DO YOUR OWN HORSESHOEING.

No. 24T990 HORSESHOERS' OUTFIT No. 1 FOR $2.65.

One Pair Flat Lip Blacksmiths' Tongs. 20 inches long.
One Double Face Horse Rasp. 12 inches long. Nothing better made.
One Adze-Eye Farriers' Hammer. Full polished, best quality hickory handle. Weight, not including handle, 10 ounces.
One Celebrated Wostenholm IXL Farriers' Knife. Every knife fully warranted.
One Cast Steel Buffer.
One Pair of Farriers' Pincers. Solid hammered cast steel, polished jaws. Length, 14 inches.
One Pair Cutting Nippers. Made of best quality tool steel. Length, 14 inches.
Two Pounds Best Quality Horse Nails. Sizes 7 and 8.
One Pound Toe Calks. Assorted sizes.
No. 24T990 Price, complete set ... **$2.65**

No. 24T992 HORSESHOERS' OUTFIT No. 2 FOR $4.75.

One Pair Flat Lip Blacksmiths' Tongs. Drop forged, no welds. Weight, 2¼ pounds. Length, 20 inches.
One Pair Solid Steel Horseshoers' Round Lip Tongs. Drop forged. Weight, 1 pound 5 ounces. Length, 12 inches.
One S., R. & Co.'s Brand Farriers' Hammer. *Adze Eye.* Round pole, full polished. Weight (not including handle), 10 ounces.
One Blacksmiths' Hand Hammer. Extra fine grade, fully warranted. Weight (hammer only without handle), 2 pounds 10 ounces.
One Pair Farriers' Pincers. Solid hammered cast steel. Weight, 2 pounds 10 ounces. Length, 14 inches.
One pair Cutting Nippers for cutting horse nails, etc., also for trimming horse's hoof. Made of solid steel. Length, 14 inches.
One Horseshoers' Buffer for cutting off or driving out nails after having been driven in hoof. Made of solid tool steel.
One Keystone Farriers' Knife. Blade can be taken out and changed in case of a breakage.
One S., R. & Co.'s Double Face Horse Rasp. Length, 14 inches.
One Buttress. Made of best grade cast steel.
One Clinch Block. A piece of cast steel used in clinching horse nails.
Three Sets Horseshoes. Best grade, any size, No. 2 to 6.
Two Pounds Ausable Horse Nails. Assorted 6, 7 and 8.
Three Pounds Toe Calks. Assorted sizes.
One Nail and Tool Box. Made of well seasoned whitewood.

This illustration shows our No. 24T992 Set.

No. 24T992 Price, complete set ... **$4.75**

OUR $14.25 OUTFIT OF BLACKSMITHS' TOOLS.

OUTFIT No. 24T995
Order by Number.

THIS KIT OF TOOLS is far superior to those usually sold, all tools being strictly first quality standard tools, such as are used by mechanics.

READ DESCRIPTION OF THE TOOLS. THE FORGE is a lever forge, built especially for farmers' use and light repairing. THE HEARTH is 18 inches in diameter. FAN, 6 inches in diameter. THE RATCHET is perfect and cannot get out of order. THE DRILL is a Standard horizontal drill, screw feed, and is furnished with chuck to take drills having square shank. THE ANVIL has a cast base with steel face and horn, same as our No. 24T975 anvils, and can be used the same as a solid wrought iron anvil. We guarantee the face of this anvil not to become detached from body of anvil; weight, 30 pounds. THE VISE is our Parallel Bench or Farmers' Vise; has steel face and screw finely finished. A good serviceable vise. Size, jaws, 3 inches. Weight, 17½ pounds. THE STOCK AND DIES cut ¼ to 3-16 right hand, 14, 18 and 22 threads to the inch, with 6 taps and 3 sets of dies. THE TONGS are dropped forged (no welds), length 20 inches. THE PINCERS are solid hammered cast steel, length, 14 inches. THE FARRIERS' KNIFE is the celebrated Wostenholm make. THE HAND HAMMER weighs 2 pounds (without handle), solid cast steel. THE FARRIERS' HAMMER weighs 10 ounces (without handle). All tools are strictly first class in material and workmanship. YOU WILL SAVE $14.25, the price of this outfit, in your own time and blacksmith bills. Shoe your horses, mend your machinery, your wagons. You can do any ordinary work. WORTH FIVE TIMES THE PRICE every year for keeping all your tools in perfect order.

No. 24T995 Our price is astonishingly low ... **$14.25**

THE FARMERS' KIT OF BLACKSMITHS' TOOLS, $25.00.

FOR THE FARMER, STOCKMAN, PLANTER AND MECHANIC.

COMPLETE FOR $25.00

There have been many cheap kits of blacksmiths' tools sold, but never before has anyone offered a kit of standard, reliable tools. Read the description of each article.

THE FORGE. We furnish a lever forge having hearth 18 inches in diameter. It is furnished with 6-inch fan. The gear is the simplest, strongest and best ever put on a forge. Only a slight movement of the lever produces the strongest blast.

THE DRILL. We furnish a self feed post drill. Will drill to center of a 12-inch circle. Spindle is bored to take in drills having ½-inch round shank. In material and finish this drill is equal to any that is made.

THE ANVIL. We furnish an anvil with steel face, accurately ground and tempered. Weight, 60 pounds. The face of this anvil is one solid piece of English tool steel, thoroughly welded to body of anvil by a patent process. The horn is covered with, and its extremity made entirely of cast steel.

ALL TOOLS furnished with this outfit are strictly first class, and are suitable for any small blacksmith's or farmer's use. You can compare this set with anything else in the market, for there's nothing offered like it.

THE VISE. We furnish a wrought iron solid box and screw blacksmith vise, with steel jaws, weighing 35 pounds.

THE SET OF STOCKS AND DIES. Cuts ¼ to 3-16-inch right hand, 14, 18 and 22 threads to the inch, with six taps and three sets of dies. The hot cutter and cold cutter are 1¼-inch cut. The hardie fits anvil. The tongs are 20 inches long. The pincers 14 inches long. The farriers' knife is the celebrated Wostenholm make. The hand hammer weighs 2 pounds without the handle. The farriers' hammer weighs 10 ounces without the handle. The buttress is 2-inch cut. The drills—We furnish 7 drills to fit drill; one each size, ⅛, 3/16, ¼, 5/16, ⅜, ½ and ⅝ inches.

No. 24T997 Our price for complete outfit, as above illustrated ... **$25.00**

33

Courtesy of Sears, Roebuck & Co.

A page from the Sears, Roebuck & Co. Catalog of 1904

welded steel blades, and froes. Sump, with his rural trade, was a blacksmith, a farrier, and a wheelwright during his career. When he does not know the answer to a question, he knows how to experiment and find the answer. Not only has he been profligate in giving me his personal experience, but he has given freely of the knowledge he gained from watching other smiths in many shops other than his own. Much of the credit for this book goes to him.

The book itself, though, has opened up numerous reservoirs of knowledge, and friendship, that were quite unsuspected when it was first published in 1969. Through all sorts of interesting circumstances, including hundreds of letters and almost as many telephone calls, I was able to be part of the founding in 1973 of the Artists-Blacksmiths Association of North America. This organization has drawn the active support of professional smiths, amateurs and scholars, has initiated regular communications among them and has provided a wealth of new information about blacksmithing. Much of the new information herein was learned as a result of writing to, talking with and watching some of the over three hundred members of the association. ABANA's remarkable growth and active support has proved that blacksmithing has a long life ahead of it, mostly as an art but also as a valuable trade. And it has demonstrated that blacksmiths are most interesting people who themselves have provided much of the mystique that surrounds a blacksmith shop.

Sump Brown is typical of most of the smiths I have met. He and the others are deeply interested in learning as much as possible about ironworking, even in retirement. All will talk for hours about techniques and the relative values of material and equipment. All show a willingness to learn, even from an amateur. With one or two exceptions, all demonstrate remarkable intelligence and insatiable curiosity. Most have had varied talents outside of smithing. Jim Whitley was a fiddler, Ernest York a horticulturist, Sump Brown a mandolin virtuoso. My research in smiths and smithing leads me to believe that the ones I have known are probably representative of smiths throughout the ages.

Jim Hood was a true intellectual. Puzzled as a young minister by certain passages in the Bible and unable to obtain satisfactory answers from Biblical scholars, he taught himself Hebrew and Greek and went to the original Bible text for answers to his questions. As a teacher, he told me, he tried to give the basics of a subject to his students, and once these were learned, he taught refinements. When he died he was working with dedication on an original theory that held that there was a mechanistic pattern to the universe. I never understood it, but he was convinced of his theory's validity.

Now, to the purposes for writing this book. They are manifold.

For one, I hope to establish, for a society dependent on mass production, the historical importance of the blacksmith in the development of civilization as we know it. The few modern people who ever think of a blacksmith think of him monotonously shoeing horses and little more. Actually, before the middle of the nineteenth century, only a wink ago insofar as history is concerned, horseshoeing was a minor, however important, part of the overall production of the smith; actually he was the cornerstone of a civilization utterly dependent on iron for tools, machines, and hardware.

Another purpose is to record at least some of the ingenious tools and techniques of the blacksmith as a help to future smiths. Of course, one book is hardly adequate; an encyclopedia equal to if not greater than Diderot's eighteenth-century *Encyclopedia of Trades and Industry* is needed to completely cover the subject. Such a work, however fascinating it may be to compile, is an impracticable dream. There are not enough people trained in the subject to seek out and write the volumes of material which my limited research indicates are lurking in the shadows of historical literature and records; there is so much to know, as my blacksmith informants demonstrate, and so few obvious sources. As a consequence, many of the techniques I describe are conjectural, based on my own experience in forging some wrought-iron item, and applied in principle to the making of an entirely different item.

Generally I have tried to describe and illustrate only the fundamental techniques of the trade, and show how these techniques were used on a few familiar items. I hope that others may find my material interesting enough to acquire the tools of the smith and actually practice his techniques to the point that some of the ancient techniques and tools will be rediscovered for the benefit of modern man. If the ancient aurochs can be reconstituted through selective breeding of modern domestic cattle, it seems possible that the ancient smith may be waiting within a few modern men.

Many of the mysteries of the prestigious armorer's craft accompanied that extinct tradesman to his grave; and there is much, admittedly, that is not known about this specialty even by such authorities as Harold L. Peterson and the few vestigial heirs of the craft who work for museums. The techniques I describe are practicable. The expert opinions of Mr. H. Russell Robinson, Assistant to the Master of Armories, Tower of London, and Mr. Helmut Nickel, Curator of Arms and Armor at New York's Metropolitan Museum of Art, have kept my imagination within bounds. Undoubtedly, however, some long-dead smiths could probably describe an easier technique in many cases.

A few very good books, shown in the bibliography, have been written in recent years about the blacksmith. This book is intended to supplement material already published and to fill some of the gaps of ignorance about the craft with new information gathered firsthand from retired and practicing smiths I have found, and from books both old and new. Conscious repetition has been avoided as much as possible. Some literature has referred in a tantalizing manner to other books that I have been unable to acquire and have not seen. Because of these references, however, I have listed some of these unseen sources in my bibliography.

My third purpose in writing this book is to give tribute to the marvelous ingenuity of man. No better medium can be found for this, I think, than the blacksmith. He worked with a material quite unlike the wood, bone, horn, stone, and copper wrought by man before the prehistoric discovery of iron. Yet once he applied his vision and imagination to the new substance, he learned to provide himself with the intense heat needed to use it; he developed the techniques needed to work it into valuable articles; he invented the tools required to bend it to his will. Many, if not most, of the blacksmith's techniques are notable for their ingenious concept more than their effect. Each, as it was developed, was an exercise in pure intellect brought forth from a vacuum of ignorance to fill a practical need. No wonder a blacksmith was granted divinity by the ancient Greeks.

Modern men are giving much attention to the thought processes of ancient peoples more primitive than themselves. A study of handcraftsmanship, indeed, leads one to suspect that primitive man may have produced, relatively speaking, more geniuses than our modern educated society. His thought processes, in ages when the reservoir of acquired recorded knowledge was small indeed, was of necessity based on pure thought and reason—on true genius, if you will. This is evident when one undertakes even a superficial study of the methods and tools of handcraftsmen.

And so to a final purpose. Perhaps to some extent the material in this book will stimulate, even inspire, modern man to better apply his magnificent mind, his inherent ingenuity, to solving intangible problems as important to our future as the mastery of iron was to the future of our prehistoric forebears.

Perhaps in the dim mistiness of the prehistoric mind there lay seeds of greatness, ready now to be planted to bear fruit for the modern world. Some of these seeds may be found in studying and using the techniques of the blacksmith. At least, the search will be interesting.

1.

THE BLACKSMITH

Fire and air, earth and water were once considered the four elemental substances of our world. Among the ancients, only the blacksmith worked with all four. His forge held the fire and his bellows controlled the air to his purpose. His material, iron, the black metal, was part of the earth, and water was essential to cool his heated iron and give temper to his red-hot steel.

Before the blacksmith there possibly were redsmiths who worked in copper and bronze, shaping these more facile materials with heat and hammer into tools and weapons. Iron, however, was the key to civilization. Once ironworking had developed, the tribes armed with iron swords and iron spearheads conquered those armed only with bronze weapons, and the people with iron axes and knives built more quickly and lived more comfortably than those who had not yet learned to make iron and steel from the ferrous ore so abundant in most parts of the world.

One is hard put to find the exact time and place that man learned to make and shape iron to his wishes. Historians feel that ironworking probably started some six thousand years ago in the Caucasus, but it quickly spread eastward and westward, and finally replaced bronze in backward Britain shortly before the Romans came.

That blacksmithing is an ancient and honorable occupation, however, is certain. So highly regarded was the smith in ancient Wales that he had a place of honor in the Prince's court alongside the priest and the poet. There was a black-smith among the gods on Olympus. His name was Hephaestus, son of Zeus and Hera, later known as Vulcan among the Romans and as Mulciber among the poets. Without him Zeus, the all-powerful, would have been less powerful, for he depended on Hephaestus to forge the thunderbolts which were hurled in anger from Olympus to tame and rule a world occupied by rebellious titans and erring men.

Hephaestus was an anomaly among the perfection of the gods. Born a cripple, he displeased his father at birth, and Zeus hurled him from the heights of Olympus, an experience that left Hephaestus ugly and misshapen. The fall, however, did not affect his art. In addition to making tools and weapons, Hephaestus also built the fine houses in which the gods lived, and he was skilled in all handicrafts. So skillful was he, in fact, that he made four beautiful golden handmaidens, endowed them with life, and used them as assistants at his forge.

It was said that Hephaestus kept his forge on the island of Lemnos in the base of a volcano which smoked and spat fire when he worked his bellows. As a divine craftsman he protected all the craftsmen of ancient civilization. When children were admitted to the city-state of Athens, Hephaestus was the god of the ceremony. Perhaps this helps explain why boys throughout the ages have been so attracted to the black-smith's shop.

There were other gods, major and minor, of other civilizations who were connected with the forge. Seth, god of evil, was the source of iron in ancient Egypt. As a consequence iron, though used, was considered an impure metal, seldom if ever placed in tombs, lest it interfere with the passage of the dead to the bright hereafter. Thor, of the Norsemen, was a smith of sorts who hurled his hammer as a weapon as often as he used it as a tool, and who caused the thunder to roll.

There were smiths with magical qualities among the ancient Germans and the Saracens. In old Russia, as in other places, the mystique of the smith was such that he was required to participate in weddings. His presence supposedly helped weld man and woman together just as he joined iron and steel at the forge.

Examination of wrought-iron and steel objects discovered by archaeologists gives evidence that the blacksmith of ancient days tried to live up to the mythical standards of divine workmanship. He very nearly succeeded, despite the fact that the ancient smith, in his small shop, was required to do most of the preliminary work that nowadays is done in huge mills. Today we can purchase our basic stock in a variety of shapes and sizes of bars and rods and almost any desired thickness of sheet iron; but the olden smith acquired his stock from a quite primitive forge that supplied a minimum variety. The smith took this rough stock and altered it to his needs. He made it smaller by repeated heating and hammering; he made it larger by welding smaller pieces together.

We often forget that the infinitive of the verb *wrought* is *to work*. It required real work in the old days to produce objects of wrought iron.

Nevertheless, iron and steel were as essential to the progress of man in ancient times as they are today in the space age. This very need spread the art of forging iron all over the civilized world, and into the primitive societies of Africa and nomad Arabia and the dark, mysterious forests of Europe. It developed into a precise art among the highly civilized peoples of China, India, and Japan, and as one region developed a new technique, it was disseminated to other lands through the twin activities of war and trade. The knowledge of working and dominating the black metal became homogeneous with the developing civilization of the ancients. It is most difficult to discover exactly how and where and when any particular technique was developed.

Perhaps the apogee of the blacksmith's art was reached during the Middle Ages in western Europe. In examining some of the intricate examples of thirteenth- and fourteenth-century armor and decorative ironwork, one marvels that man could conceive such design, much less execute it in as stubborn a material as iron or steel. Of course, some beautiful work is still done by a few vestigial experts who serve museums and furnish the ceremonial armor of European elite army and police units, but there is an interesting difference between medieval armor and that made since the eighteenth century, when rolling mills were developed. The use of calipers reveals that the old pieces were made of great hand-hammered sheets which originally were massive bars of iron; sometimes they were produced by welding together narrow strips of sheet iron that had first been thinned by hand.

About the only labor-saving raw material available to the medieval smith was wire. The Germans developed a machine for drawing wire through hardened-steel dies about the thirteenth century. (The process has not changed essentially in the last seven hundred years.) When first developed it saved the smith untold hours in providing wire for chain mail and other small items and appendages for wrought ironwork. Theretofore, for about five thousand years, the smith had made his own wire by twisting small flat strips of iron and smoothing them with the hammer.

Until the last years of the eighteenth century, the blacksmith and the various specialists of the trade, such as the armorer and the cutler, used hand labor to transform raw ironstock into items of beauty and utility. The ingenuity and powers of visualization required for this transformation were truly wondrous. While fundamental techniques did not change over the millennia, the smiths throughout the centuries did develop techniques of skill that would well suit a metal sculptor.

Too often ironworking is referred to as a trade rather

than an art. Actually it is both. Utility articles of iron were so important to the progress of society all over the world that the trade aspects of the blacksmith's work dominated the aesthetic aspects in the public eye. Only so many men had the talent to be good blacksmiths, and, regardless of how artistic their inclinations, they were needed to supply the tools and weapons and hardware of society.

That smiths were needed is attested by any modern telephone book or city directory with its pages upon pages of Smiths, most of whom are descended from blacksmiths.

In the twentieth century, particularly in its latter half, civilized societies take our iron- and steelwork so much for granted that we seldom consider its impersonal source. Until the middle of the nineteenth century, however, and in some areas into the first quarter of the twentieth century, the source for ironwork was not impersonal: it was the village smith, and every village and crossroad had at least one. Large or small, his shop was the key to beautiful houses in the community, to fine craftsmen in wood and soft metals and stone, to industry and transportation, and to security against criminals and hostile forces. When one thinks of the almost innumerable articles for which ironwork was required in the old days, one quickly sees the importance of the village smith, a man who learned his trade, or art, through long years of apprenticeship and experience. Unfortunately, most of the smith's education was by word of mouth, and few if any texts on the subject were written until the 1890s, continuing until about in 1930 in America, when blacksmithing seemed headed for oblivion.

Imagine trying to live without an available smithy before 1860, or even later in some communities not readily reached by rail or ship. It simply could not be done without reverting to the Stone Age. Certainly, many of our pioneers learned to substitute wood for iron in many instances, but even this would have been virtually impossible without the irreducible minimum of iron and steel tools such as axes and knives and hammers.

The traditional blacksmith's most important function until mass production replaced him as a tradesman, was supplying the tools of civilization and war. In a large city or a small backwoods settlement he would make, according to his own design or that of his patrons, the hammers, axes, adzes, plane bits, knives, sickles, scythes, auger bits, files, chisels, carving tools, spears, swords, arrowheads, and all other necessities of the various farmers and craftsmen found in a community. All craftsmen were basically dependent on the blacksmith's skill and availability.

He was no less essential to transportation. His skill and techniques were absolutely required to weld and fit wagon tires and hub rings, to shoe horses and oxen, and to make and fit all the metal accoutrements of wagons, carriages, and sleighs of a horse-drawn society. Possibly among the most skilled in the trade were the ships' blacksmiths and armorers who shaped iron precisely to the intricate needs of ships subjected to the continual motion and buffeting of the world's oceans possibly for years before returning for repairs and refitting. Each warship and later whaling ship generally carried its own blacksmith or armorer, with his small forge and anvil and stock of iron and steel adequate to make at sea all necessary repairs on fittings and guns. The ship's smith manufactured grappling hooks or made and sharpened harpoons. Anyone who read Melville's *Moby Dick* will not forget the gory scene of making a special harpoon for the great white whale; a weapon tempered in blood, instead of oil or brine.

In regard to transportation, the village smith was even called upon to furnish the ice skates of the village children, as well as toy wagons and doll carriages.

Perhaps it was the householder, from the most modest to

the most gracious, who, until the middle of the nineteenth century, best appreciated the presence of a skilled smith in his community. Without the knowledge and skill of ironworking the comfort of a man's home could barely have exceeded that of Cro-Magnon man.

There is hardly a way, even when using morticed and pegged frames, to build a fine house without iron. Some nails are necessary, and these plebian articles were handmade until a nail-cutting machine was developed around 1790. Usually they were produced, in all the special forms of the eighteenth century, by an apprentice or journeyman in the community smithy at the rate of a couple of thousand a day. The variety included tiny carpet tacks as well as huge, hand-forged spikes 6- to 8-inches long. The spikes were used sparingly when it was inconvenient to use wooden pegs in construction; the smaller finishing nails, brads, and tacks were necessary for the delicate assembly of stairways and doorways, and for the attachment of fine molding. Of course, all of the older nails were square, and because of this they seemed to bind with the wood into which they were driven.

Iron hardware, too, came from the smith, made to traditional design or to the special tastes of the housewright or his customer. This included hinges, large ones for large doors, and small decorative tulip, rattail, and butterfly hinges for cabinet doors. Shutter fasteners were all handmade, and usually locally produced until the end of the eighteenth century, and were needed for every house, large and small. Even a modest house required iron door latches, window fasteners, footscrapers, and so on.

There was but one source of decorative ironwork for a fine house. The secure wrought-iron gates and fences, the spikes for the tops of brick walls—all were procured from the local smith, or one fairly convenient, who specialized in decorative work.

Perhaps where the blacksmith contributed most to civilization, provided the basic wherewithal for happy marriages, and made the servant's life more pleasant, was in the kitchen. Civilized nations of the eighteenth century and before, and until the twentieth century in remote areas, did most of their cooking over an open fire. Special utensils were required, most of them made of durable iron by the local blacksmith. The variety one finds nowadays in antique shops is amazing, some of it so specialized as to be quite unidentifiable, though most intriguing in shape and construction.

Fundamental, of course, were firedogs and later andirons. Many of these were made of cast iron from the sixteenth century on, but most were wrought, sometimes into beautiful curves and shapes, nearly every one unique. Another essential piece of cooking equipment in the old days was the iron crane, mounted into the walls of the hearth so that it could be swung over the fire and off the fire. On this crane were hung all the assorted kettles and boilers needed by the cook. When the skill and inventive talent was available, some kitchens had marvelously intricate cranes that were adjustable as to height and lateral position as well as designed to swing out for placing a kettle over coals or flames, depending upon what was cooking. In more modest homes and backwoods cabins the fireplace crane was dispensed with in favor of a simple iron bar from which were hung a variety of pothooks, long and short, to place utensils closer to or farther from the fire. Often it was the job of the blacksmith's apprentices to turn out these graceful S-shaped hooks to fit the specifications of customers.

Other basic equipment needed in the kitchen were the poker and shovel, log tongs, and of course a variety of shapes and sizes of forks, spoons, ladles, strainers, and spits for roasting meats. Some spits were merely long iron rods with a crank formed on the end; others were elaborate affairs that were turned by a clock mechanism actuated by weights; still others were turned by the draft of the chimney moving a small propeller connected by a chain to the spit; and some were turned by a small dog walking patiently on a treadmill. (In fact, in some areas in America and the British Isles a species of stocky, short-legged dog was bred especially to operate the spit. They had not the status of long-legged hounds, but they eased the job of the cook who prepared the game caught by the hounds.)

In addition to basic cooking equipment, the local smith also provided many refinements such as trivets and toasters and toasting forks, kettle pourers, which enabled a cook to pour water from a kettle without removing the vessel from the fire, and pipe tongs, often exquisitely wrought, to enable gentlemen to pick up coals from the fire to light their churchwarden pipes. Pipe tongs, however, were usually found only in a fine house; common folk merely wet thumb and forefinger and picked up a coal with bare hands.

One can imagine how busy a local blacksmith was in supplying the manifold wrought-iron items needed by even a small settlement. It is true that a well-made item would last for generations, and replacement, except in the case of horseshoes, was seldom a big factor in building a smith's trade. Nevertheless life would have been much cruder without the day-by-day availability of at least the elemental skills of ironworking.

By and large, however, most men who chose to follow the trade of forging iron and steel were competent. The botcher (which is derived from the same root as *butcher*) simply could not make a living for long. No customer could afford to continue trading with a blacksmith who ruined a horse's foot because of bad shoeing; people would not continue to order ugly wrought ironwork or poorly welded wagon tires. The consequences of poor ironwork in a largely backward nation such as America, much of it hostile frontier, simply could not be tolerated. And once in England, so the story goes, a kingdom was lost for lack of a horseshoe nail.

There is another factor, also, which helps the blacksmith maintain high standards of quality in his work. A blacksmith is not wholly dependent on brawn; he must have brains and imagination and the powers of visualization as well. The lack of uniform quality in iron and steel requires unusual personal attention from the smith. His ability to improvise, to make do with what he has, has been an important characteristic of the good smith down through the ages. A stupid, unimaginative fellow is generally a poor smith and will not do well in his chosen craft.

There were some easily understood differences in the blacksmith's trade in Britain and Europe and in America. In Britain and Europe, with their larger cities fairly close together and with good communications, the ironworkers tended to specialize. Possibly this specialization began to occur during the Middle Ages, that time of consummate hand-craftsmanship, before America was discovered. Armorers, real artists in forming and decorating iron, were the most respected specialists. Then there were farriers, who specialized in shoeing horses and, eventually, in curing sick horses as well. In addition there were cutlers, who made only knives, swords, and scissors, all requiring especially developed skills in welding steel and iron together and in tempering steel.

There were specialists in forging and finishing small items such as bridle bits and harness buckles, as opposed to large shops employing many men who forged the separate pieces of huge wrought-iron ship anchors and welded the pieces together on great anvils, using half a dozen men wielding 20- to 35-pound sledges. The pieces of an anchor weighing several tons had to be heated for hours before welding heat was attained, and shops specializing in such heavy work were equipped with large iron-bound wooden cranes to move the sparkling pieces together over the anvil. Such work was directed by a master smith who tapped the work with a rod to indicate where the hammerblows were to fall.

In America, on the other hand, until the middle of the nineteenth century most blacksmiths catered to a general trade, with a few specialists being found only in such cities as Boston, New York, Philadelphia, Charleston, Savannah, and New Orleans. The typical village smith in early America was called upon to turn his hand to any job connected with iron. This status was maintained until the development of steam power finally reached a point where huge steam-driven trip-hammers were used to produce all manner of tools through mass production. When that point was reached, around 1840, much of the beautiful detail of everyday American life was lost for several generations.

The village blacksmith, with his tradition of fine workmanship, could hardly hope to compete in price with the factory where one man could turn out fifty hammers or axes a day, instead of the maximum two or three a day possible for a smith working at his forge.

The factories, however, came into being at a time when the country's population was burgeoning, when vast new lands were being opened for settlement as the Indians were removed from most of the country east of the Mississippi, and when the resources of the local smiths were taxed to supply the ironwork for all aspects of transportation and the repairs of new machine tools and equipment, new tasks for which an individual craftsman was still absolutely necessary. He hardly had time to do all this and make the axes, hinges, and hair curlers needed by the new millions.

During this period the blacksmiths began to think in more commercial terms. Time became more of a profit factor than it had been since the beginning of the world, and the ratio of production to effort began to follow modern concepts of time-use relating to profit. For instance, the smith, as did his customers, found it less expensive to buy factory-made hammers and tongs than to make them. He retained his ability to make his own tools, mind you, but it simply took too much time away from more profitable work. After the Civil War the blacksmith was no longer so essential to as many fields, but he had more work to do. When steel plows came into general use, for instance, the blacksmith was needed to sharpen them. It was dull, pedestrian work, but it was profitable, and generally in America he made enough money sharpening one plow to buy a pound of sow belly or 2 or 3 pounds of corn meal.

During this time, too, the smith's sources of supply became more productive and his raw material easier to acquire. In the 1830s and 1840s new, more efficient methods were evolved for making iron and steel, while the development of railroads and canals greatly facilitated delivering raw iron-stock to hitherto isolated communities. The smith was no longer so dependent on his scrap pile for stock, and a larger portion of his time could be spent in actual fabrication and repair rather than in preparing his stock for work.

Large new industries in Europe and America also employed many blacksmiths, while other industries, notably tool making, were started by smiths of vision and foresight.

The railroads, for instance, had great need for smiths in their repair shops. Here, in huge buildings equipped with monstrous steam-driven trip-hammers, great cranes, and large furnace-type forges, the captive smiths of the railroad straightened axles, repaired the ironwork of boxcars, and made many of the special tools needed for the maintenance of tracks and rolling stock. Also, they employed expert tool makers who, with the usual anvil, hammer, and forge of the village smithy, made and re-dressed chisels, hammers, picks, and other items by hand, as in the olden time.

Probably one of the strangest results of the research and

development activities of the steel industry was that they finally created instructional literature for the blacksmith's trade. Until the last couple of decades of the nineteenth century the blacksmith learned his trade only through oral instruction and experience as an apprentice and, later, a journeyman. During the period roughly between 1890 and 1920, however, when trade schools were being established, a number of books on the techniques of forging were published in Europe and in America. These volumes, about the first definitive literature on the subject since Diderot's great *Encyclopedia on Trades and Industries* was written in 1767, dealt mainly with the techniques of using mild steel to make tools and machine parts used in industry. They are valuable to the student of antique wrought ironwork, however, because many of the basic techniques they described are as ancient as the trade itself, and many of the books describe the techniques of working wrought iron as a departure point for describing the better qualities of mild steel. Some of them are quite well-written; others are so poorly composed that only the diagrams and illustrations have any instructional value.

Unfortunately the books on blacksmithing came at the end of the blacksmith's long era of preeminence in metalworking. They were too late to maintain the trade as it had been, in face of the frighteningly, but excitingly, rapid development of industrial mass production of shaped metal objects, welding by oxyacetylene and electric processes, and the cost of handcraftsmanship.

The blacksmith in one way or another continued to be an essential and familiar part of every community until World War I. After that, because of motorcars and the continuing developments of mass-production techniques, his trade began to languish. It almost followed the long road to oblivion down which such ancient and honorable craftsmen as the flint chipper, the fletcher, the coachmaker, the weir maker, and others had virtually disappeared in western civilization.

There are few general blacksmiths left. Some are found in cities and towns, older men who work alone. Most do blacksmithing as a sideline, with nostalgic affection. Their livelihood comes from the repair of mass-produced machines.

The decorative-wrought-iron industry employs a few workers who call themselves blacksmiths, but their skill frequently could have been surpassed by a three-month apprentice a hundred years ago. There is a growing number of farriers. A good farrier working at a race track can make more money than most corporation executives in the United States, and a six-week course in horseshoeing costs about $1500—no negligible tuition for a trade school in the 1960s. Farriers, however, while they use hammer and tongs, forge and anvil, are not general blacksmiths.

One can expect to see the general blacksmith disappear entirely before the end of the twentieth century. Probably he will pass unnoticed and unmourned by most. After all, during the past hundred and fifty years he was so much a part of the everyday scene that he was taken for granted by most; and while intelligent, he was usually too poorly educated and too modest to publicize his importance in a community. Yet his passing has a poignancy about it; we should not be the civilized technicians, the travelers, the warriors, the artists we are today without the individual blacksmith's presence and infinite skill over the thousands of years of progress since the beginnings of his trade in the Caucasus.

His fire, however, has been passed to the artist. For the young blacksmiths of the late twentieth century, the artists who have rediscovered the fascination and psychic satisfaction of ironworking, are growing in numbers. This enthusiastic band will save the sounds, the smells, the visual joys of the blacksmith shop as a human heritage for generations to come.

2.

THE BLACK METAL

Practically all the craftsmen of the ancient and the modern world, until recently, were dependent on the blacksmith for their tools. The smith made their tools as well as his own and was quite independent of all craftsmen but one, the iron-maker. It's possible that the earliest blacksmiths smelted their own iron, but it's highly probable that iron making became a special occupation long before the dawn of history.

One can only speculate how and when iron was first discovered. It is the most plentiful of the earth's useful metals and the most ubiquitous; there are vast deposits of iron on every continent, and the supply so far has been inexhaustible.

Unlike copper and lead, silver and gold, however, iron is a reluctant substance, a quality that makes it as valuable in use as it is difficult to acquire. Copper, for instance, can be found lying on the ground in its pure state, ready to be picked up and wrought by any hunter with no more equipment than a hot campfire and a couple of stones for hammer and anvil. So can lead and silver and gold. So can zinc and tin, which easily combine with copper to make bronze, the predecessor of iron for tools and weapons.

Iron, though, is seldom found in a pure state. Occasionally a meteorite is found on the surface of the ground, but so rare is the occurrence that less than a thousand meteorites have been found in the United States since the country was first colonized. Bog iron is fairly common around the world. It is a type of iron pyrites found in various-sized lumps in swamps and shallow ponds. The first iron furnace in the

American Colonies was supplied by bog iron dredged from the coastal swamps of Massachusetts in quantities of 300 tons a year. Bog iron, however, is limited in supply and its qualities are inferior. The modern world would never have been built if bog iron had been its only source of ferrous metal.

The world's real supply of iron, the infinite potential wealth of knives and axes and spearheads; the miles of railway rails and the fleets of ships; the mountains of skyscrapers and the noxious hordes of automobiles; the Eiffel Tower and the Golden Gate Bridge; the batteries of cannons and the numberless armies of rifles—all were locked in the rocky vaults of the earth's surface back when the world began. Man somehow discovered such wealth when sticks and stones comprised his only digging equipment. Somehow he found that ferrous ore when brought to a high heat would release its iron and provide man with his most common, and at the time his most valuable metal.

The process of smelting ore must have been discovered by accident, just as the process of vulcanizing rubber and the secret of the X ray were discovered in our own time. Possibly man first found it after a forest fire which had been fanned by the seasonal high winds of the spring or autumn solstice to a degree of heat that released the substance from its ore. He had found the source of a metal that would provide him and his tribe with material advantages not realized before the discovery, and he soon devised a method of controlling the smelting process to his needs.

Probably the first iron furnaces were merely pits dug in a steep hillside with a tunnel dug from the bottoms of the pits out of the base of the hill in the direction of the prevailing wind. The ironmaker built a roaring fire in the pit when the wind was steady and strong, and piled his iron ore on the fire. As the fire burned down he retrieved the lumps of iron from the ashes and shaped them to his purpose.

Not all of this primitive iron production was usable. Some

was dirty, brittle cast iron, impossible to shape even when red-hot, but a few lumps from every smelting were probably free enough from carbon to be malleable. With these he made superior spear heads and axes, which allowed him to live better and to enslave the men of tribes armed only with stone or bronze and set them to work digging iron ore and smelting more iron.

Now, of course, men who lived in flat country also wanted iron. With no hills in which to dig a deep pit they built their own pits aboveground in the shape of stone towers. Since they had to be fed from the top, these first towers were probably no more than 6- or 8-feet tall, with a draft hole at the base. Very simple, very wasteful, these furnaces were built near the sources of ore and were abandoned when the ore became too difficult to mine. Probably the fuel first used was plain firewood, such as was used in the home fire. This is substantiated by the fact that blacksmiths in the North Georgia mountains used green chestnut wood in their forges instead of charcoal or coal until the 1920s, and with it generated enough heat for welding.

Such early methods of smelting iron lasted well into the historical period on some European farms, providing individual farmers with enough iron to satisfy their needs for simple farm tools.

These prehistoric methods were used in our own time to help bridge the gap between an agrarian and an industrial culture. In the early 1960s in China the demigod Mao Tse-tung organized backyard iron refineries in western China which were no more than crude stone towers, 6- to 8-feet tall, with a draft at the base, fed from the top with fuel and raw iron ore. In these crude furnaces the Chinese peasants produced a low-grade pig iron to feed the modern steel mills of the nation. A determined explorer could probably find a few such crude furnaces operating in the hinterlands of Africa and Asia.

In time ironmasters learned to transform the useless cast iron into wrought iron by resmelting it in a deep fire, burning out excess carbon and beating out the impurities. Such refining was made much easier by the invention of valved bellows around the fourth century. The value of this simple but ingenious device was increased still further by harnessing waterpower for sustained operation of giant bellows. Until the thirteenth century, however, there was little control over the quality and type of iron produced in the crude furnaces of the day. Some of the product would be cast iron, some wrought iron, and some carbon steel, depending upon circumstances of fire, fuel, and ferrous material. Cast iron, which contained more than 2.2-percent carbon, was useless for working; wrought iron, which contained less than .3-percent carbon, was the product most in demand for agricultural tools, nails, horseshoes, and other utilitarian items for everyday use; steel, an iron that had absorbed from .3-percent to 2.2-percent carbon, was invaluable for making tools, weapons and springs because it could be hardened, then tempered, by heating it to the proper degree and quenching it in water. The latter two forms, wrought iron and carbon steel, were the only materials worked by the blacksmith. They comprised the "black" metal, as opposed to shiny silver, gold, copper, and brass, which the ironworker would "smite" with his hammer. So he became known as the "blacksmith."

In the thirteenth century iron making became an organized industry and its processes began to be controlled in a modern sense. In Spain, when seignorial anarchy was being subdued for national stability, when the ignorance of the Dark Ages was exposed to the light of the Renaissance, the Catalan furnace was developed. Its greatly increased productive capacity and elimination of waste at once provided the material to arm national military organizations and provide a base for national economic power.

The Catalan furnace, a hearth-type facility developed

about 1292, was used in conjunction with the eighth century Osmund furnace to offer double-stage refining. The molten "ball" from the Osmund furnace was reheated in the Catalan type, resulting in a "bloom" from which much of the carbon had been removed by heat and oxidation. The bloom was then forged, or later rolled, into bars and sheets of quite high quality wrought iron.

Also invented in the thirteenth century was the stuckofen which, when married to the Catalan furnace, became a direct ancestor of modern blast furnaces. The stuckofen, however, yielded a new metal, cast iron, too brittle to be forged, but plastic enough when molten to be cast in many shapes.

Cast iron, which had always been a waste product and something to be avoided, was the desired product of the blast furnace. It was produced in a large stone or brick tower, 30- to 50-feet high, lined with ceramic brick to form a generally pear-shaped cavity.

The blast of air that entered the base of the cavity was generally provided by water-driven pairs of bellows. In France, however, an ingenious blower consisting of long tubes into which air was sucked by falling water and forced into the furnace by rising water from an enclosed housing was sometimes used, as described and illustrated in Diderot's *Encyclopedia.* The tower and bellows were enclosed in a large building properly equipped with raised walkways from which the fuel, iron ore, and purifying agents, mostly limestone, were fed into the top of the preheated furnace.

There was a special technique for feeding the furnace and controlling the amounts and alternation of the fuel, ore, and limestone. This was important not only to the quality of the iron and the longevity of the furnace lining, but also to the life and safety of the workers. A clogged vent or an untoward gas pocket within the stock could suddenly explode with the force of a volcano, spewing coals, molten iron, red-hot limestone, and brick over a large area. Whenever the blast of hot air and gas through the top of the furnace ceased to be steady, and the flames within the cavity died down then leaped upward alternately, it was a sign of imminent explosion. The workers, on beholding these signals, acted accordingly—they ran.

As with ancient furnaces, molten iron in the blast furnace filtered down through the fuel and slag and collected in a basin located below the air pipes of the bellows. Usually it took from twelve to fourteen hours from the time the furnace was lit until the basin was ready to be tapped. Tapping allowed the molten iron to flow into sand molds, the ash and slag floating on its surface being removed as the metal flowed.

In England, the cooled cast iron was known as pig iron because it was molded in a series of trenches that resembled a sow and her suckling pigs, the central mold being known as the sow, and its tributary smaller molds as the pigs. French ironmakers generally molded an 8-foot long triangular bar of iron known as the "slut."

Charcoal was the fuel used in early blast furnaces. Prodigious amounts of it were needed and its production for the iron and steel industry had its effect on the history of the Western world.

A charcoal burner's life was lonely and dirty. He spent most of his existence living in temporary quarters deep in the wilderness. Half his time was given to endless cutting of wood, cord upon cord of it, which was hauled to the cleared spot in the forest where the coal was made. So much wood had to be continually cut and hauled, indeed, that charcoal burning necessarily took place deep in the forests close to the source of raw material.

One can understand the growing concern of European monarchs for the preservation of timber after the fourteenth century when iron production took a sharp increase. As much or more charcoal was needed to produce a ton of iron as was iron ore. For instance, in America, where the supply of cordwood seemed inexhaustible, an iron furnace producing 15 tons of pig iron a week consumed the wood of 4 square miles of forest each year. Such voracious consumption of woodland by the iron industry led to an edict by Queen Elizabeth of England that limited cutting of forests in certain areas of her realm in the latter years of the sixteenth century. She needed the timber to build the ships for her navy. Other monarchs followed suit in succeeding generations in all civilized lands except America, Scandinavia, and Russia, until the utilization of coal and coke for iron furnaces was perfected in England during the eighteenth century.

In Europe and in America especially, the lowly, lonely charcoal burner was far more responsible for clearing the great forests than hardy pioneers or great lords wanting more land for agriculture. Much of the land in the eastern areas of the United States was cleared to feed the iron furnaces. The bloody battlefield of the Wilderness, fought over so stubbornly by Union and Confederate soldiers in the Civil War, was land that had been cut by the charcoal burners and had since grown back into the tangled second-growth jungle, floored with dry, dead tree tops, which made the Wilderness battlefield so difficult.

After hauling his wood to the burning place, the charcoal burner stacked it into high piles, the logs being placed roughly perpendicular to the ground, and he covered this mass of wood with an airtight blanket of dirt and charcoal dust mixed together and packed over a layer of leaves or pine needles. Draft holes were opened in several places around the base of the pile and a chimney hole was left in the center of the top.

The fire was lit from a nest of shavings and kindling at

Burning charcoal

the bottom of the chimney hole. When it was burning merrily
the draft holes and the chimney were covered and the burner
kept a careful eye on the process by occasionally digging
small holes in the blanket of dirt, to see how the burning was
progressing.

The burners tended the fires for days, the length of time
depending on the amount of coal being produced at one burning. Such supervision was needed to close or open draft holes
and chimney to regulate the supply of oxygen to the fire.
Without such constant care the quality of the coal suffered
either burning into ash or not charring completely. Also, the
burner guarded against gas pockets forming in the mass of
wood. These could build up unknown to a careless burner and
suddenly explode, tearing a great hole in the dirt blanket and
requiring emergency action to cover the wood quickly to
continue charring.

There may still be a few small furnaces that use charcoal
to make iron. The last known source of old-fashioned wrought
iron (charcoal-smelted), however, was the ancient firm Ramnaes Bruks, AB, of Ramnaes, Sweden.

Of interest to the historian of blacksmithing is the fact that Ramnaes Bruks made iron with charcoal from 1590 until 1964. Its product was known to the world as "Swedish iron." For the last century the furnaces used were adapted from a type developed in England, and the iron produced in the furnace and rolling mills was known in Sweden as "Lancashire iron." Strangely, this ancient-type charcoal iron is useful in electrical devices. Because of its properties, due largely to charcoal smelting, Swedish, or Lancashire, iron is most suitable for relays and other parts of telephone, telegraph, and radio installations.

The last American source for wrought iron disposed of its inventory in 1974. England is known to produce some wrought iron but ships it in minimum quantity of 1,000 pounds. Some iron and steel supplier in America might possibly stock this material. Wrought iron was used in the U.S. for bridges well into the 1960s. Some scrap wrought iron might be found occasionally in junkyards.

Forging Swedish charcoal iron demonstrates why it was the favorite of Colonial smiths. It seems to mold more easily under the hammer, due no doubt to the inclusion of slag during its smelting. Also, it welds easily. When cold-forged, it draws out without splitting and separates into two distinct layers, such as is observed on cold-forged plate armor. Altogether it has certain indefinable qualities made for the blacksmith, qualities not present in mild steel or in the pure wrought iron produced with coal, gas, or electric fuel. Charcoal makes a difference in ironmaking, but its cost is too high for modern society.

Charcoal was essential in the production of carbon steel, too. In early times steel was usually a fortuitous by-product of making malleable iron. After the fourteenth century, though, in the West most steel was made deliberately from wrought iron, just as wrought iron was made deliberately from cast iron. The transition from iron to steel was quite simple. Pure iron rods or bars were packed in charcoal dust in a tight iron box or furnace and the dust was then fired and blown with bellows for a varying period of time, depending on the size of the iron being treated. Once the iron became white-hot it began to absorb carbon from the charcoal at a rate of ⅛ inch of absorbtion every twenty-four hours. Accordingly, small bars of iron turned into steel in a day's time, while larger, thicker bars needed longer treatment. As might be expected, the degree of carbon in the center of the bar was less than on the outside surface, but generally iron made into steel by this primitive method contained from 0.3-percent to 2.2-percent carbon and could be tempered, though the tempering of each piece was slightly different from others.

This product, so invaluable for making tools and weapons, was generally called "blister steel," because the high heat over hours and days gave it a blistered appearance. Some called it "shear steel," because its main uses were in making shears and other cutting instruments that required a hardened edge. It was easily welded to iron, so that old axes, plane bits, drawknives, and scissors were made of the more plentiful soft iron with a steel edge welded on. The quality of blister steel was uneven and undependable, necessitating testing to determine the proper tempering heat for each individual piece being used. The finest came from Sweden and Holland, though all the European countries and their colonies produced some for general use.

While Europe and its New World colonies suffered the inconvenience of blister steel for centuries, in the Orient, particularly in India, another type of greatly superior steel had been in use since early in the Christian era. This was known as Wootz steel. It was the finest steel in the world, with even texture and carbon content. The fabulous swords of Damascus were made of Wootz steel.

It is possible that Europe became familiar with Wootz steel during the latter days of the Roman Empire, when there was a considerable amount of trade with the Near East. Undoubtedly the professional warriors of Europe noticed the superior quality of Saracen weapons during the Crusades and brought back samples of Wootz steel to their personal armorers during the eleventh, twelfth, and thirteenth centuries. When European nations established colonies in the East during the period of exploration after the fifteenth century, Wootz steel became an important article of commerce. The British developed a good market for the superior metal after its subjugation of India. Despite wide use over the centuries, however, the secret of making Wootz steel was not discovered until the nineteenth century.

As with blister steel, Wootz steel was made by carburizing pure iron. Instead of using charcoal as the source of carbon, however, the Oriental steelmakers used molten cast iron with a high carbon content.

A faggot of pure iron plates was immersed in a crucible of molten cast iron. By capillary action the highly carburized cast iron was drawn between the thin plates of pure iron, and as the pure iron was heated almost to a melting point it absorbed more carbon. The mass was allowed then to harden into an ingot, which was worked into tools and weapons.

Wootz steel, though more easily tempered, was hard to forge, which may clarify the oriental technique of shaping swords, axes, and knives with a minimum of smiting. European smiths found that Wootz steel could not be worked below a blood-red heat; if it was, the metal "red seared," or cracked, just as with pure iron when worked at any heat between a blue and a sunrise red.

Modern analysis, through the science of metallography, shows that Wootz steel is composed of a mixture of granules of soft iron and carbon steel. This composition explains the beautiful patterns found in true Damascus swords, patterns never truly duplicated by European smiths who made artificial Damascus sword blades by repeatedly twisting and welding steel and iron rods together into the stock.

About 1740 Mr. Benjamin Huntsman of Attersea, England, frustrated by the uneven quality of the blister steel he used for clock springs, did some serious thinking about the problem and chanced upon the secret of "cast steel." Huntsman took the blister steel he had been using, chopped it into fine pieces and remelted it in a crucible where it was kept from further carburizing from contact with the fire. When the steel was molten he cast it into ingots that, when cooled, were wrought into clock springs.

Huntsman's discovery provided him with a steel of which every ingot was carburized evenly throughout, and in which the air pockets and blisters of the old steel were eliminated.

Huntsman kept his trade secret for a number of years despite covetous competitors and the demand for superior steel for gun springs and weapons. The secret was finally discovered through a ruse. A supposedly drunken farm laborer begged sanctuary in Huntsman's shop one cold, rainy night and was invited in by an indulgent foreman. While pretending to sleep off the results of his excessive drinking the pseudolaborer observed the complete process of making cast steel. Thus one of the early examples of industrial espionage carried Mr. Huntsman's process to the world, where it notably improved the quality of guns, swords, knives, clocks, and cutting tools for the next century and a half. Upon cast steel was founded the reputation of Sheffield, England, for making fine cutlery.

It is known that many casings, drive rods, and smaller machine parts in the nineteenth century were made of wrought iron and case-hardened by carburizing and then tempering the outside surface. Carburizing was effected by packing the item in charcoal dust and raising it to a white heat for eight to twelve hours, just long enough for the surface to absorb enough carbon for tempering. One may suspect that certain blacksmiths, particularly those making iron and steel articles for the Indian trade in America, may have case-hardened knives after they had been forged. This method would have produced a soft-iron knife with a steel surface which could be tempered. If the speculation is valid, it explains the curious custom of some American Indians of sharpening their knives only on one edge, rather than on both edges; a case-hardened knife holds an edge only on the outside surface.

Until about 1860 the iron- and steelmakers of the world merely evolved improved methods of producing the black metal of olden times. Whether it came from a simple rock tower built near a primitive village, with perhaps a ton of iron produced each year, or whether it came from a late eighteenth-century blast furnace with a volume of from 15 to 30 tons a week, wrought iron was wrought iron, the pure element with special immutable characteristics.

It was soft, yet tough. For instance, it could be bent double without breaking. Indeed, many farriers in the old days tested horseshoe nails by bending them across the forehead to determine softness.

As with wood, pure iron had a sort of grain, a fibrous quality due to silica content, which influenced the methods by which it was worked. These fibers become quite apparent when examining old pieces of wrought iron that have been exposed to the elements, or buried in some ancient warrior's grave. The fibers may also be seen at the end of an iron rod which has been worked at too low a heat, for the force of the hammerblows separate them until the iron resembles the frayed end of a wooled thread. Making too sharp a bend, even when hot, weakens the fibers, so that old pieces have

Wrought iron, showing fibers

rounded corners where bent, and old anvils had a section of a corner rounded for forming bends.

Wrought iron is practically indestructible, except by the elements. Even under the elements, however, pure iron deteriorates from oxidation less readily than the modern steels. For this reason it was still used in the 1960s for wrought-iron fences, gates, and other items in coastal locations, where the corrosive action of salt air quickly destroys modern steel.

It is almost impossible to burn iron in the forge no matter how hot the fire is blown. Of course, it oxidizes to some extent, but, except for the smallest pieces, iron melts before it burns. For this reason it is relatively easy to weld, and the joint, when properly done, literally makes two pieces as one. So little does iron oxidize that it can be welded without a flux most of the time, whereas modern steel must be treated with a deoxidizing compound before the molten surfaces of two pieces may be joined together.

When subjected to enough heat pure iron may be formed into the most intricate shapes with the most simple tools. Beating it, however, hardens it by packing the fibers so tightly together that the material becomes brittle when hammered cold. Once subjected to heat again it becomes as malleable as in its original state. There is some evidence to indi-

41

cate that where steel was unknown certain primitive tribes hardened pure iron weapons and tools by cold-forging them. This is a delicate process, for one blow too many after the iron is packed causes the fibers to separate.

Carbon steel, particularly the blister steel of olden days, was quite similar to pure iron in its working qualities. The main difference between old-time steel and iron was that the carbon content of steel, small though it was, made the steel more susceptible to burning. Since it oxidized more readily steel often required a flux for welding. It welded at a lower heat than iron, and while it could readily be joined to pure iron by an expert smith, each metal had to be brought to its own proper welding heat at exactly the same moment. Cast steel was worked exactly the same as blister steel, its only difference being that it was much easier to temper.

In the middle of the nineteenth century the supply of raw ironstock in many forms had been plentiful for a couple of centuries. It was still precious, however, because distribution channels were hardly improved over what had been used during the Renaissance. Smiths in the small farm villages of Europe and the backwoods communities of America before 1860 were dependent on a few canals, incomplete railroads, and slow wagons for their supply of iron fresh from the furnace. Because of transportation iron was costly, and steel more precious than rubies. As a consequence the smith became a junkman; he searched for small bits of scrap iron and steel as though hunting for the widow's mite, and his scrap pile became an important source of supply for the iron needed in a community. Worn-out gun barrels were made into tomahawks. Old horseshoe nails were welded together and twisted and further welded to make shotgun barrels. Discarded horseshoes were drawn out and eventually made into nails. Pieces of scrap iron left over from making wagon tires were used to make rifle barrels or axes or adzes. Every smith had a pile of scrap iron behind his shop whence he regularly drew material for his jobs. Farmers and farm lads carefully saved any bit of iron, old nails, bolts, and horseshoes found along the roads of their communities.

Any iron article turned out by a smith before 1860 might well be made of scraps which had long histories. It is said that every bottle of good Spanish sherry contains a few drops of the wine first put into the casks three hundred years ago when sherry was first produced; and that each European gold coin probably contains a tiny bit of the gold mined in ancient Babylonia and Egypt. So it was, to some extent, with iron items fabricated by the smiths of many an isolated village.

Pure iron and its derivative, carbon steel, were the only raw materials of the blacksmith for untold generations. With primitive machinery and cheap labor the ironmongers and smiths fashioned it into its basic forms, bar, rod, and sheet, and from this supplied the needs of a growing population all over the world. This held true until about 1860 when new,

Hunting through the scrap pile

greatly improved methods of ironmaking were developed and "mild" steel appeared on the market to gradually replace wrought iron for almost all purposes. Such replacement took a couple of generations. When it finally came, the world was a different place, and the tocsin of the traditional village blacksmith was already sounding.

Essentially the iron produced by modern methods is smelted in a crucible in the manner developed by Benjamin Huntsman. The fuel used is gas, coke, or electricity. Modern coke furnaces are far more efficient than the old blast furnace because they utilize the hot gases that formerly escaped up the chimney. The iron produced is known as "mild steel," though it is actually not steel, but high-quality iron. It is slag-less and free from the impurities of old-fashioned wrought iron, and it contains a small portion of carbon, but not enough to allow it to harden when heated and suddenly cooled. Though it is cast into ingots and then rolled into various forms, it is not the same as the old-fashioned cast steel upon which the Sheffield steel industry was built.

As the modern steel industry developed, so did the transportation and distribution of steel in the Western world. After 1860 the blacksmith could depend more and more on a ready supply of mild steel fresh from the mill.

There were problems in its use, however. Mild steel just did not work like the old iron. It burned when too hot, and it was practically impossible to weld as dependably as wrought iron. In fact, a Mr. Casterlin, who had been a blacksmith for forty years before he wrote a book on the subject in 1890, stated unequivocally that mild steel would not weld. He said that the best a smith should expect was a good "glue job." Certainly the smith had to be more careful in welding wagon tires and other articles of mild steel. A good flux was essential, and as welding heat was arrived at just before the burning point, a smith had to be quick to remove his iron from the fire before it was consumed in a flurry of incandescent sparks.

The smiths of the world might not have liked mild steel, but after about 1900 they had little else available. They had to learn to work it or else not work at all. Some smiths continued to make old-fashioned articles from mild steel, but these can usually be detected by appearance and "feel." Mild steel never packed like pure iron, so that it bent more easily, even after forging. Since it had no fibers, it could be bent into more acute angles without weakening. On articles such as eyebolts the lack of fibers allows the eye to be punched, while the eye in an iron bolt must be bent around the horn of the anvil and then welded. Mild steel rusts and corrodes more easily than iron, but no fibers are apparent in rusted steel as in wrought iron.

Mild steel was only the beginning of a bewildering variety of special steels available to the modern blacksmith. The one closest to wrought iron in forging and welding quality is called "10-20 hot rolled." This is available at most steel supply houses. Other types of mild steel, however, may be used when 10-20 hot rolled stock cannot be found.

In addition to common mild steel, there are countless types of ferrous metals which can be shaped cold, which will not rust, which need not be tempered for tools. All of these may be used to make beautiful and useful functional items.

Scientific and historical circumstances have combined to make the true black metal, wrought iron, almost obsolete. Yet some of the same impersonal circumstances have produced a social need for the blacksmith's art to enhance our modern lives. The fascinating, ancient mystique of the smith remains, fortunately, a continuing factor in society.

The modern blacksmith has met the challenge of new technology by learning to work mild steel almost as well as his forebears worked black iron.

3.

THE BLACKSMITH SHOP

No wonder old-time blacksmith shops were so interesting. Each had an atmosphere all its own, reflecting the personality of the smith and the character of his community. Its appeal and demonic mystery was comprised of an infinite number of details, visual, auditory, and olfactory.

Blacksmith shops, until the end of World War II in many areas, had so long been a part of almost every community in the civilized world that they were more than a current necessity; they were a solid link with the past, a constant reminder of man's slow struggle upward from animal oblivion by his own ingenuity. They provided a sense of stability because they had always been there, and a feeling of humility because without them civilization would have vanished in a few short years.

For those who recognized the blacksmith as a real factor in the history of civilization there was atavistic symbolism in the glow of his forge and the ringing rhythm of his hammer. To those few people the blacksmith's fire was an eternal flame, the dawn-light of history, the source of material progress, the hatching heat of the facile labor and the leisure which spawned man's intellect.

Like other craftsmen and artists, the blacksmith was no better than his tools. Unlike other artists and craftsmen, however, he was unique in being able to make his own tools. As the circumstances of his trade changed over the centuries, so did his tools. Old designs were adapted to new uses, or new designs were executed as needed. Consequently, any well-equipped shop was likely to have a fascinating variety of tools, some mysterious in shape and ingenious in construction, the uses of which could be explained only by the smith who made and used them. Despite the variety of individual tools, however, there were only five or six categories of tools and equipment, all of which were necessary to the smith down through the ages.

Forge and bellows, anvil and slack tub, hammer and tongs, swage and cutter, chisel and punch, file and drill— these were the basic categories of equipment. Of these the forge, or hearth, was fundamental because iron, unlike copper and other soft metals, simply could not be shaped or formed with any ease or control without the application of intense heat.

Forges over the world varied in size and in the material of which they were made, but all were identical in that they contained the fire.

Most were made of brick or stone, usually about 30-inches high and from 24- to 40-inches square, although some were rectangular and a few were round. The smith who did welding, and most did, made certain his hearth was as deep as it

Brick forge

Wood and clay forge

was wide: the deeper the fire the more oxygen from the bellows was consumed, and the less oxygen to oxidize the iron being welded. Sometimes the forge might be made of wood standing on four stout wooden legs, the hearth portion a wooden box thickly lined with clay. Some smiths maintained that such a forge held the heat better.

Most city shops in the old days had hoods of brick or metal over the forge connected with a large chimney to carry out the smoke and fine ash. In the country, though, the smoke from the fire was often allowed to drift out through the myriad openings in a shingle roof, and the ash was allowed to settle where it would. In the days of charcoal fuel, smoke was not really a problem once the kindling had burned away, but in the latter days of blacksmithing, when bituminous coal was adopted, it was necessary to provide a flue for the heavy smoke released by green fuel.

About the middle of the nineteenth century a number of patent forges appeared on the market. Usually these were made of heavy cast iron with the manufacturer's name molded on the front. They came in a variety of sizes suitable for the farm blacksmith shop or the industrial shop. About the only advantage they offered over the brick and stone hearths was a certain mobility.

All forges, of course, even the elemental types built of clay around a hole in the ground, found even today in parts of Africa and the Orient, were equipped with an air pipe which led from the bellows. This was known as the "tuyere" in sophisticated circles, but with true Anglo-Saxon usage was corrupted into "tweer" or "tue iron" in England and America. Sometimes the tue iron led directly to the fire from the side of the hearth. More frequently it was connected with a grate, often called a "duck's nest," a device of cast iron that was mounted in the center of the hearth and designed to be cleaned periodically of ashes and cinders which dropped into it from the fire.

In primitive areas the tue pipe was sometimes no more than a small tunnel hollowed in the earth from the air source to the ground-level forge.

On the front and sides of the forge were racks for tongs and tong rings to hold the handles of the tongs together when

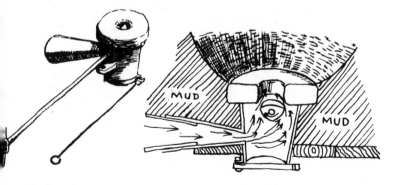

Left: The duck's nest, made of cast iron. Right: How the duck's nest operates.

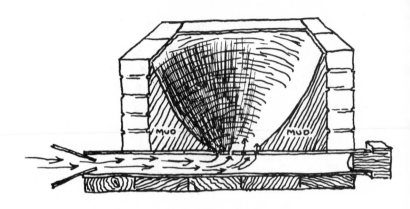

A simple pipe grate

gripping a piece of iron in the fire. Of course, almost every forge had space on top not taken up by the fire, and this was usually put to good use as a place to put special pieces of iron or steel that the smith expected to use in the near future, or on which to lay his tongs so they were handy for instant use when his iron reached the proper heat. There might have been a few isolated smiths who were so well organized that they replaced tongs and iron and hammer, each in its proper place, after each phase of a forging operation, but such smiths were few indeed. Consequently the top of the average forge was usually piled haphazardly with all manner of scrap and tools that only the smith could lay his hands on quickly.

No fire in the forge burned properly, though, without its necessary adjunct, the bellows, a marvel of ingenuity and efficiency. The great bellows, preferred by many smiths even after the invention of the "squirrel-cage" blower, was a combination of wood and leather and valves and pipes and levers and counterbalances. Evidence from old illustrated manuscripts indicates that bellows constructed with simple valves must have appeared about the fourth century, during the last tumultuous years of the Roman Empire. The importance of the invention is better understood by considering the vague and shadowy history of devices that preceded the bellows.

First of all, one may assume, the primitive smith used a fan of some sort, possibly a bird's wing such as the turkey-wing fan our American backwoods forebears used to fan their cooking fires and make them burn hotter. Perhaps eventually the blast from the fan was directed through an earthen tube or tunnel that concentrated the increased oxygen to a spot in the fire where it did the most good. This principle is illustrated by the ruins of a unique smokehouse in the Colonial ghost town of Old Brunswick, near Wilmington, North Carolina. Here smoke was forced by a fan through a short brick tunnel from an outside fire into the smokehouse, possibly at the suggestion of a Negro slave who remembered a primitive forge in an African village.

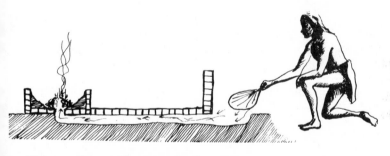

How a fan might have been used—as indicated by a smoke house at Old Brunswick, N.C.

After the fan, and probably simultaneously with it, the more progressive smiths of ancient times might have used a blowpipe. This simple device, like the fan, is still used in certain primitive societies to make the cooking fire burn brighter. In ancient days when slaves were plentiful one can visualize a master smith working at a forge around which

Presumably the first tuyere

several deep-chested slaves were blowing the fire through brass or reed pipes, and certainly this would have created welding heat in a short time.

There are references in the Bible to "treading the wineskin" to heat metal for tempering, indicating that probably the wineskins of the Mediterranean countries were adopted by smiths at an early time to serve as the first mechanical airblowers. One is hard put to figure out how a wineskin was used efficiently as a blower unless it was enclosed between two boards, as indicated in ancient Egyptian art. Pressing an inflated skin to force air through a pipe to the fire is easy to see, but one wonders how the skin was then easily reinflated. Egyptian paintings indicate that it was operated with string, but a hole would have been needed through which to suck new air, and this hole must have been closed during the process of deflation. The smiths' apprentices during the era of wineskins probably exercised some special dexterity which qualified them to open and close holes with heels of hands or feet while operating the wineskin.

Possibly there were other devices for forcing oxygen into

Treading the wineskin—as it might have been

the fire. Years ago a motion picture with an African setting gave a glimpse of a savage blacksmith at his forge. Near him was a helper operating blowers consisting of two sheets pegged to the ground over holes connected presumably with the ground-level forge by two earthen tunnels. The apprentice lifted and lowered the two sheets alternately to supply a constant stream of oxygen to the fire. Controlling such a primitive device, which experiment has proved to be workable, required considerable technique and two enduring arms.

A most ingenious bellows is made by covering the mouths of two special jars with loose skin which has been tied tightly around a hollow tube projecting through its center. Clay pipes lead from the bottoms of the jars to the fire. A blast is created by alternately raising and lowering the skins, the thumb placed over the end of the hollow tube when pressing, and being released when raising, in effect creating a hand-operated valve.

The invention of the air valve, however, led to one of the most fascinating machines of all times, the bellows, a machine that retained its basic form and efficiency for sixteen hun-

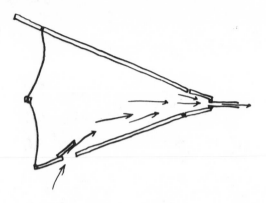

The single-action bellows—invented about the fourth century.

dred years. It was cast aside when the smith's traditional functions were taken over by machines.

An air valve is a simple device operated by air pressure. It is nothing more than a hinged flap covering a hole. Air coming through the hole from a direction opposite to the flap forces the valve open and admits air. When air comes from the direction of the flap, the valve is forced over the hole, making it airtight.

The earliest bellows equipped with valves were single-chambered affairs like the well-known bellows used to blow the den fire. They were made of two teardrop-shaped boards, one having a hole and a valve on the inside, the other solid, with leather tacked around the edges of both boards to make an airtight chamber. Separating the boards created a vacuum that filled with air through the hole, the valve automatically opening; pressing the boards together closed the valve and forced air out of the chamber through the blow pipe into the fire.

How long the single-chambered bellows was used by smiths and ironfounders is uncertain. Until the seventeenth century and later it was used by ironfounders in tandem, since this was the only way it provided a constant blast of air. Blacksmiths used it in tandem for the same reason, until it was replaced at some unknown date by the great double-chambered bellows.

Essentially shaped like the small fireplace bellows, the improved bellows used by smiths from about the sixteenth century, or perhaps earlier, consists of three flat boards, the lower and middle having air valves, and all connected at the smaller end to the tuyere. When enclosed with leather, kept taut by one or two ribs in each section, it has, like Congress, an upper and a lower chamber which together dispense a constant stream of air.

Its principle of operation is quite simple. The center board is fastened by a pin on either side to uprights close to the forge. Both upper and lower boards are hinged to a box that holds the tuyere. Valve holes, from 3 to 6 inches in

How single-action bellows were mounted in team— according to an illustration from the Weisz Kuenig, *sixteenth century*

diameter, are cut in the bottom and center boards, each having a valve of leather or thin board on its upper surface.

When mounted on the uprights the lower board falls down of its own weight, being held by the leather casing, and the upper board rests on the middle partition. When the lower board is pulled upward by means of a chain fastened to a lever above the bellows, all the air in it is expelled through the middle air hole to inflate the upper chamber automatically and push a stream of air through the tuyere.

Once the upper chamber is inflated the lever is released; the lower board then falls down, allowing the lower chamber to fill with air, and the upper board descends by its own weight, closing the middle valve automatically and forcing more air through the tuyere. The weight of a piece of iron or a brick on the upper board increases the pressure of air through the tuyere. An adjustable counterweight prevents the board from descending too quickly, thus controlling the

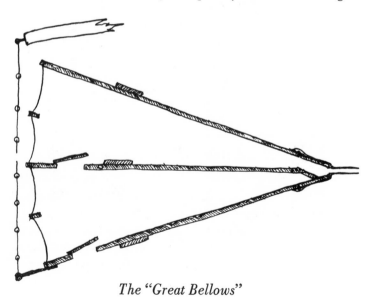

The "Great Bellows"

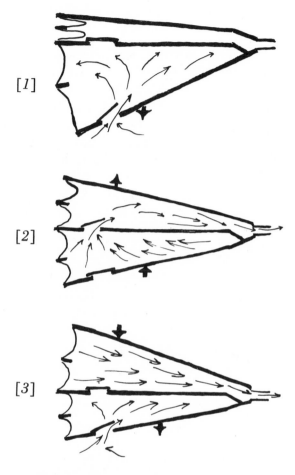

How the "Great Bellows" operates: [1] Bottom board drops, allowing chamber to fill with air through lower valve. [2] Lever and chain lift bottom board, forcing air through upper valve to upper chamber and out through the tuyere. [3] Bottom board is allowed to drop and chamber is refilled. At the same time, upper board drops of its own weight, forcing air from upper chamber through tuyere. A continuous stream of air is ejected while the bellows is in operation.

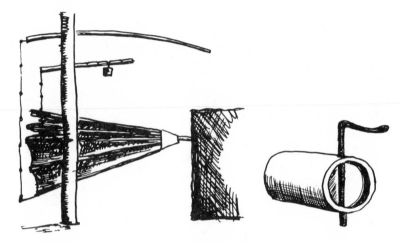

Left: Some smiths controlled the blast by counterweighing the upper board of the bellows. Right: Later smiths resorted to a simple butterfly valve in the tuyere to control the volume of air.

force of the blast. A simple butterfly valve in the tuyere, adopted in later days, serves the same purpose.

There are few variations in the construction of these marvels. They vary in size from 6 or 7 feet for large forges to 3 feet for the average blacksmith shop. A good bellows has enough leather so that when both chambers are extended the height of the leather at the back is equal to or greater than the width of the boards at their widest points. Some have both chambers connected to the tuyere, but the better and more efficient ones have only the upper chamber opening into the forge.

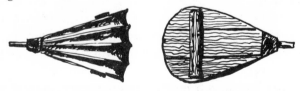

Depth of leather should equal width of bellows

This latter design is better because it prevents "blowback." When the lower chamber is connected to the tuyere and reinflated it sucks in a little inflammable gas from the fire as well as air through the lower valve. Sometimes the gas ignites and explodes in the lower chamber, bursting the leather loose, if not splitting it, and requiring a shutdown for extensive repairs. A well-trained smith with the less-efficient bellows thus guards carefully against the threat of explosion. His warning comes when the lower board descends as far as it goes. If at this time the smith hears a muffled pop, as though a wine cork were being pulled under a cloth, he leaps for the lever and pumps vigorously for a few seconds to expel any gas that may have entered the lower chamber. Blowback can be prevented by lowering the bottom board gently, instead of allowing it to fall by its own weight, or by installing a counterweighted lever to slow its action, but it happens occasionally to even the most diligent worker.

Operating the old-fashioned double-chambered bellows is a comfort and a joy. Some technique is needed to maintain a constant stream of air, but this is soon acquired, enabling one to create a subtle, low-decible, natural music. Blowing the fire causes it to roar mightily, and against this Wagnerian theme can be heard the point and counterpoint of a creaking lever, the thump of lower and upper boards as they come in contact with the immobile middle board, and the muted tapping of felt-padded valves inside the chambers.

As a stage setting for this symphony the fire brightens and sparks from the charcoal fly, dancing up the chimney, while the iron gradually turns a brighter red, then white, until welding heat is reached, and a whole corps of tiny white incandescent sparks, like fleas of Hades, leap from the semimolten iron to perform an airy ballet in the heated air above the fire. No wonder the old-time blacksmith shop was such a popular gathering place in towns and villages. Nowhere else could a bored loafer find such bright, continuous entertainment.

It is recommended that bellows be placed in a corner of the shop whenever possible. This position protects at least one side from having holes punched in the leather by a careless apprentice with a bar of iron. An even safer position is to mount it in a frame hung from the ceiling, with a long pipe going to the tuyere and a long rope or chain attached to the lever for floor-level operation.

Some maintenance is needed on a bellows. When the leather gets old and stiff the smith washes it off with a damp cloth and liberally applies neat's-foot oil. Occasionally the

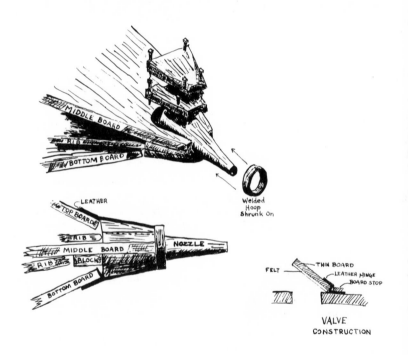

Bellows construction

caulking between the joints of the wood boards has to be replaced to avoid loss of air pressure. Otherwise a good bellows lasts literally for generations if protected from damp and rot.

The great bellows was never entirely replaced by more-modern devices, but it was displaced to some extent by the rotary squirrel-cage blowers which appeared in the latter half of the nineteenth century. While the blower was the most modern machine available for creating a stream of air when it was invented, actually it reverted back to the earliest, the fan. It is nothing more than a series of small fans mounted in a circle to blow air constantly through the tuyere. They are used widely in air-conditioning units, home and automobile heaters, vacuum cleaners, and portable hair dryers. In fact, a hair dryer can easily be converted to use with a small forge in any home workshop.

A blower is not nearly so colorful as a bellows, but it is efficient and it had the advantage after 1890 of being operated by electric power. Even then, though, many smiths preferred hand operation to effect better control of the blast.

Blowers were homemade in rare instances. Factory-made

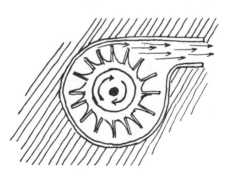

The most modern air machine, the rotary blower, is merely a series of fans mounted on a wheel

blowers were used in the blacksmith shop at the Carlisle Indian School in Pennsylvania, when Bird Partridge, a North Carolina Cherokee, went there to learn blacksmithing. When Bird returned to his home on Goose Creek in the Smoky Mountains, however, he had no money to buy a blower. Undeterred by lack of capital, he made his own blower out of hand-sawn boards and thin sheet iron, and it worked well enough for him to make a living at his forge.

Sumpter Brown, a skillful professional smith in Cobb County, Georgia, improved his factory-made blower with the insight that has characterized master smiths from the beginning of the craft. First of all, he electrified his hand-operated blower when he could not find a helper. Then, needing a way to instantly stop the blast when doing certain types of work, he designed a cover that fitted tightly over the intake hole in the blower casing. Fastened to a lever that pivoted from a screw mounted on the casing, this cover is adjustable to control the blast to a delicate degree or to shut it off instantly. He used his native intelligence to determine that no more air can come out of the tuyere than is allowed to go into it. In doing so he demonstrated the type of simple, pragmatic thinking which has always made the blacksmith a superior craftsman in developing necessary techniques.

A tub of water is necessary in every smithy, of course, to cool hot iron so that it can be handled or tempered. Water is made readily available by the slack tub, sometimes called the slake tub, which strongly indicates the good, honest Anglo-Saxon derivation of the term. Sometimes a special chamber is built into the end of the forge and kept filled with water. More often the slack tub is half of a great whiskey or wine barrel located between the forge and the anvil; its rim is a handy place to store horseshoes.

The smith who makes or sharpens tools, or makes springs or cutting weapons, needs tempering baths and special slack tubs. Brine and oil cool steel a little more slowly than plain water, providing a more delicate temper. Brine is used for larger pieces such as axes, and oil for small knives and springs. The brine, of course, is mixed in the shop and generally carries a high proportion of salt. The oil used was whale oil in the nineteenth century, and before that usually refined tallow, kept warm and liquid in a jar or a bucket placed near the heat of the forge. Later, of course, petroleum oil, even motor oil, has been used.

For tempering the old-time smith often used a double tempering bath consisting of a small tub filled with brine, fastened between two sticks, which in turn rested on the rim of a larger tub of clear water. The brine was used for tempering, the clear water for rinsing off the salt from the steel immediately after tempering. Brine did not freeze in cold weather, but a careful smith inserted a 4-inch-square stick in the clear water to keep the barrel from bursting in freezing weather.

A double tempering bath. The small tub is filled with brine, the large tub with clear stagnant water.

Also in the forge area is that other traditional and essential piece of equipment, the ringing anvil. "Ringing" is not an idle description, for unless the steel face of the anvil rings as a bell when struck it is often considered inferior.

Anvils used to be available in a large range of sizes, expressed in weight, from 25 pounds for craft shops where small tools were made, to 800 pounds or more for the shops that specialized in extra-heavy work. The usual size was from 100 to 200 pounds. In 1975 there are no known anvil manufacturers in America. Fine anvils are available, however, in Germany, England, Sweden and other countries.

In one form or another the anvil has been part of the blacksmith's shop equipment since the beginning of the craft. Archaeological studies show that the Vikings sometimes used a large, flat-topped stone as an anvil.

But by the seventeenth or eighteenth century it had become somewhat standardized in several shapes, all based on the prototype "mousehole" anvil, so named because of the hole put in its stubby waist for handling purposes. Cheap anvils were forged from pure iron, but these did not hold up. As early as medieval times good anvils were made of wrought iron with a steel face, of from ½ to 1½ inches, welded onto the iron and tempered to a straw color. The bonding of steel and iron prevented the hard face from cracking.

About 1848 in America a means was devised for casting anvils and welding a steel face to the casting while it was still molten. These anvils, however, did not ring. While apparently they were quite serviceable, many smiths disdained them because of their lack of a traditional musical quality.

Old illustrations indicate that many of the anvils of medieval times were almost square. Some of them had a horn or beak projecting from one or both sides and others did not. For general forging during any period, though, it seems that a horn or some substitute for it must have been necessary for

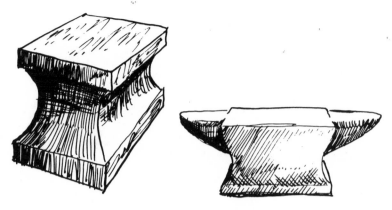

Left: A medieval square anvil. Right: A double-horned anvil used by medieval armorers.

shaping curves. It seems, also, that armorers, especially the craftsmen who made helmets and plate armor, must have had special curved anvils, sometimes listed as "maides," on which to shape the intricate forms of a steel suit.

Except for certain small stake anvils, this basic tool of the smith was usually purchased from special anvil makers' shops. Max Segal, who worked with the great Samuel Yellin, recalls that in his family's seventh-generation blacksmith shop in Poland, all of the tools except the anvil were made in the shop. Anvil making, however, required forges and trip-hammers far larger than was required in regular shops, hence the reason for buying them from an outside source.

Appropriately for such an ancient tool, the anvil has its own nomenclature. The forged iron that constitutes the mass and weight is called the "body." It is shaped to a narrow rectangle on top, called the "face," which extends to a smaller rectangle, called the "table," which further extends into the cone-shaped pointed "horn." Its square "heel," or "tail," is the portion of the face opposite the horn that protrudes over

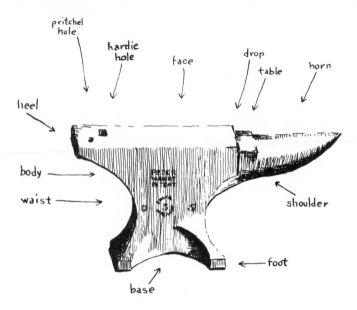

The London Anvil—the most popular form since the eighteenth century

the "base." At the bottom the iron is spread by forging into the base, and this is further extended in each corner into the "feet." Between its top and base it is shaped into a narrow portion, called the "waist." The base generally contains a hollow space about 4 inches in diameter, penetrating into the iron about 3 inches. Some anvils also have a 1-inch hole in front and in back of the waist into which a bar can be inserted for carrying or handling.

The rectangular steel face is welded to the top of the wrought-iron body in a position that leaves a ½- to 1-inch drop from the top of the face to the top of the table. Opposite the horn the face is punched with a hardie hole, from ½- to 1-inch square, depending on the size of the anvil, and a round pritchel hole, usually ½ inch in diameter. All anvil tools, from hardie to halfpenny snub-end scroll, fit into the hardie hole; the round hole is for punching or making boltheads or for inserting a rod around which hot iron can be bent when hammering over the horn is unsuitable.

Appropriate to such an ancient tool is the method of marking the weight of English and American anvils, a method so illogical that we can be sure it came unaltered from the ancient Anglo-Saxon standards of weights and measures. Each anvil is stamped on the waist with three numbers. The first designates the hundredweight, which, it must be remembered, is 112 pounds. The next number marks quarters of a hundredweight, and the third designates simple pounds, the sum of the interpretation of these three stamped numbers being the weight of the anvil.

For instance, an anvil stamped 1–2–3 weighed 171 pounds: the "1" standing for 112 pounds, the "2" standing for two quarters of 112 pounds, or 56 pounds, and the "3" standing for 3 pounds—total, 171 pounds.

There are several basic designs of anvils, the differences rather minor. Most British and American smiths have always preferred the English or London pattern in various weights. A 100-pound English pattern is about 22-inches long from tip of horn to heel. Its face is 2 ½ inches in width and about 15 inches in length, punched with hardie and pritchel holes. Most have only one horn, but some, called farrier's anvils, have a horn at each end. Smaller farm shops and specialty shops often used stake anvils. These were designed with a sharp point to replace the normal flat base, the point being driven into the log mounting block. Some had a flat face; others had specially shaped faces for special work.

Another pattern popular on the continent is the Lièges design. In overall appearance it is much like the London pattern, but it frequently has only the hardie hole in its face, and only sometimes a pritchel hole. The Lièges pattern, too, is available, with one or two horns or no horns at all.

Any object of iron and steel weighing from 100 to 300

A Lièges Pattern Anvil—found mostly in continental smithies

pounds is practically indestructible, but even anvils must be used carefully and maintained regularly. Blows with too heavy a sledge can break off either horn or heel and greatly limit the usefulness of the anvil. Cheaper ones with a thin steel face of only ⅜ inch or less will, after constant pounding, become swaybacked in the middle and useless for precision work. Even the good ones on occasion develop uneven faces, or have the corners of the face chipped or rounded.

When this happened in the early days a careful smith dressed the anvil face on his own forge to restore its pristine quality. It took an hour or more, depending on the size of the anvil, to bring it to the orange heat necessary for dressing face and corners with hammer and flatter. Some smiths during this process delayed hardening the face until they had filed and rounded the corners in certain areas for special uses such as forging the edges of chisels. Then another hour or more in the forge brought the face to the cherry-red heat for hardening under a stream of water, and the smith was in business again.

After 1845 there were a number of anvil manufacturers in America and in Europe. The Eagle, Columbian, Haye and Budden, Swedish American, Peter Wright, and a few other brand names became symbols of dependability to nineteenth-century American smiths. Before 1845, when anvils were first manufactured in New Jersey, all American smiths procured anvils made in England, Sweden and Germany. These may have varied in cost and quality, but all were of forged wrought iron with a steel face welded onto it. Diderot illustrates the welding of the face onto the body of the anvil in his *Encyclopedia*.

This traditional method of making anvils was followed in England, Sweden and Germany until recently. Modern technology and metallurgy, however, have allowed anvil manufacturers to cast or forge whole anvils of steel which may be hardened and tempered as readily as the face of a wrought iron anvil. Such anvils are of high quality, in function and ringing.

An anvil is usually mounted on a huge section of log

Relative position of anvil and forge in most shops. The anvil may be placed closer to the forge when small work predominates.

fairly close to the forge. For working on small articles it is better to have it placed close to the forge, so no heat is lost in moving work to the anvil. For large, heavy pieces, however, which hold heat for a long time, the anvil is placed farther away to provide plenty of elbowroom.

There is a rule of thumb for determining the mounted anvil's height. The smith should have the face of the anvil reach the knuckles of his hands as they hang by his side. This height allows him to use the power of gravity and the full weight of his hammer on his work without straining and without bending his back. Even the arm holding the work by tongs can be held in a natural position without strain, thus providing better control in turning or moving the work as forging proceeds. When a shop's work requires a great deal of punching or heavy hammering by a helper, however, the anvil is mounted at a lower height, to receive the full value of the downward momentum of the helper's sledgehammer. Gen-

The top of the anvil should reach the smith's knuckle

erally the smith places the anvil with the horn at his left and the heel at his right.

While not of critical importance, there is difference of opinion in the type of log used for mounting the anvil. Some old smiths maintained that elm was best because it was difficult to split, while others swore in the solidity of post oak. Some would have the log rest on the floor, while others thought the log butt should be buried at least 2 feet in the ground. Most used a natural section of log with the anvil held in position by large nails at the feet, but those with a sense of orderliness often squared the log to the exact dimensions of the anvil's base.

A few smiths eschew logs and heavy timbers completely and make their anvil stands from four heavy planks joined into a narrow, truncated pyramid, designed so that only the feet of the anvil rest on the four corners of the stand. Modern machine shops equipped with anvils often mount them on a

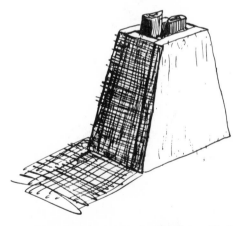

An anvil stand made of two-inch planks nailed together. The anvil is held in position by the two semi-cylindrical boards, its feet resting only on the corners of the stand.

steel stand which is bolted to the floor. Really, the only principle involved is to provide the anvil with the solidity of the earth or a building. When an anvil is not mounted solidly, when it bounces slightly or wobbles with each blow of the hammer, part of the force of the blow is lost.

Often when logs are used the smith will tack a strip of leather around the circumference of the log to hold his hammers and punches and other tools needed quickly.

In the old days the anvil was used on holidays such as the Fourth of July, or Christmas Day in the South, for a purpose far removed from blacksmithing. Men still alive today can remember as boys the excitement of "blowing" the anvil in the street in front of the blacksmith shop on a gala day. Two anvils were needed for this operation. One was laid on the street face down, and the cavity in its base was filled with black powder. Another anvil was placed rightside up on the

Blowing the anvil

base of the first so that the cavities of the two coincided. A fuse was then placed between the two and was lit while the expectant boys and men, standing at a good distance, watched with eager anticipation as a small cloud of smoke indicated the progress of the fire through the fuse. Then suddenly there was a roar, a flash of orange flame, and a cloud of white, odoriferous smoke. Ringing merrily the upper anvil was thrown several feet into the air before falling to the ground. The whole exciting business was then repeated as long as the supply of black powder lasted.

Blowing the anvil will not be successful if the bases of the two anvils used do not fit tightly together. Any space whatever between the two must be tightly caulked with clay or mud to insure an exciting event. Otherwise the explosion merely blows smoke and flame out the crack, while the top anvil remains inert.

4.

HAND-TOOLS AND OTHERS

The blacksmith's basic shop equipment, his forge and bellows, anvil and slack tub, are practically immovable and are used only in a stationary position. These tools, however, are of no use without the endless number of other tools, mostly hand tools, which a blacksmith collects or makes for himself to fit a variety of needs over the years.

First of all, the smith needs some special tools for his forge—pokers, shovels, and rakes. Pokers usually are no more than ¼-inch rods with a ring handle formed on one end. If used to test the surface of iron while welding, the poker may be a ⅛-inch rod drawn out to a fine point on the end. Ordinary pokers may have the end flattened for 3 or 4 inches, and many have the end drawn out to a blunt point and bent at a right angle 1 inch or 1½ inches from the end. For brazing, the smith's poker is flattened and dished for 2 inches on the end to form a "spoon," used to apply brass or copper filings to the surface of the iron to be joined with brazing.

Most smiths keep a small shovel at the forge side to rearrange the coal or to pack the coal by pounding it with the flat of the shovel. A rake, merely a poker with a crossbar and three or four teeth, or sometimes a flat crossbar, is also convenient for smoothing the surface of the fire or piling coal, especially charcoal, over the top of a piece of iron to be welded.

When anthracite coal is used, the smith requires a watering can. Some use a regular garden sprinkling can, but most make their own out of a tin cylinder, with a thickly perforated bottom and a wire bail. This may be filled from the slack tub, and the water from the perforations may be directed where needed on the fire to wet the coal for packing, or to control the extent of the fire for special purposes. It may also be used to shrink wagon tires in the absence of a slake trough.

In effect the blacksmith's anvil is his workbench and as such has an endless variety of ancillary tools needed for shaping, cutting, and bending hot iron. These are known as "anvil tools." In the old days they were made by the blacksmith himself, and as each smith had special needs from time to time he made special tools that sometimes defy identification and motive. They are linked with the anvil only by the common occurrence of a square shank designed to fit into the hardie hole.

Most essential of the anvil tools is undoubtedly the "hardie" itself, or "cutter," an inverted chisel which allows the smith to cut off or split barstock without a helper. There are hot cutters, ground with a sharp edge for cutting hot iron, and cold cutters, sharpened to a more obtuse edge to stand up under cutting cold iron. Hardies are as universal as hammers and anvils in all shops.

Another widely used anvil tool is the "bottom fuller," which, when one thinks about it, is hardly named for its function, to make iron thinner. In appearance a fuller looks like a blunt hardie with a rounded edge. One holds the iron over the fuller and hits it with a heavy hammer, creating a dent, and this is repeated along the length of the stock to be thinned. After fullering, the corrugated surface of the iron is smoothed with the hammer or the flatter. The fuller is also used in shaping, as when a rounded shoulder is being formed. Special fullers are used by specialists such as armorers and cutlers to form blood channels on swords and daggers.

One such fuller is known for some reason as a "cheese

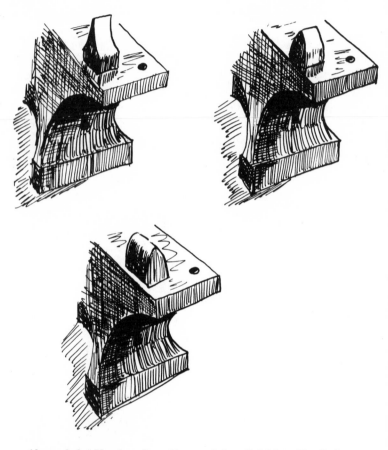

Above left: Hot hardie. Above right: Cold hardie. Below: Bottom fuller.

fuller." It has a wide, semicylindrical face, rather than the wedge-shaped face with rounded edge found on the regular fuller. Decorative-wrought-iron craftsmen and armorers use the cheese fuller for special shaping and dishing rather than the drawing-out process.

The other main group of anvil tools consists of "swages" of infinite size and variety, usually used in sets of bottom and top swages. A well-equipped smithy has a set of round swages for making square rods into round rods in any dimension from ⅛ inch to 1½ inches. There may also be oval swages, square swages, diamond swages, octagonal and hexagonal swages, depending on the type of work in a particular smithy. Special swages are made and used to give a smooth finish to cross welds and T welds, and others are used to save time in scarfing the ends of rods or bars to be welded.

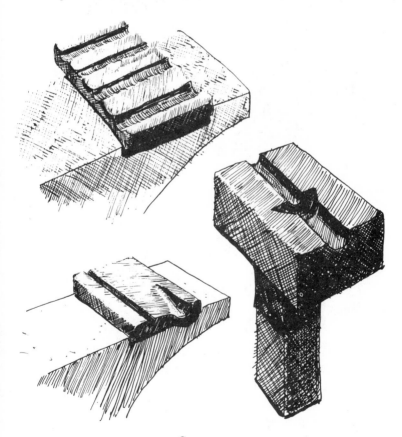

Swages

Very special bottom swages that sometimes fit into the post vise instead of the anvil are the "monkey tool," for forming tenon shoulders on a rod, and "nail-" and "boltheaders," for forming nail- and boltheads. In the twentieth century swaging, in combination with powerful automatic steam, hydraulic, and pneumatic hammers, has become the only means of forging hammers, axes, chisels, tongs, and other tools.

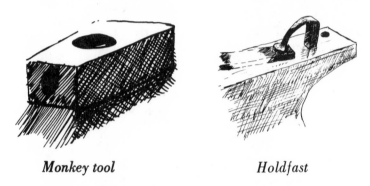

Monkey tool   *Holdfast*

Additional anvil tools are legion in number, form, and use. Some are merely miniature anvils with curved surfaces for gentle bending; others hold a slight circular depression for finishing the rough spread ends of rivets. The halfpenny snub-end scroll, the leaf tool, and the crimp tool are used by British wrought-iron artists for their delicate scrollwork. Also nearly every good smith makes himself an "anvil beak," or "bick," no less than a miniature horn that fits into the hardie hole. A square shanked "holdfast," which jambs into the hardie hole, is useful for holding a piece of hot iron when both hands are needed to work it. The "fork," in various sizes, is used for bending rods or bars.

Good smiths, the real professionals, take good care of their tools, especially the anvil, about the only piece of equip-

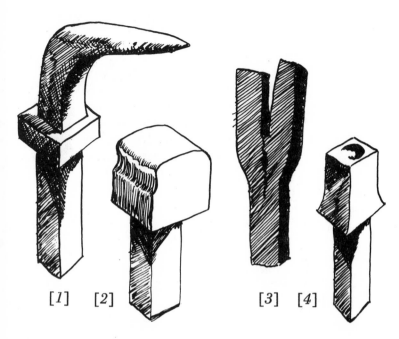

[1] *Anvil bick.* [2] *Halfpenny snub end scroll.* [3] *Fork,* [4] *Rivet header.*

ment they can not make themselves. While the table of an anvil is used for splitting or cutting with a chisel, it soon becomes so rough from repeated cuts by the chisel that it can not be used for delicate work without marring the work. The careful smith generally has a "chisel plate," no more than a flat ⅛-inch-thick piece of iron plate bent to fit over the anvil face to protect it from the chisel. Of course, a chisel plate is easily made and can be quickly reversed or replaced when its surface becomes too rough for fine work.

Possibly one of the worst disadvantages a smith suffers is the limitation of having only two hands when another is needed to hold stock for quick work, such as welding, before the heat is lost. To make up for this lack a well-equipped shop has some special racks and stands, either standing close

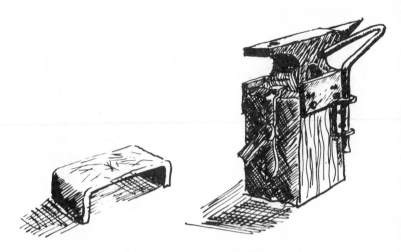

Left: Chisel plate. Right: Anvil block with support.

to the anvil or mounted on the anvil block. Sometimes such auxiliary devices are made of a stout bar mounted to the anvil lock and fully adjustable as to height and distance from the anvil. Then, in preparation for lap welding two separate pieces, for instance, the smith adjusts his stand carefully. When his two pieces are brought to welding heat at the same time, both are taken from the fire. One piece is supported by the rack, with its heated end on the anvil and the tongs dropped. Then the smith can pick up his conveniently placed hammer while holding the second piece with another pair of tongs and join the twain before the sparks stop jumping. No doubt thousands of blacksmiths over the ages made and used many ingenious devices for this sort of work, and probably some interesting inventions regretfully have been lost in the limbo of prehistory. Movable stands, which hold a long piece of stock while one end is being heated in the forge, are known as "blacksmith's helpers."

Another piece of equipment which stands on the floor near the forge is the "mandrel." It is no more than a cone of cast iron some 2- to 4-feet high on which the smith shapes circular

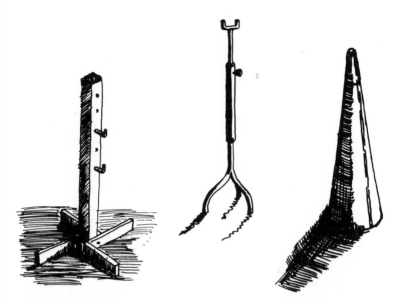

Left: Wooden blacksmith's helper. Center: Steel blacksmith's helper. Right: Mandrel.

objects such as nose rings for oxen and hub bands for wagon wheels. The better mandrels have a slot running from point to base on one side into which the tongs can be inserted while holding the piece of work. Some also have a removable tip with a shank that can be taken off the mandrel and placed in the leg vise or hardie hole for convenience.

No less essential than his anvil is the blacksmith's "hammer." Any halfway decently equipped shop has a bewildering choice of hammers of every shape and weight. Some are hard and some are soft, and while most are made of iron and steel, some are made of copper and lead for special work.

The blacksmith instinctively learned the physicist's formula "force equals mass multiplied by acceleration" long before physics was a developed science. By controlling his mass through the use of hammers of different weights and controlling his acceleration through the applied strength of

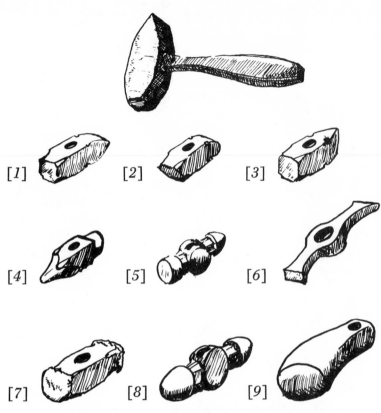

The hammer and types of hammerheads: [1] cross pein, [2] tool dresser, [3] straight pein, [4] chisel makers, [5] ball pein, [6] double faced, [7] soft, [8] round faced, [9] file makers.

his arm, the smith is able to summon the force for whatever job is required, whether it is welding a 1000-pound ship's anchor or forming a delicate iron leaf for a gate.

Probably the most frequently seen hammer in most shops is the 4-pound cross-pein hammer, a mass of iron square or octagonal in cross section, punched in the middle to receive a hickory or ash handle, with a flat face on one end and a wedge perpendicular to the handle on the other. Some preferred the same weight hammer made with a straight pein, that is, the axis of the wedge is parallel to the axis of the handle.

In the old days, before 1850, this hammer, like most others, was hand-forged of wrought iron with a tempered-steel plate welded to the face. Generally it could be used for several years before the face cracked, usually into three wedge-shaped pieces if properly tempered. When this happened the smith replaced the steel face and had, for all practical purposes, a new hammer. After 1860, in increasing numbers, the smith bought factory-made hammers of steel throughout. They were somewhat tougher than the old variety, but a few misplaced blows chipped the edges of the face, and the smith then had to suspend operation long enough to remove the hammer handle and dress the face by heating it, reshaping the edges, tempering it in brine, and replacing the handle.

Not all hammers have tempered-steel faces. Some are kept soft for special work, such as repairing cutlery and weapons, when a hard face will mar the already-finished surface, requiring extra work to smooth it.

While a 4-pound hammer seems to provide the best force with the least acceleration on most jobs, no two jobs are ever alike. As a consequence, for each job the smith selects the proper hammer, ranging from a ½-pound leaf hammer to a 35- or 40-pound two-handed sledge wielded by an apprentice.

Some of his hammers have ball peins, a type still commonly used today in machine shops and garages, which range in weight from about 1½ pounds to 3½ pounds. Others of his hammers are double-faced of different weights; and still others are peculiarly shaped for special jobs, such as those with angled peins or angled faces for dressing chisels, or with an angled face for making files. The point is that the hammer, considered primitive man's first devised tool, the first extension of his hand, is shaped and adapted in the smithy to all sorts of special and peculiar uses more varied than surgeons' scalpels. In this day of mass production the variety of hammers available has dropped considerably, but a good smith, equipped with his fire, his anvil, one hammer, and iron, can make his own hammers for any use.

Since in the hands of a skilled smith the hammer becomes a precision instrument controlled by coordination of eye and muscle, hammer handles are as important as hammerheads. The olden smith usually made his own, out of hickory or ash or maple in America, and out of ash in Britain and Europe. Handles are made to fit the smith's hand and the peculiarities of his arm action. Some are thin for small hands and others thick for large hands. Some are short and some are long. Sometimes light hammers are given long handles to provide more leverage, or heavy one-hand hammers are given short handles to make it easier to lift them. Any hammer over 5 pounds is usually considered a sledge requiring two hands to wield, and of course all sledges are equipped with handles 30-inches long or longer. Heavy sledges, incidentally, are usually the province of the apprentice, who strikes where the master smith tells him to strike in forming or welding heavy work.

Any modern full-time smith, however, will acquire a mechanical "power hammer" of from 50 to 200 pounds force, still manufactured in America. It saves time and doesn't talk back.

It is safe to assume that the first blacksmith devised some sort of tongs, perhaps from sticks of greenwood. Undoubtedly tongs were forged of iron early in the game, and by the Middle Ages they were made in as many or more different forms as the hammer. Tongs vary in length from 15 inches for those used in light work to perhaps 36 inches for large two-handed tongs used to lift heavy pieces from the fire, the extra length being needed to keep the smith's hands away from the searing heat of white-hot metal. Most variation is found, however, in

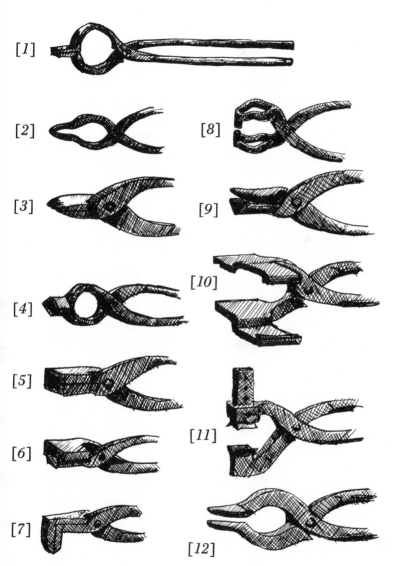

Tongs: [1] *straight lipped,* [2] *pickup,* [3] *straight lipped,* [4] *bolt,* [5] *box,* [6] *semi-box,* [7] *side,* [8] *hammer,* [9] *wedge,* [10] *side,* [11] *adjustable,* [12] *round nosed.*

85

the shapes of the jaws, the short section forward of the rivet which holds the two tongs together and allows them to pivot.

For general work the jaws are straight, like a pair of pliers, or the jaws are curved from the lips to the rivet. This curve, which forms a circle when the jaws are shut, provides a springy tension that allows the lips to hold more steadily; it also allows the lips to be easily adjusted for different thicknesses of metal, again to improve the grip.

Straight-lipped tongs, however, simply do not grip a round surface, nor do they grip a large flat surface tightly enough. Therefore the smith, typically adapting his tools to his needs, always has a number of tongs, some made with curved lips, or nose, to hold round stock, some with squared lips to hold square stock. Others have T-shaped lips with vertical extensions at each end to pick up heavy rectangular stock.

Special tongs are made for making hammers, axes, and other eyed tools. Usually these are designed to fit into the eye vertically so that the smith can hold the work tightly while he turns it from one side to the other in shaping blade or face on the anvil. In other cases the lips are offset to one side to grasp a long piece of stock that extends beyond the rivet, parallel to the handles. Offset lips, too, are used to hold the blades of mattocks or adzes while being dressed. In the latter days of blacksmithing, almost every country smith had several pairs of plow tongs, tongs with one lip flat and the other formed with a downward extension, made to fit in the bolt hole of a plow blade to hold it securely while being sharpened. The general types of tongs are straight, box, semi-box, side, hammer, bolt, wedge, and plow.

The use of some peculiarly shaped tongs found in long-abandoned shops will be conjectural for all time, except that one can know some long-dead smith shaped them that way so that he could turn out more precise work on some article.

A few smiths make adjustable tongs with replaceable jaws, but most adjust tongs the easy way: they merely heat the jaws red, pick up the stock intended for the next job, and hammer the lips of the tongs precisely to fit the stock. Such instant adjustment is necessary for safety and efficiency. Nothing is more exasperating than to strike a red-hot iron that is not gripped securely and to see it fly off the anvil and land in a pile of shavings which catch fire, or under a tangled pile of scrap iron, or perhaps on the smith's hand or arm, leaving an excruciating burn.

Smiths who do decorative ironwork have a special pair of tongs called "bow tongs," with rounded jaws which clamp collars on gates and fences without damaging them.

Possibly the simplest of the smith's tools are "chisels" and "punches." He needs quite a number of these for punching holes of various sizes and for cutting, splitting, and carving iron.

Punches and chisels, along with "flatters," "top fullers," and "top swages," are often mistaken by the uninitiated collector for a form of hammer because they are eyed to receive handles. Handles for all set tools, however, are for keeping the hand away from hot metal and for preventing being accidentally hit by the hammer. As a consequence, they are not formed or fitted with the care of hammer handles. Frequently they are made of an unsmoothed piece of sapling or a broken wheel spoke.

In some cases the handles for set tools of all descriptions are made by wrapping a ¼-inch iron rod or a withe of oak, hickory, or witch hazel around a groove forged in the tool. These very flexible handles keep the blow of a heavy hammer from vibrating the handle uncomfortably. Tools with this sort of handle are termed "rodded" tools.

Punches are easier and quicker to use than drills and are used whenever possible, almost always on red-hot iron, but occasionally on cold sheet iron when the stock is thin enough.

Punches come in two basic forms, handled and unhandled. Those without handles are usually at least 2-feet long, so that the hand grasping it is far away from the hot iron. Usually they have a section of tempered steel welded to the face of the punch. They are available in a number of sizes ranging from about ¼ inch up to 1½ inches in ¼-inch sizes. Most are tapered so that as they are driven through the iron the hole is slightly enlarged, which makes them easy to withdraw. Whenever close tolerance is needed in a punched hole it is just punched a bit smaller than necessary and then reamed to a precise size. This was especially true before the advent of post drills and twisted-drill bits after the 1860s. When these mechanical advances were universally adopted the smith forsook his punches for the drill when accurately sized holes were required.

Part of the equipment of a smith who makes decorative items, such as cooking tools, lighting appliances, footscrapers,

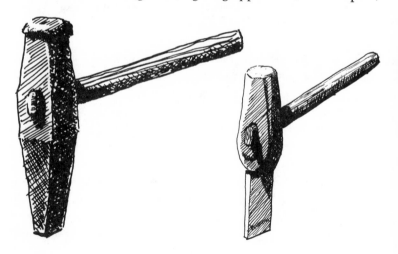

Handled punches

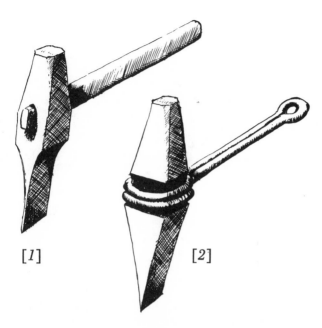

Chisels: [1] *handled,* [2] *rodded.*

and so on, is a set of special punches of diverse shapes. These make heart-shaped holes, square- and diamond-shaped holes, and holes shaped like arrowheads or fleurs-de-lis. Often the work of a particular smith can be identified by the special designs of punches he used job after job during his career. Most of the special punches are used in conjunction with a punch plate containing holes that fit the shape of the punch.

No less varied than punches are the chisels, also called "sets," needed in a good shop. There are usually a number of cold sets with short shanks and obtuse edges to cut cold iron. Hot sets with handles, or with long shanks and sharp edges, are used exclusively for cutting hot iron. Hot and cold sets are made in all widths from about ½ inch to 2 inches. As with punches, hot and cold sets have tempered-steel edges, or, in most cases after 1860, they are made entirely of carbon steel.

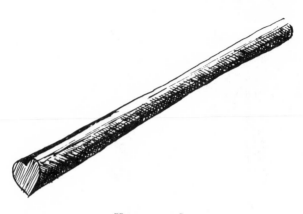

Heart punch

Not only are the types of chisels manifold, but the names applied to various types are sometimes so different as to confuse even the knowledgeable smith. For instance, a cold set is also known as a "cold chisel," a "cutting chisel," or a "flogging chisel." "Cape chisels" are known as "key chisels," while round cape chisels are sometimes known as "gouges," all of them designed essentially to cut grooves in iron as wood chisels and gouges cut in wood. "Chipping chisels" are ordinarily rather wide-bladed and often equipped with handles. They are used to smooth stock or to chip away unevenness after a weld. Hot chisels or hot sets are also called "splitting chisels." Of all things, there is even a "cow-mouthed chisel" for carving round corners in a cavity in a cast-iron or wrought-iron block.

As with punches and anvil tools, there is no limitation to types of chisels, and there are only a few general rules in their overall design. Any smith can create a new type of chisel for a new use, keeping in mind that cold chisels cut better when the shank is short, no more than about 7-inches long, and that handled hot sets need a rounded butt end to concentrate the force of the hammer down through the body of the chisel to its edge.

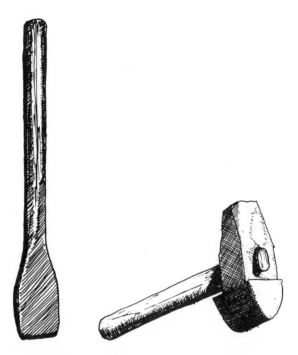

Left: Small fuller. Right: Top fuller.

Much like a chisel in appearance is a "small fuller." This is a rod of tool steel about 1-foot long, shaped on one end to a rounded edge to serve the same purpose as the lower fuller. Its edge is never more than 1-inch wide, for it is used to fuller small stock when drawing it out to smaller size and to make neat shoulders for a projection.

For bigger work the large "top fuller" is used. This weighs about 3½ pounds, has an edge 2- to 3-inches wide, and is equipped with a handle. It is used for exactly the same purpose as the small fuller, but on larger stock.

A companion piece to the fuller is the "flatter," or "slick." By the very nature of its shape and function the fuller leaves iron somewhat corrugated. This roughness is smoothed to some extent with hammering, and then the flatter is used.

91

It looks as though it should be called a "flatter." Like many punches and chisels it has a handle, and resembles a hammer to the ignorant, but its face is much larger than that of a hammer, being usually about 3-inches square with a slightly rounded surface, and it is made of tempered steel welded to an iron head. In use its face is placed on the hot rough iron and is then struck with a sledge by an apprentice. As the iron is moved following each blow of the hammer the surface becomes as smooth as though it had been produced by a rolling mill. The rounded surface eliminates the chance of an impression from the edges of the face.

Flatter

A few expert smiths can get the same smooth effect with a hammer, making the iron look as though it has been planed and sanded when they are through. Most cannot, however, and the battered heads of most slicks now found by collectors indicate that this tool was frequently used.

Similar to the flatter in appearance is the "set hammer," misnamed and often wrongly identified. Some look like a hammer with a broad face, and some look like a flatter with a small face. They are used to shape a neat shoulder in iron, and they are struck on the back, just as other set tools. Their faces are flat instead of having the rounded face of the flatter,

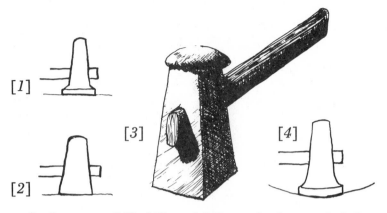

Set hammers: [1], [2], *and* [3] *are flat bottomed.* [4] *is curved bottomed.*

and it is by this small difference that they are often identified. They are equipped with handles usually, as are other set tools.

Lower swages have been described among the anvil tools, and most lower swages, pronounced and sometimes spelled "swedges," had their counterparts in upper swages. They, too, are set tools, each with a handle.

Often a blacksmith whose work is fairly general equips his shop with a set of upper swages, or makes them himself, and substitutes a universally useful "swage block" for the lower swages. He is not qualified to make this tool himself, but he can make a wooden pattern and have it cast at the nearest iron foundry.

Swage blocks are generally 2 ½- to 3-inches thick and anywhere from 6- to 18-inches square, depending upon the versatility required. Usually two of the sides are serrated with semicylindrical depressions ranging from ⅛ inch to 2 inches in diameter. When the block is placed on the anvil, or on a separate wooden block or stand, these depressions are used to shape round cape chisels or used in place of lower swages.

The remaining two sides of the cast-iron block are usually

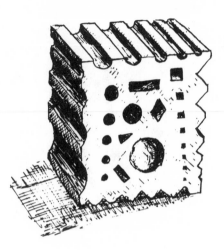

Swage block

devoted to V-shaped depressions of successively larger sizes which serve as lower swages for shaping square stock. Sometimes, however, depending on the needs or whims of the smith, the edges provide half-ovals, half-rectangles, half-octagons or hexagons, or half of any special shape a particular smith may need.

There is no waste of space on the flat sides, either. They are pierced with all sizes and shapes of holes—round, square, rectangular, heart-shaped, whatever—to provide a precise variety far beyond that offered by the pritchel and hardie holes in the anvil. Such holes go entirely through the mass of cast iron, but often on both sides the swage block has semispherical or semiegg-shaped depressions for shaping ladle and spoon bowls, for in eighteenth-century America and Europe the smith provided these items to other craftsmen and households.

Toward the end of the eighteenth century, decorative wrought ironworkers in England began to use special swages, or "dies," to speed production of leaf and flower finials for bars in fancy fences and gates. Before the adoption of dies it might have taken a master smith half a day to shape one iocanthus leaf properly and to his satisfaction, since it required precise forging with special hammers and many heats. After the introduction of dies the smith could, of course, turn out a leaf in one heat. Production was increased, but the hammered sculptured beauty of real handwork was lost, foreshadowing the stiff sameness of machine production.

What a pity, however, that dies, however efficient, sent into oblivion such a delightfully named device as the half-penny snub-end scroll!

Belonging to the swage family, though not really set tools, are "drifts" and nailheaders.

Drifts, in effect, are internal one-piece swages used to furnish proper shape and finish to the eyes of hammers, axes, adzes, tomahawks, and other eyed tools. So simple are they that today a collector may well pass them over as unfinished pieces of scrap iron. Some are almost round, some oval, some elliptical, and some rectangular, depending on the shape the smith who made them wished to give the eyes in other tools he made. They always have a short taper at one end, the end struck by the hammer, and a long taper on the

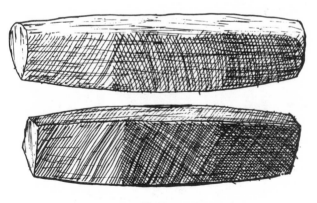

Drifts

end inserted into the partially formed eye. In common with decorative punches, their shapes often identify an individual smith's handiwork, particularly in the case of tomahawks made for the Indian trade. Usually drifts are made of hard, but not brittle, tempered steel with a fine finish, to make it easier to drive them through an eye, and to furnish a smooth finish on the inside of an eye.

Nailheaders and boltheaders were found in practically every country or city forge before the end of the eighteenth century, after which they began to disappear in America because handmade nails could be bought more cheaply from Europe at the time. Before then, though, and before the introduction of cut nails about 1790, most blacksmiths kept nail- and boltheaders in a variety of sizes for producing anything from large bridge spikes to tiny upholstery tacks.

A nailheader is made of a bar of steel forged with a raised portion at one or both ends. Most are about 6- or 8-inches long and perhaps 1-inch wide, with raised portions about 1-inch deep and the strip connecting them ½-inch thick. The raised portions are pierced with a tapered square punch that starts at the bottom of the header and projects through its top to a point where the cross section of the punch matches the size of the square nails to be headed. The top or rounded side of the punched hole is shaped to form the nailhead; it has an inverted pyramidal depression for horseshoe nails, a slight rounded depression for roseheaded nails, and a flat surface for tacks and broadheaded nails. With the variety of sizes and types of heads needed on handmade nails one can imagine the number of separate nailheaders in a well-equipped blacksmith shop in Colonial times.

There is no difference in principle between nailheaders and boltheaders. In design the boltheader differs only in its straight round hole and the shape of the depression that forms the head. Some bolts, of course, have round heads, some

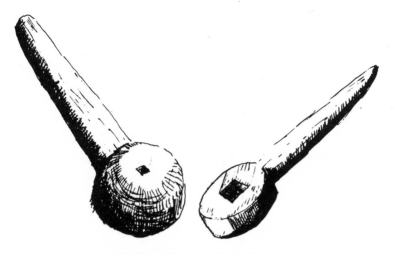

Left: Nail header. Right: Bolt header.

square, and some hexagonal. Most have square shoulders, but some machine bolts have bevel heads, and carriage bolts have round heads and a protruding square shoulder. Whatever type head is needed, the boltheader is made to form it.

Boltheaders and nailheaders generally are used over the pritchel hole, but carriage makers used a header designed to fit into a vise, to take care of longer bolts than the height of the anvil allows.

During the eighteenth century, specialty smiths devised and used a "milling cutter" for squaring and finishing the shoulders of small bolts and screws used in small machines such as gunlocks, doorlocks, and clocks. Made of steel with a hard temper, these milling cutters are no more than a tube with cutting edges radiating from the aperture on one end, in essence a circular file. Held in the vise, these cutters receive the forged screw after a slot has been cut in the head. The smith then rotates the screw with a screwdriver bit held in a brace and gives its shoulder a fine, level finish.

Milling cutters are named for the resemblance of their cutting teeth to the grooves on a millstone. They are con-

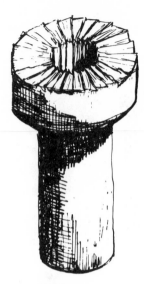

Milling cutter

sidered the first step in the development of that indispensable piece of equipment in modern machine shops, the milling machine, the original of which was observed in France by Benjamin Franklin during the American Revolution. The milling machine, though inspired by blacksmiths, was the only device developed in thousands of years that invaded the smith's domain by mechanically shaping metal without the use of forge and hammer and anvil. It was established in American industry when used by Eli Whitney for the first example of mass production, manufacturing contract muskets for the United States Army early in the nineteenth century.

There are other tools for heading nails and bolts, though they use the same principle. Shops that specialized in nail making, such as Thomas Jefferson's nail manufactory at Monticello, frequently replaced anvil and separate nail-header with a stake anvil resembling a shoe last, made with a fixed hardie for cutting off the nails and pierced in the small end of the anvil's face with a heading hole.

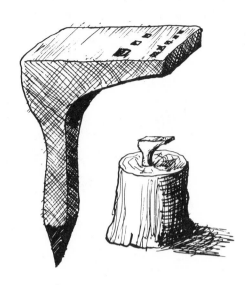

Nail maker's stake anvil

In regard to making bolts and screws, there is more to it than forming. Threads have to be cut on bolt ends and nuts, and threads have to be cut in the holes of plates to receive bolts. All of this work, too, was formerly done by the blacksmith, who maintained a variety of sizes of taps and dies.

There are records of thread-cutting tools in seventeenth-century blacksmith shops; possibly they were used before, although most early tools and weapons used rivets instead of screws.

Most thread cutting since 1900 has been and is done on the screw-cutting lathe, which was invented toward the end of the eighteenth century but not widely used until the second half of the nineteenth century. These were largely unavailable to the country smith, however, and he continued to use hand tools for this purpose.

"Taps" are used to cut threads on the insides of holes, and the blacksmith often made his own in the old days, before the adoption of standard threads. They consist of a threaded tool-steel rod tempered very hard, with three or four flutes cut into the rod to provide a cutting edge to the threads. The shank is squared to fit into a handle for screwing the die into holes as the threads are cut. This tap is then used to make a matching "die," a plate drilled with the proper-size hole in which inside threads were cut. Sometimes the hole in the die is intercepted by three or four smaller holes drilled around its periphery and intruding into the threaded hole so that the threads are also drilled through, again to provide a cutting surface. Instead of the separate dies universally used since the 1870s, most old-time smiths used a "screw plate," made of flat, tempered tool steel, which contained several dies and often had iron handles welded to the ends for easier turning.

Some smiths used a more primitive die called a "jamb plate," which was a flat piece of hardened steel containing several sizes of threaded holes with no cutting edges on the threads. This was merely jambed and twisted on the end of a bolt to cut threads for a short distance. It worked fairly well on small iron screws, but it may be conjectured that for large bolts the ends were heated red hot and the jamb plate was used to compress rather than cut threads.

Punched holes are accurate enough for rivets, but where bolts and screws are used in ironwork the smith usually drills his holes, or cuts a punched hole to specific size with a reamer. Accordingly, every shop should be equipped with one or several drilling devices.

From time immemorial the smith used two ancient-type drills for making small holes in fairly thin plates. One of these was the "pump drill," which is still used by certain primitive tribes. It is merely a rod, usually of wood, with a crude chuck at one end. Above the chuck is a circular flywheel of metal, stone, or wood to provide momentum. Action is begun by a string attached to the top of the rod, with both ends of

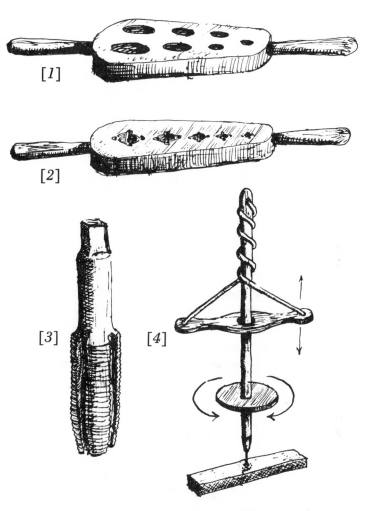

[1] *Jamb plate.* [2] *Screw plate.* [3] *Tap.* [4] *Pump Drill.*

the string attached to the ends of a flat handle board some 6-inches long, pierced at its center so it can move vertically up and down the rod. To operate, the rod is turned until the strings twist tightly around it, drawing the handle board up as high as possible. Then the operator pulls the handle down with force as far as it goes, untwisting the string and turning the rod. The motion is continued by the centrifugal momentum of the flywheel until the string is twisted in the opposite direction and the handle again draws up as high as it may go. The process is then repeated by rhythmic pumping of the handle. The drill point, of course, drills first in one direction and then in another, scraping rather than cutting a hole through the metal plate.

As with many hand tools, the pump drill needs a sense of rhythm which, once acquired, gives an elemental pleasure to its use that is never found in using modern power drills.

The "bow drill," common in many craft shops from earliest times to the nineteenth century, is as simple in operation as the pump drill. It consists of a chuck, usually of wood, attached to a free-turning spindle held by the operator and a plain bow, sometimes with a handle at one end, furnished with a linen or leather string which is wrapped one time around the spindle. It is operated in the same backward and forward motion as the pump drill by moving the bow back-

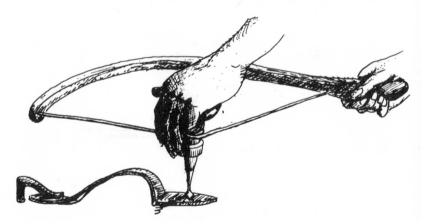

Bow drill

ward and forward horizontally. Since the operator can apply more pressure with it than with a pump drill, the bow drill is used for making holes in fairly thick plate.

For cutting holes with a continuous circular motion the blacksmith employs a regular "brace," exactly like that used by a carpenter or cabinet maker. With this he can drill a sizable hole in fairly thick plate by exerting pressure with his muscles or the weight of his body.

Very heavy work sometimes needs to be drilled, however, and for this the olden smith adopted another ancient principle, that of the Archimedean lever, in combination with the continuous circular motion of the brace, creating the "drill press" or "beam drill."

Simple in principle, but most effective, the beam drill allows almost unlimited pressure to be applied to the drill bit while it is turning. Its beam is a heavy, strong piece of timber, 7- or 8-feet long, often a straight sapling with the bark removed, fastened to an upright pole by a bolt at one

Beam drill, or drill press, in use

end. On the opposite end of the beam is fastened a heavy weight of stone or scrap metal attached with wire or chain or even rope. About 2 feet from the fastened end, a metal socket is mounted to the underside. Into this is fitted a metal brace rounded on one end to fit into the socket and pierced with a square hole at the other end to receive the square shank of a drill bit. Under the beam is a narrow, strongly braced bench, usually with heavy legs set into the floor.

When a heavy piece of metal is placed on the bench and the brace, with drill bit in place, is fitted into the socket, the smith turns the brace while the weighted beam exerts pressure downward. The pressure can be increased by pulling on the weighted end of the beam with one hand while the smith turns the brace with the other.

This primitive drill press was universally used in smithies until about the middle of the nineteenth century, when it was gradually replaced by the "post drill," a well-designed machine attached to a stout post and operated by turning a wheel.

A cast-iron framework gives rigidity to the post drill, and a series of cogwheels operates the ½-inch "chuck," in which drills are inserted and secured by tightening a screw. Downward pressure is exerted through a threaded spindle operated with a ratchet. A cammed lever, actuated by the operating wheel on the side of the frame, turns a cogwheel that threads the spindle downward an adjustable degree with each turn of the wheel. With the advent of the far more convenient post drill, the old beam drill disappeared from the smithy, and the post drill remained, eventually to become converted to an electrically driven drill press in many instances.

Until the post drill was introduced most smiths made their own drill bits of tool steel, most of them being what are called "flat bits," that is, no more than a shank flattened at one end, pointed at an angle of 45 to 60 degrees, and sharpened at an angle of about 30 degrees on the two edges of

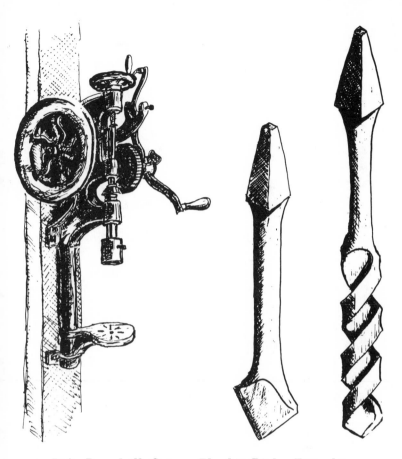

Left: Post drill. Center: Flat bit. Right: Twist bit.

the point. Of course they are tempered very hard, just short of being glassily brittle. The era of the post drill introduced twist-drill bits, but these are difficult to make by hand and old smiths usually bought them, in sizes from $\frac{1}{64}$ inch up to $\frac{1}{2}$ inch. Because of the limitations of the post-drill chuck, which only takes a $\frac{1}{2}$-inch shank, old smiths bought special post-drill bits of all sizes, each with a $\frac{1}{2}$-inch shank. Many, though, later fitted an adjustable chuck into the post-drill chuck to accommodate all sizes of hand-drill bits.

105

About the time the post drill became universally adopted, the blacksmith replaced his pump and bow drills with small "hand drills" and larger "breast drills." The hand drill is a simple mechanism still available in nearly every hardware store. The breast drill, on the other hand, has almost been cast into the limbo of forgotten hand tools. It consists of a metal rod with a revolving adjustable chuck, fitted with a cogwheel and turned by another larger cogwheel mounted on the side of the rod. On the upper end of the rod a breastplate is mounted, while a handle is screwed to the rod almost opposite the larger cogwheel. The breast drill allows a smith to drill holes up to ½ inch in diameter when he places the breast plate on his chest and uses the weight of his body to exert pressure on the drill point, at the same time steadying the whole machine with the side handle.

"Reamers" were also made by the smith in most cases. Unlike machine-made reamers with a number of cutting edges placed radially around the axis, homemade reamers are nothing more than flat forged bars, tapered slightly at one end to facilitate starting in the hole to be enlarged, and filed and honed to furnish two cutting edges with angles of about

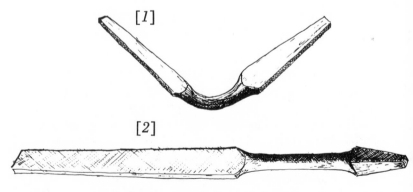

Reamers: [1] *hand,* [2] *flat.*

70 to 75 degrees. The reamer shank is round, sometimes with a square section on the shank end to insert in the chuck of a brace or beam-drill brace. Sometimes the smith may forge a simple reamer on both ends of a rod, bending the rod to a 90-degree angle in the middle and providing himself with two reamers which are turned by hand.

Of course, as with any craftsman, the blacksmith requires some sort of "workbench." The smith's bench is not unlike that of the cabinet maker, coppersmith, or carriage maker in construction, made of heavy planks that will hold steady under pounding and heavy weight. In most cases the bench has one corner fairly close to the forge so that one of the main bench tools, the vise, is handy for red-hot iron. A standard piece of equipment, some form of vise was found in nearly every smithy from ancient times until the present.

Named for the heavy post which sets in the floor, the "post vise" or "leg vise" is made of forged iron. Its jaws, of steel plate welded to iron are 4 to 7 inches wide. The back jaw is a continuation of the post. The front is hinged to the post about 2 feet from the top. With a hinged joint, of course, the post vise does not have vertically parallel jaws, but it holds well nevertheless. Its jaws are closed by a 1-inch screw with a sliding-bar handle inserted in the outside end. At the hinge, a large flat spring mounted between the post and the outside jaw spreads the jaws automatically as the screw is loosened.

In later years the bench might also have a smaller machinist's "bench vise" with vertically parallel jaws for smaller work.

Vises are mounted so that the top edge of the jaws is even with the smith's elbow. This is the proper height to allow him to file evenly and squarely without strain.

Many of the other bench tools are quite similar to the equipment of a modern machine shop, except that before the

Post vise

era of mass production the tools were almost always made by the smith himself. There is a set of "screwdrivers." "Pliers," which in the old days resembled tongs rather than our modern machine-made pliers, are there in various sizes and shapes, including needle-nosed and broad-jawed.

Also there are "clippers" in several sizes, for cutting everything from wire to large bolts. Some of these may have scissor jaws, and from the 1870s on they might have been factory-made with additional power from leverage built in at the pivot point. For clipping nailheads and boltheads they are designed like pincers, with the cutting edge perpendicular

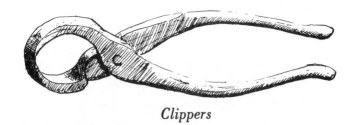

Clippers

to the handles so that the jaws can be easily forced under the nailhead or bolthead.

Since about 1790 most smiths have had a "hacksaw," a more convenient and accurate tool for cutting small bars and rods than the cold chisel, which had been used for that purpose until that time.

Many shops are equipped with "bench shears" for cutting sheet iron up to ¼ inch in thickness and with "shear cutters" mounted on the floor for cutting heavy bars and rods, either cold or hot.

Bench shears are shaped like a huge pair of short-bladed scissors or tin snips, the blades being from 6-inches to 1-foot long. Each blade extends into a heavy handle some 2- to 3-feet long, one of which is bent at one end to a right angle that fits into a hole in the workbench. Often two men are required to operate bench shears: one to hold the sheet metal and the other to close the shears.

Bench shears

109

Leverage supplies the power to operate the shear cutter. It is comprised of two heavy steel blades 12-inches long, with a hard temper, the lower mounted solidly in the floor and the upper pivoting at one end to provide shearing action, again like scissors. There is a hole in the outside end of the lower blade, and a bolt through this provides a pivot for a 6-foot lever that stands perpendicular to the floor. The upper blade has a ½-inch slot some 2- or 3-inches long in its outside end, punched to slant upward toward the outside upper corner. A bolt through this to the handle provides a camming action when the handle is pulled forward, pivoting the upper blade downward to shear the iron placed between the two blades. Sometimes a heavy weight is shrunk onto the upper end of the handle to add the power of momentum to the power of leverage. There are a number of different designs for shear cutters, all operating on the same principle.

Of course, the bench holds a legion of "files," of every shape and size and degree of coarseness, matching in number all the files found in hardware stores in the 1960s and, since the smith can make his own, others of special design for special jobs. While the competent smith can usually put a fine finish on a piece of work with his hammer and flatter, he often must file small pieces to make them fit properly, and on some items it is easier to file than to forge. Francis Parkman, writing of his visit to Naples in the 1840s, described passing the smiths' quarter of that largely medieval city and hearing the industrious screeching of files from every shop up and down the street.

File making requires some special bench tools, including the crooked hammer used for this special work and a leather clamp which holds the file blank flat on the bench while the teeth are being cut. Leonardo da Vinci invented a mechanical file cutter in the sixteenth century, but it was never widely adopted, and files were cut by hand until very recent times.

There are many kinds of files: "rasps" with large pointed

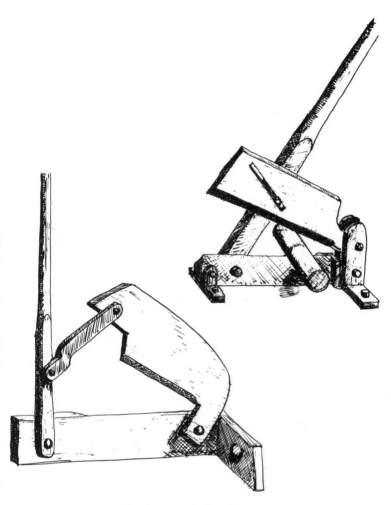

Two types of shear cutters

separate teeth, named with a degree of onomatopoeia; "mill files," so named because the cuts resemble the grooves on a mill wheel; "mill bastard files," possibly named because the slanting cuts follow the direction of the bar sinister in medieval heraldry.

111

The ingenuity of the individual smith in designing and making his own tools reasserted itself after the era of mass production and automatic machinery began. One who visits the few remaining smithies found in small towns is impressed by the small machines designed and built in the shop to circumvent the lack of helpers in the latter days of the trade.

Of course, there is a long tradition of simple machinery in the blacksmith shop, most of it in the large shops that made large articles such as ships' anchors and anvils.

Shops located in piedmont regions or in the mountains were often placed near a stream to take advantage of waterpower. With a stream available the large smithy could harness the water to drive a waterwheel to operate his lathes and his large "trip-hammer" for extremely heavy work.

A trip-hammer operates on the simplest principle. It consists of a large hammerhead weighing 100 or 200 pounds and is mounted on a piece of timber as big around as a man's leg. This in turn is pivoted on a horizontal iron bar between two upright posts sunk in the floor, so that pressing the hammer "handle" downward raises the hammerhead a couple of feet.

Power to depress the "handle" and raise the head is transmitted from the waterwheel with a large drum, either

The principle of the water-operated trip hammer

mounted on an extension of the waterwheel axle or turned by a belt connected to the axle. Four or five pegs mortised in the drum are positioned so that as the drum turns the pegs depress the "handle" and raise the head. As a peg rotates it passes over the end of the "handle," releasing it so that the head can fall downward on an anvil placed directly below it. The same type of trip-hammer was used in the early bloomeries which converted pig iron to wrought iron.

In coastal towns where falling water was unavailable for power, large trip-hammers used to forge anchors and large chains were operated by manpower in the old days. The hammer, in this case, was raised and lowered by two gangs of men pulling alternately on a large rope. The rope, in turn, operated a cog that raised the head a certain distance, then released it to fall on the anvil.

Such a hammer is illustrated in Diderot's *Encyclopedia*. It employs the principle utilized by Leonardo in the design of his horse-operated pile driver. It is quite conceivable that some large smithies in the olden days also used horses instead of men, depending entirely, no doubt, on which was cheaper.

After the introduction of electric motors and small gasoline engines, many smiths made their own trip-hammers to replace an absent apprentice or a striker. Some of these were designed on the principle of the pile driver, but electric power was used to lift a large hammerhead in a frame to a point where it was tripped and it fell onto an anvil. Others made their automatic hammers on the principle of the old water-powered trip-hammers, utilizing a sledge with its handle, the hammerhead rising when the end of the handle was depressed with power from an internal-combustion engine.

Some, like the hammer in Sturbridge Village, were equipped with wooden springs and operated by foot power.

The real professionals, however, of the late nineteenth and the twentieth centuries, purchased power hammers from the Little Giant Company of Mankato, Minnesota, Champion of Lancaster, Pennsylvania, and other makes both foreign and

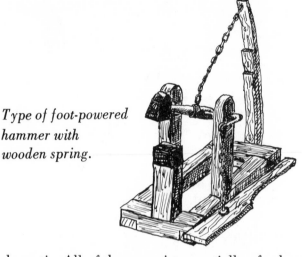

Type of foot-powered hammer with wooden spring.

domestic. All of them consist essentially of a heavy cast iron frame, a heavy flywheel with an eccentric bearing which operates the hammer and a treadle clutch for controlling the speed and force of the hammer. Both the anvil and hammer face may be removed for the insertion of swages, cutters or punches. Power is supplied by water, electricity, steam or an internal combustion engine. The smallest of these hammers is of 50 pounds force; the largest, such as used in railroad shops, of several tons.

Power hammers are still manufactured by the Little Giant Company. Used ones can be acquired sometimes from industrial supply houses.

In America, until World War I, most blacksmiths were also wheelwrights; they made and repaired all manner of wheeled vehicles, from wheelbarrows to Conestoga wagons. This occupation, considered a specialty in England and Europe, requires a number of additional tools not directly connected with the tools of forge and anvil. Indeed, most of them are for working wood and making hubs, spokes, and felloes, as well as wagon frames and bodies.

Perhaps the most dramatic of the wheelwright's tools is the "lathe" for turning hubs. In Colonial times it was often the "great wheel" lathe, which is so frequently illustrated and can

114

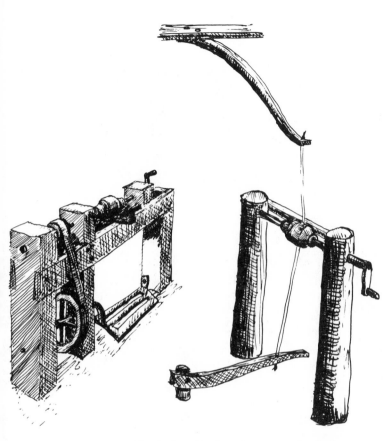

Left: Foot-treadle lathe. Right: Spring-pole lathe.

be seen at a number of Colonial museums, such as Williamsburg. At times a primitive "spring-pole" lathe with backward and forward rotation was used. This is the early type which gives the machine its name from the lath used as a spring to tauten the belt and return the piece of work to its original position after it had been rotated by pedalpower. Later shops in the early 1800s might have had a "foot-treadle" lathe, which provided continuous motion, as did the big wheel, and where a small stream was convenient the lathe was turned by waterpower. This equipment was also used by the smith or his helpers to turn handles for the drawknives, screwdrivers, and wood chisels that he made for his general trade.

The wheelwright's bench includes a number of "wood planes," "spokeshaves," "felloe saws," "rasps," "wood chisels," and "augers" for making and fitting the parts of wheels and bodies. Among the smaller tools are "tenon cutters," inserted in a carpenter's brace to cut tenons on the ends of spokes where they fit into the felloe.

Also there are "tiredogs" and "spokedogs" for prising tires and spokes into place, and there are "boxing engines," "calipers," and "samsons."

Outside the shop the wheelwright generally has an old millstone lying flat on the ground, to use when shrinking a hot tire on a wheel, and a cooling trough, for cooling the tire quickly after it has been fitted.

An important tool for the wheelwright is the "traveler," a 6-inch iron wheel with a handle. No more than a measuring device, the traveler is run carefully around the perimeter of a wagon wheel and the revolutions are counted. This measurement is then transferred to the tire iron so that the tire can be cut accurately before welding.

Some travelers are more elaborate than others. Many are homemade, some with a wooden wheel, and these usually have only a single mark on the wheel's rim that is placed on a premarked spot on the wagon wheel. The revolutions of the traveler are carefully counted, and any excess portion of a revolution is marked with a piece of soapstone. Others have the wheel marked every ⅛ inch around the rim, with a pointer mounted on the pivot to show the distance over a full revolution.

For hub bands the wheelwright sometimes uses a small 3-inch traveler with an offset handle, which allows him to insert the traveler wheel inside the hub band to check its size after welding.

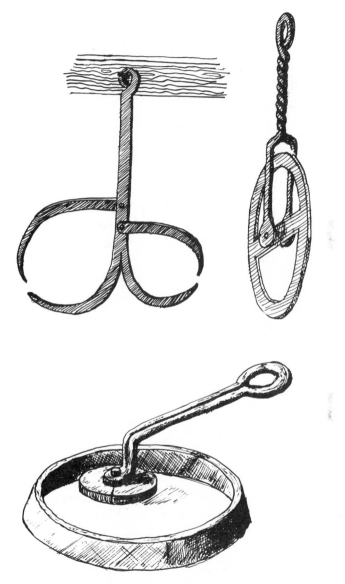

Top left: Wheelwright's double caliper. Top right: Sump Brown's homemade traveler. Bottom: Sump Brown's hub-band traveler.

From 1870 on, the wheelwright's profession became less demanding of skill and experience because of the many wheel and wagon parts made in factories. About that time, for instance, factories began to furnish bent felloes, two to a wheel, to replace the sawn felloes of six or seven to a wheel, which had been handmade by the wheelwright since prehistoric times. Factories also began to provide hubs and spokes of standard sizes, which the wheelwright had only to bore and fit.

Foundries, about the same time, began to manufacture cast-iron bearings for hubs and cast-iron sleeves for wooden axle ends, each of which needed only to be fit into the hub or onto the axle, saving the wheelwright-blacksmith the labor of forging these essential accoutrements.

There were new mechanical helps, too, that appeared in blacksmith and wheelwright shops in the closing years of the nineteenth century. These included "hub borers" to provide more accurate holes, bored and reamed to a conical shape in one operation; "tire benders," adjustable to any size tire; and "tire" and "hub-band shrinkers," a real labor-saver. The shrinkers allowed the wheelwright to make a misfitted tire or band smaller without the effort of cutting it and rewelding. This was important, as most wheelwrights guaranteed their tiring. The careful ones refused to retire a wheel in rainy weather, or even if the wagon had forded a creek on the way to the shop, as moisture swelled the wood in the felloes and made it impossible to do a good tiring job.

Practically every blacksmith in the old days was a farrier, and the bulk of trade for many was shoeing horses. Additional special tools were needed for this exact art. Farriery, however, is a growing trade in 1967, and farrier's tools today are almost exact duplicates of those used by ancient Roman and Middle Eastern farriers. Unlike the tools of general blacksmiths and wheelwrights, all of the farrier's tools are available today from a number of suppliers.

The farrier's tool kit in the old days was usually hand-made, sometimes resembling a carpenter's homemade tool-box with a carrying strap, sometimes made from half of a small keg with partitions for different-sized horseshoe nails and for space to stow the tools of the trade.

Tools include pincers for removing old shoes, a "buffer" for cutting off the clinched ends of old nails, and a rasp for making the hoof flat to receive a new shoe. A "hoof-cleaning knife" with a crooked end is needed to clean and trim hoofs around the frog, and a pair of "hoof parers," resembling clippers, but with one jaw sharpened to a cutting edge, is used to trim the outside of the hoof to size. The "shoeing hammer"

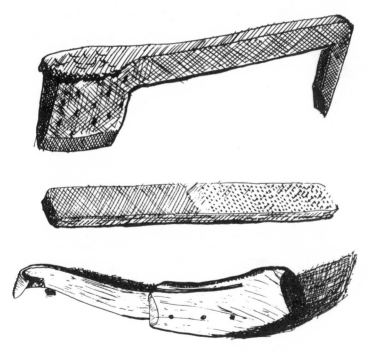

Top: Buffer made from a worn out rasp. Center: Rasp. Bottom: Cleaning knife.

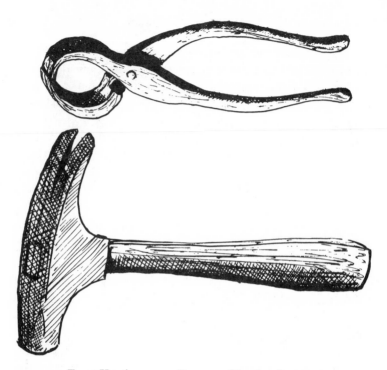

Top: Hoof parers. Bottom: Shoeing hammer.

is a light claw hammer, easily mistaken for a carpenter's hammer, used to drive in the nails, the claws being useful in pulling nails that are crookedly driven.

As in general forging, the farrier needs forge, tongs, anvil, and hammer to make his own shoes, often specially weighted to correct a gait, or to fit factory-made shoes, which often require cleats turned with a cat's-head hammer. The farrier's anvil is usually smaller than the shop anvil, but otherwise exactly the same.

Those adults who remember the smithies of childhood generally recall an older smith working alone or with a single helper. In olden days, though, blacksmithing was a veritable industry, and while some small country shops may have operated with one or two helpers, the smithies in towns and cities often had ten to fifteen apprentices and journeymen working away in a large shop with several forges and anvils. The great Samuel Yellin of Philadelphia employed as many as one hundred smiths in his shop at the height of demand for his artistic work during the first thirty years of the twentieth century. His shop is now kept by his son as a museum.

As had been the case since the days of medieval guilds, a man usually became a smith only after several years of apprenticeship, traditionally seven years in England and Europe and perhaps three or four years in America. After such training he became a journeyman who, in Colonial America and in England, was furnished with a suit of clothes and the essential tools of his trade and was sent out to seek his fortune. As a journeyman smith he traveled around working in different shops, gaining experience in the trade and observing the techniques of a number of master smiths. Many worked to accumulate enough capital to open their own shops and become their own masters.

Being an apprentice was not easy work. It required brains, brawn, initiative, and patience, and the lad who started as a blacksmith's apprentice was really no more than another piece of preautomation equipment. His job was to blow the fire, pull off old shoes from fractious horses, and strike hot iron with a heavy sledge when and where the master told him to strike. Often his instruction was of the negative sort, a cuff when he did something wrong, rather than motivation and direction to do his simple tasks properly.

Apprentices should be diligent in learning the use of the ancient hand tools regardless of what improved equipment they may use to make a living. For hot iron is still the same as it has always been. And modern equipment is merely a technological evolution of hand tools. Those who learn to use the old tools will find that such basic knowledge gives them a much better understanding of modern tools in meeting the continuing challenges of smithing.

5.

GENERAL TECHNIQUES

In the old days a blacksmith in his lifetime might have made ten thousand or more of a given item, such as horseshoes or nails or chisels. Each item of a kind might be an exact duplicate, to all appearances, of the others. While making the items the smith might conceivably have struck a million hammerblows. Yet, despite his experience and skill, each hammerblow was different; each had a different effect on the hot iron being worked; each was followed by a blow different in sequence from the blows used on the previous item. As with marble and clay and precious metals, the working of iron comes from the eye and the intellect rather than from some rote action of the hands. In better work, no matter how utilitarian, the force used to shape the iron comes from the soul. Forging, in its best examples, is indeed an art.

There are few rules to be stated in teaching an apprentice to shape iron and steel to his will. Perhaps this explains the absence of instructional literature over the centuries. Teaching the art depends largely on demonstration, and learning depends on doing. General principles only can be explained with any lucidity. A text on the subject may guide, but it cannot guarantee.

Shaping iron is essentially a molding process. Molding requires controlled force and delicate technique in the application of that force. Before the force or technique can be used with any control the iron must be brought to a plastic state by heating it. As with every other facet of ironworking, heating requires knowledge, and experience, too.

What happens to iron and steel when subjected to heat is easily observed through the use of a sewing needle and a common match. When the point of the needle is held in the flame of the match an immediate change is seen in the steel. First the point turns to a pale yellow, then straw yellow, then purple, then blue, then gray, finally a dull red. These colors run up the needle from the heat as it is conducted through the length of the steel. The red color indicates that the metal has become plastic to some degree, and can be bent without breaking. If held longer in the flame the red color changes in intensity. Following the dull red it changes to a sunrise red, the color of a sunrise on a winter morning. From that it turns a cherry red, then a bright red, then light red, almost orange, then white. A continued heat turns white heat into an incandescent white, then to a liquid incandescent yellow which indicates that the surface has become semimolten. When subjected to further heat it will erupt with tiny incandescent sparks

Welding temperature on soft iron

that show the metal is burning. At this heat it is too hot to be worked if it is steel, but it can be hammered if it is pure iron.

As color is a somewhat relative condition, it is difficult at times to determine the color of heated iron in bright daylight. Many old-time smiths solved this problem by keeping a small keg or box near the forge. A heated iron could be thrust into the darkness of the keg and gauged more accurately than in daylight or in the light of the forge fire.

The phenomenon of iron and steel is that they can be worked at any of these stages between sunrise red and the time that sparks erupt without damaging the basic structure of the metal, and the hotter it is, the easier it is to work. If hammered below sunrise red, or at a blue color, the iron becomes brittle, which is corrected only by reheating or further cooling. Of course, some modern sheet steels are made for cold forming into all manner of shapes, but heavy bars and rods, even of new types of steel, require heat for working.

The blacksmith refers to each time the iron is made red-hot as a "heat." He tries to finish each item with as few heats as possible, particularly items made of steel. Too much heating of steel affects the quality of the metal. Also, too much heat on either steel or iron oxidizes the surface, making it rough and covering it with scale so hard that it sometimes refuses a new file. So thick does the scale become after too many heats that when it flakes off it can affect the dimensions of a wrought item up to 1 percent loss by weight per heat.

Iron, when hot enough, can be transformed into almost any desired shape. A large 2-inch bar, for instance, can be eventually drawn into wire the diameter of a straight pin. Thin rods can be made into thick rods. It can be bent and twisted, pinched and cut, molded like clay, joined permanently together, if it is first made plastic by heat from about 1,400 to 2,800 degrees F.

Blacksmithing, or to the purist, forging, has its own simple terminology. "Fullering" is using the fuller to draw out a bar by first making a series of impressions in the bar with the fuller, then hammering it smooth. To "draw out" means to make a thick rod or bar thinner. To "upset" means to make a thin bar thicker. "Flattening" is using the flatter, or slick, to smooth a bar after fullering.

"Punching" is merely using punch and hammer to force a hole through a piece of hot iron. "Drifting" is enlarging or shaping the hole with a drift. "Cutting" or "cleaving" means cutting off a bar or rod by hammering it over the hardie, or hammering a hot or cold set through it. "Scarfing" or "chamfering" or "beveling" is hammering the end or edge of a bar or rod to create a diagonal surface. "Welding," of course, refers to joining two pieces together after the surface of each has been heated until it is molten. There are several types of welds.

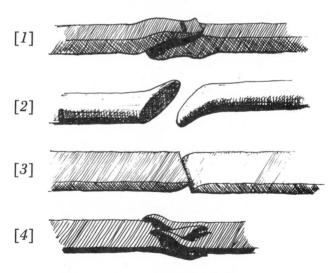

Scarfing: [1] *normal scarf,* [2] *butt scarf,* [3] *simple scarf,* [4] *scarf for thin stock.*

"Lap welding" is nothing more than lapping the scarfed end of one bar over the scarfed end of another to join them together at welding heat. Wagon tires, for example, are lap-welded. "Butt welding" is welding the ends of rods or bars together butt to butt, instead of scarfing them for a lap weld. Also a rod may be butt-welded perpendicularly to a flat bar. This is a form of "jump weld," as when two separate pieces are brought from the forge and joined on the anvil. To "T-weld" is to join a rod or bar perpendicularly to another at a point away from its end.

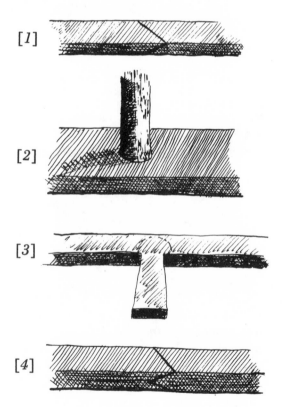

Welds: [1] *lap,* [2] *butt,* [3] *"T",* [4] *tongue.*

A "tongue weld" is accomplished by splitting one piece of iron and tapering the piece to which it is to be joined, then inserting the taper into the split before welding.

There are other methods of joining separate pieces of iron besides welding. "Shrinking" is done by inserting a cold piece into a hole in a hot piece of iron. The hot iron shrinks as it is cooled and holds the cold piece almost as tightly as

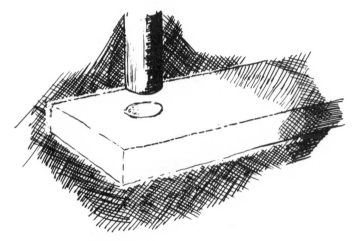

Shrinking as a means of joining

a weld. "Riveting" is using rivets inserted through holes in two pieces of iron, the rivet then being bradded on both ends. "Bradding" is upsetting the end of a rod inserted in a hole to prevent it from being pulled out. "Banding" or "collaring," used mostly in decorative wrought iron, is bending a small strip of hot iron around two pieces of cold iron.

"Packing" is hammering iron or carbon steel at a low heat, usually sunrise red, to pack the fibers of the metal together. "Shaping" is exactly what it sounds like, shaping or molding a piece of hot iron as desired by hammering, swaging, fullering, or whatever.

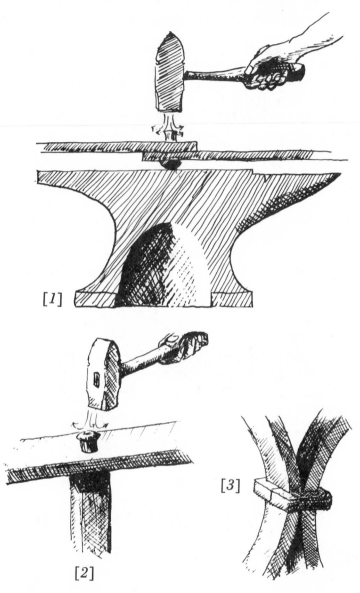

Other means of joining: [1] riveting, [2] bradding, [3] collaring.

128

"Dressing" is reshaping a tool that has been battered out of shape.

The "shoulder" is the lower surface formed by the difference in height of surfaces on a piece of iron; the higher surface is known as the "boss." "Tenons" are the same as tenons in woodwork. A smith who specialized in decorative wrought iron formed a round tenon on the end of a square or rectangular bar with a monkey tool; the tenon was then inserted in another bar and bradded.

"Flux," often referred to as "welding compound," is powdered borax or a mixture of borax and sal ammoniac used for welding mild steel and carbon steel. Some smiths also mix drill shavings with the borax. These tiny bits of steel heat quickly and absorb the oxygen, lessening the effects of

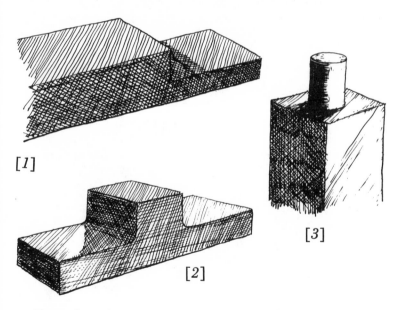

Examples of forming terms: [1] *shoulder,* [2] *boss,* [3] *tenon.*

oxidation on the iron being prepared. The function of flux is to glaze the surface of the metal to prevent the oxidation which makes it impossible to join two pieces of iron even at welding heat. The melted flux also washes away any oxide formed before the flux was applied. Wrought iron, with its silica content, and some mild steel, can often be welded without a flux. Old-time smiths, however, to insure a good joint, frequently used salt or clean sand as a flux for iron. Some said that salt helped keep the fire clean, as well as preventing the formation of oxide.

This brief glossary is useful reference in describing the techniques of forging. It is quite impossible, though, to precisely define the exact techniques employed by any particular smith in making any specific item. Each smith was a different person with different muscular and mental characteristics; each had different equipment and different training; each, generation after generation, developed his own techniques. The absence of textbooks and hard-and-fast rules made the development of individual techniques a fascinating study. Some fundamental techniques, of course, were employed by all smiths, but the application and order of elemental methods, the tools used, and the methods of tool use varied greatly from forge to forge.

There is another factor controlling the technique of iron-working, a factor that has plagued the smith since his art began. That factor is the iron itself. Iron and steel are stubborn, reluctant, exasperating materials. Even modern controlled methods of steel making fail to turn out rods and bars exactly the same. In the old days, the smith found far more differences in the iron and carbon steel available to him. As a consequence, each piece of iron he heated in his forge offered a unique challenge, a new adventure, as it were. Every job he undertook required constant visualization, constant decision, based on the material the smith had on hand, the equipment in his shop, and his own innate skills and weaknesses. He had to do the best he could with what he had, physically, spiritually, and mentally.

His techniques, then, have of necessity depended on individual experience and personality from the time he started his fire until the last wrought-iron item of the day was cooled, hissing, in the slack tub. As a consequence, forging was a living dynamic art, based on a few fundamental principles, but depending largely on meeting the exigencies of any given moment. Perhaps it is good that few textbooks have been written on the subject. Had books been written and disciplined methods been established centuries ago, we should probably miss the delightful variety that old wrought iron offers to the modern world, and the subject of ironworking would not be so fascinating.

One of the underlying principles any old-time smith learned as an apprentice was the importance of his fire. His fire had to be clean, and the first job of an apprentice each morning usually was to clean the forge of ashes, slag, and small pieces of iron that had been lost in the fire. Then he laid a new fire, his method depending somewhat on the first job to be done that day. For tempering or working small pieces he made a fairly shallow fire, packed flat on top. For heating large pieces or welding he planned a deep, narrow fire.

In the days when charcoal was the blacksmith's fuel the fire was made differently from later fires of coal. Though no record has been found of the exact method of laying charcoal fires—the old fuel has not been used generally for at least a century—experience shows that charcoal requires a deeper fire than coal. On the one hand, it burns more quickly; on the other, it cannot be packed as coal into a virtual oven that concentrates the heat by preventing the escape of hot gases through the top of the fuel.

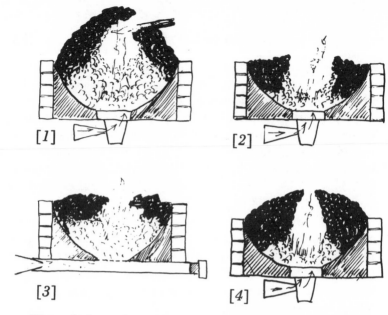

Fires: [1] *welding,* [2] *trench,* [3] *charcoal,* [4] *pot.*

In starting a charcoal fire the smith places a handful of wood shavings and kindling in front of the tweer or above the duck's nest and lights them. When the blaze has caught he pumps the bellows to create a very slight blast. Once the kindling is burning merrily he dumps a half-bushel of charcoal around the blaze and pumps the bellows more vigorously, pushing the charcoal into and over the blaze as he pumps. When the charcoal is lit he puts on more, breaking up larger lumps with the hearth poker or shovel, packing it as best he can around the fire. As the kindling burns away he then arranges the fire for its purpose, spreading it wider or piling on more charcoal to make it deeper, depending on the job to be done. As jobs change during the day the smith may clean out the forge and build a new fire, again to suit his special purpose.

A coal or coke fire requires a slightly different starting technique. First the coal is shoveled around the perimeter of the forge, leaving the duck's nest clear. Kindling is placed and lit, and as it catches fire coal is pushed closer to the blaze. Sometimes, to make the fuel more amenable, it is wet thoroughly with water, which helps the mass stick together. Then as the coal catches fire it is pushed toward the duck's nest. Soon coke forms around the core of the fire, and the coal may be packed with the poker to form a tight vessel filled with heat. Coke left from the old fire should be saved to facilitate starting the next fire.

When a coal or coke fire is built for welding, a different starting technique is used. First of all a short log, 4 inches in diameter, or a short piece of 4 x 4 timber, is placed on and over the grate. Coal is shoveled around this to a depth of 8 or 10 inches, then it is wet thoroughly and packed solidly around the log. After the log is withdrawn a fire is lit in the bottom of the cavity formed. As the coal catches fire the upper surface is packed over the top of the cavity until an oven is formed. The iron to be heated for welding is then placed near the top of the cavity to be heated with a minimum of oxygen.

Once the fire is started the smith takes care to keep the hearth box full of fuel, which actually insulates the fire and saves fuel in the long run. When the fire eventually burns "hollow as a gourd's neck," to quote Sump Brown, it must be built up with coke from the walls of the fire, not green cool. This is done by striking the outside of the coal with a heavy poker or tongs to force coke from the inside to fall on the hearth, or by picking the side coke off with a poker.

The smith's fire is essential equipment. One cannot underestimate the importance of using a high quality "shop" or "metallurgical coal" in efficiently producing professional ironwork. Shop coal is bituminous. It must have a low sulfur and phosphorus content. In addition, it must have a "coking button" of 7 to 9, so that the coke forms into a hard mass. Ash content must be extremely low and the coal should not flame once it has turned to coke. Ordinary stoker, or "steam," coal is simply not suitable for smithing.

These specifications from the Geological Survey of Alabama may be used in ordering shop coal:

Moisture	2.5%–3%	Volatility	25%–35%
Ash	3%–6%	Carbon	55%–65%
Sulfur	1%–2%	BTU	13,500–14,500

It is important, especially for welding, to clean the fire every two or three hours and remove any clinkers. These hard, glassy objects are the residue of sulfur and other impurities which sink to the bottom of the hearth and are blown on the iron, making welding impossible.

Heating iron, even large bars a couple of inches square, takes a surprisingly short time in a good fire. It is the mark of the beginner, however, to heat too quickly. To do so requires a strong steady blast of air, and while air makes the fire burn it also oxidizes the iron, creating more problems than quick heating can solve. With charcoal, heating is hastened by covering the iron with fresh charcoal. With a coal fire, however, the iron heats more quickly if covered with pieces of coke saved for the purpose from previous fires, or picked from the top of the fire.

For simple bending the iron is heated to an orange-red, perhaps to a white heat on smaller pieces that will not hold the heat long. When at the proper color the iron is removed from the fire, with tongs if short, but a long piece is handled with the bare hand for better control.

A rounded bend is shaped over the horn. The iron is rested across the horn parallel to the floor and is bent downward with hammerblows which move perpendicular to the floor. If the iron is to be bent into a circle the smith moves it across the horn as he hammers in order to keep the direction of hammerblows perpendicular to the floor.

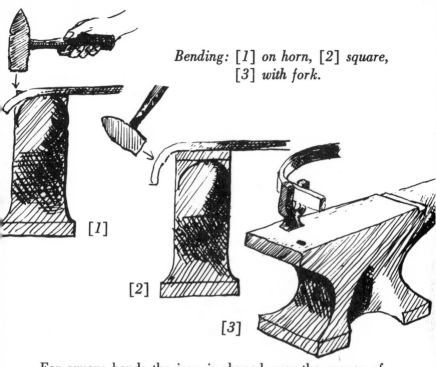

Bending: [1] on horn, [2] square, [3] with fork.

For square bends the iron is shaped over the corner of the anvil face or in the vise. Steel can be bent into quite sharp angles, but iron should be bent over the round corner of the anvil face so as not to break its fibers.

When the horn is too large to make a very tight rounded bend, the smith resorts to bending it around a rod stuck upright in the pritchel hole or held in the vise, or else he uses the large hollows in the swage block. Very small thin pieces can be bent with another pair of tongs as a start, the bend then being trued up on the horn or around a rod. When the color of the iron dies to sunrise red it should be reheated before further working.

Drawing out requires a more practiced eye than bending. A small piece of iron is easily drawn out with a hammer, usually of 4-pounds weight. The iron is heated to orange-red, then laid across the face of the anvil and struck with the hammer, taking care that the hammer face strikes the iron parallel to the anvil face. Slow, well-placed blows of the hammer are more efficient in rough drawing out than a series of quick blows, which are reserved for smoothing the iron after it has been shaped.

The fuller comes into use when drawing out large pieces. It is used to indent the orange-red iron along the surface to be drawn out. After fullering the uneven surface is smoothed with a heavy hammer or with a flatter. When only part of a bar is to be drawn out, leaving a boss, the fuller is driven into the hot iron where the shoulder is to be, then down the iron as far as desired. When a square shoulder is wanted, either the set hammer is employed or the iron is turned over and the shoulder is squared on the edge of the anvil.

It must be remembered that while iron is being drawn with a hammer along its length, it also becomes wider than it was originally. Consequently the smith, when drawing out a bar, must continuously turn it on its side for a blow or two to maintain the original width. The good smith observes

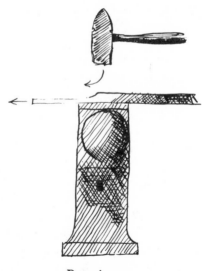

Drawing out

Left: Use of fuller. Right: Making shoulder.

the effect of every hammerblow, keeping in mind always the shape he is working toward. As a piece widens, therefore, he turns it on its side to contain the width while the iron is still hot at that point. This is much easier than reheating the iron to dress the width later on. When a fuller is used the iron does not widen with each blow nearly so much as with a straight hammerblow.

A bar of iron or steel must sometimes be beveled or drawn out to an edge, as when making knives or chisels. Generally this is done only with the hammer. When the iron is hot it is placed across the anvil face where the corner is rounded or else along the top of the horn. It is molded by a rolling motion of the hammer, which molds the metal as desired. At times the beveled edge is molded with the pein of the hammer.

Thinning a knife edge also pushes the steel to the side, and after a few blows it begins to curve along the edge, giving the edge a convex shape. If the edge is not too sharp, the bar can be placed concave side downward on the anvil face and straightened while hot. It is easier, however, to compensate for the spreading before drawing out the edge. To do this the smith bends his bar into a gentle arc before draw-

Knife blade with compensating bend before chamfering edge

ing out the edge, placing his bevel on the concave side. When his drawing out is completed, then his bar is again straight.

Drawing out, if properly and easily done, requires recognition of the plastic qualities of hot iron. A direct hammer-blow pushes the metal out from the point where the hammer strikes, like throwing a flat rock in a shallow puddle. Many of the hammerblows, though, should glance off the hot surface. Such glancing blows move the hot metal in the direction of the hammer, molding it rather than stamping, providing maximum degree of control.

One of the minor techniques of shaping, the ringing of the anvil, has found its place in song and literature. When a piece of iron is smitten on the anvil face there is no real ring, for the iron mutes the bell-like sound from the tempered face. Ringing results from the light taps of the hammer directly on the face beside the hot iron. Experienced smiths usually hit the anvil face once for every two or three blows on the iron. The reason is to give the arm a momentary rest from lifting the heavy hammer, for the tempered hardness of anvil face and hammer face makes the two surfaces so resilient that the hammer bounces upward like a rubber ball when tapped on the anvil, thus giving the smith a headstart in lifting his hammer for the next blow. Such is the practical reason for wasted, ringing blows.

One may suspect, however, that at heart nearly every smith is an artist, and that the bell-like tones of unproductive blows provide some aesthetic satisfaction. There is reason behind this presumption. A great part of the pleasure of working with any hand tool is the reflection of the body's natural rhythm in a saw stroke, a file stroke, the regular twisting of a screwdriver, or the blows of hammer and ax and adz. In the smithy this natural rhythm is accentuated by the pure musical note of the ringing anvil. It furnishes every smith with his own built-in music, and it anticipated by centuries the newly discovered psychological benefits of wired-in music for offices and shops and dairy barns.

There are other elemental pleasures, physical and artistic, in hammering red-hot iron. First of all, there is the changing color of the iron to watch. When orange-red it has an almost transparent quality that gradually thickens as the constantly cooling metal changes its color eventually to a dark, dull red barely perceptible in daylight. There is the action of hot oxide scale which violently detaches itself from the iron with every hammerblow, shooting off in all directions like miniature meteorites. The smith develops a feeling of accomplishment and power as he sees the normally intransigent material change its shape under each determined blow, and he discovers a confidence born of control over the elements themselves as their natural integrity is broken and molded into a form preconceived by the smith. Sometimes his hammer coaxes; at other times it forces. With some exceptions black-smiths are often described as gentle, tractable men. If this is so it might be explained by the smith's opportunity to release his innate human hostilities through pounding iron. Forging seems to soothe the soul as well as please the eye and strengthen the arm.

Drawing out may be considered the main technique used in working iron simply because it is, in most cases, easier to reduce the dimensions of iron by pounding than to make those dimensions larger by upsetting. In some cases, however, upsetting is vitally needed. This technique is not really any more difficult than drawing out, but it requires more delicacy and develops more frustration.

Perhaps the widest application of upsetting in olden times was to thicken the blunt end of a nail to create a head. Since this was done with a swaging device, which held the shank while the nail was being headed, there was not the usual problem with the technique. But in upsetting the end, or particularly the center section, of a thin rod or bar the smith has to place his blows with great accuracy.

Always the iron being upset is given more heat than the orange-red required for most other forging operations; it is brought to a white heat to provide maximum plasticity. There are several approaches to upsetting the end of a rod or thin bar. When long enough, the upsetting can be done by holding the bar perpendicular to and a few inches above the floor or anvil face and dropping it straight down repeatedly until the end has spread sufficiently for its intended purpose. Of course, before dropping the bar to the floor the smith places a piece of sheet iron or a flat rock where the rod is to be dropped to act as an anvil. On shorter pieces the smith may hold the hot end of the iron upright on the anvil face and hammer the other end to spread it. Or he may hold the hot iron across the anvil face and hammer on the hot end.

Both of these methods must be done with the utmost care

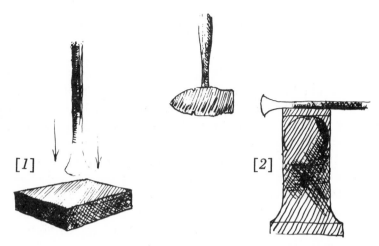

Upsetting: [1] *dropping,* [2] *hammering across anvil.*

to prevent the white-hot iron from bending, for when the axis of the blow or the drop does not exactly correspond with the axis of the softened rod, bending occurs, requiring straightening before another blow can be dealt. Sometimes a short rod is held upright on the anvil, hot end uppermost, and is upset with the hammer; sometimes it is held in a vise. It all depends on a particular smith's peculiar methods. Usually a minimum number of hard, well-directed blows are more effective for upsetting than many quick, light blows. Often a smith will cool the first ½ inch of the white-hot end of a rod by dipping the end in the slack tub, thus giving him a solid point on which to hammer.

Because of the likelihood of bending, upsetting a section of rod some distance from the end is quite difficult. When performing this feat the smith brings the section to be upset up to white heat and then follows the same procedure used to upset an end.

Scarfing the end of a rod or bar preparatory to butt welding is a special form of upsetting, differing from the regular form only in forming a diagonal face on the upset end.

Though not really considered forging operations, punching and cutting are important aspects of ironworking, and neither is so easy to do as it may appear on the surface. When cutting, for instance, a bar is brought to orange or white heat, depending on its size, placed over the hardie, and hammered down on the hardie's edge until it is severed. This requires care for the last two or three hammerblows, for if too much force is used it will part the iron so quickly that the hardie's edge will be battered and dulled and will require redressing for future use. When a chisel is used for cutting large, heavy pieces of iron, the relatively soft anvil table is used to support the iron, or a cutting plate is placed on the anvil face to protect its polished surface. Again, as with cutting with the hardie, care must be taken with the last few hammerblows to prevent the chisel from unduly scarring the table or plate.

Splitting, or cutting iron parallel to its long axis, and along the fiber structure of pure iron, can be done with the hardie, but a chisel is preferable. When using the hardie for splitting it is impossible to see the split being made, since it is on the bottom side of the iron. Consequently, a split longer than the width of the hardie edge, which requires lining up a series of cuts, can often result in a crooked or overlapping split that weakens one or both sides of the split at a critical point.

Because pure iron is comprised of long parallel fibers, a hole is often punched in the iron before splitting, at a point where the split will end. The hole prevents the split from continuing inadvertently when the iron is being worked later.

The main problem with punching is to line up the punch on top of the hot iron with the hole invisible beneath the iron. As the punch is tapered, juxtaposition of punch and hole does not have to be exact, but a fairly close alignment of the two is necessary.

Punching can be quite easy on thin sheet, often being done cold over the end grain of a block of wood. For punching any

Splitting soft iron after hole has been punched at end of split

stock over ⅛ inch, however, heat is required (unless the smithy has modern, hydraulic or mechanical punches which will punch ½ inch stock cold). The spot to be punched is marked with a center punch when cold. After bringing to an orange heat, the piece is laid on the anvil face, the punch is placed in position and set with a heavy blow. After being set, it is driven three quarters through the iron, the smith being careful to quench its end after every three blows to prevent the end's getting hot and upsetting in the hole into a ball. When the hole is three quarters through, the iron is turned and the hole started on the other side at a spot which has darkened from the cold end of the punch. It is set again and driven until the smith feels it penetrate. Then quickly it is placed over the pritchel or hardie hole, or a hole in the swage block and driven through. It may be drifted after punching.

There is a special danger from punching for small barefooted boys who may hang around a blacksmith shop. Punching over the pritchel hole allows the punch to cut a small round plug from the iron. This small piece drops through the pritchel hole into the ashes and dirt around the anvil block, and it retains its heat for several minutes. Beware, then, to the barefoot boy who steps upon one of these plugs! The result will be burning pain, a yell, a foot thrust quickly into the slack tub, and a blistered sole.

Perhaps the most glamorous of the smith's operations is welding, to take two separate pieces of iron and make them one. To the uninitiated it is akin to the medical miracle of restoring a severed limb successfully. Most competent smiths master welding, but a few never seem to learn how, regardless of their skill in shaping. Once mastered, however, welding is such an easy thing to do that the smith uses it in making all manner of objects, from horseshoe-nail rings to twist-steel shotgun barrels, from tongs to axes. Probably the most difficult welding job is to join the two different substances of carbon steel and pure iron, each of which welds at a different heat, but even this becomes second nature to most master smiths. Old-timers frequently observed that even a fool can weld soft iron, but such an observation is not always accurate.

Of course, a high-enough degree of heat is the basic requirement of welding, enough heat to bring the surface of the iron to a semimolten state. The real secret, however, is to prevent oxygen and other impurities in the fuel from coating the iron, making it impossible to weld. The unitiated usually fails in making a proper weld in two areas: the form of his fire and the lack of restraint with which he pumps his bellows or blows his blower.

The fire has to be both deep and tight. Fuel is built up from 5 to 8 inches from the grate when coal is used, and to a depth of 12 inches with charcoal. The iron is placed over the fire on top of the coal at these prescribed depths, then more fuel is heaped above the iron to form a sort of oven.

Since charcoal by its nature is difficult to pack, and burns out quickly, a charcoal fire for welding requires a mass of fuel. To insure that too much heat did not escape upward through the loosely packed charcoal, the old-time smith would sometimes lay a piece of sheet iron over his fire, with the iron to be welded placed directly underneath.

When using coal the latter-day smith wets the fuel thoroughly with water and packs it with blows from the flat of the hearth shovel. When he sees a viscous white smoke emerging from the coal surrounding his fire he sprinkles on more water and packs the mass more tightly to keep inflammable gases contained within the fire.

Now a fire can be brought to welding heat within a minute or so if the bellows are pumped vigorously, but such action also pumps an excess of oxygen in the fire, too much oxygen to be burned up before the heat reaches the iron. When this is done the iron oxidizes so thickly that a weld is impossible regardless of how soft the iron becomes; it cannot join under these circumstances. Patience, then, is the word. The air is fed to the fire slowly and with restraint, until the fire grows incandescently white, a blistering fire which sears the eyeballs if looked at directly for more than a couple of seconds.

The iron, of course, is scarfed before the welding process starts. It is important to have the scarfed surfaces convex rather than concave, so that any flux and oxide is forced from the joint with the first hammerblows. Otherwise the joint welds only around the edges of the scarf.

Now for the iron. It is placed at the top of the fire until it turns red, then it is removed and flux is sprinkled over the surface to be welded. Flux not only coats the iron; it melts and flows into the tightest cracks, removing any oxide already formed.

Back into the fire the iron goes. Bellows are pumped slowly and steadily at a speed that keeps the fire incandescent. Slowly the iron grows lighter in color. As the smith pumps he watches the color, keeping the iron immobile so as not to disturb the fire, applying additional flux to the joint at times with a spoon. When the iron approaches welding heat he may increase the blast to speed the process. Often he pokes a small hole in the side of the fire so that he can look down into the midget inferno to observe the state of the heat.

It is possible after long experience to know that iron has reached welding heat by observing its color and the texture of its surface. Pure iron can be welded in a state from an oily, almost white yellow to incandescent white with tiny sparks erupting from the surface. You may also weld 10-20 hot rolled mild steel at sparkling heat, but other mild steels and carbon steels seem to weld best at an oily yellow heat. Cold rolled mild steel is particularly difficult to forge/weld and often requires experimentation to make it join.

It takes a good eye to determine welding heat by color alone, especially when the smith is gazing into a cavern of fire so hot that it seems to penetrate his eyeballs. In view of the difficulties involved many smiths resort to a more practicable method of determining welding heat.

They use a small probe—no more than a ¼-inch rod drawn out to a paper-thin chisel edge. As the iron grows hotter the smith sticks this rod into the fire and probes the heated surface of the iron. Having a thin edge, the end of the probe heats instantaneously. When the surface of the iron is molten, the sharp edge of the probe reaches the same state, so that when it touches the iron it sticks and the rod has to be twisted to disengage it. This sticking demonstrates conclusively that welding heat has been reached. Then the iron is taken quickly from the fire to the anvil, and the joint is made.

Welding is hardly automatic after proper heat has been reached; a prescribed technique is required in hammering the two molten surfaces into one. First of all the joint is hit smartly in the middle to drive the two convex surfaces of the scarfs together and to force flux and oxide out around the edges. Next the thinned edges of the scarfs are joined with light, quick blows, for the edges, being thinner, lose welding heat quickly. The last stage of hammering is to hit every spot of the surface with quick blows to complete the joint. Then, while the iron is still a bright red, the smith smooths the completed joint with hammer and flatter.

There are several additional tricks of the trade in welding. In joining two flat pieces with a lap weld, the lower piece should usually rest at a slight angle on the edge of the anvil face. This is to keep as much of the iron as possible from the cold anvil, which draws the heat quickly. Of course, the first blow flattens the iron on the anvil, but the first blow also joins the two pieces.

Because loss of heat happens so quickly once the iron is drawn from the fire, the smith who welds small pieces, such as bridle rings or harness buckles or cabinet hinges, has his anvil close to the forge. Often he makes his joint while resting his iron on a preheated bar. For wagon tires, gun barrels, and heavier work the anvil must be a step or two from the forge.

The smith without a helper must resort to a technique called "dropping the tongs" when welding two separate pieces into one. For this, a little planning is needed. The hammer must be laid beforehand on the anvil block, ready to be grabbed with no loss of time. Two pairs of tongs are required. When the irons reach welding heat, the smith takes a pair of tongs in each hand and lifts the irons simultaneously from

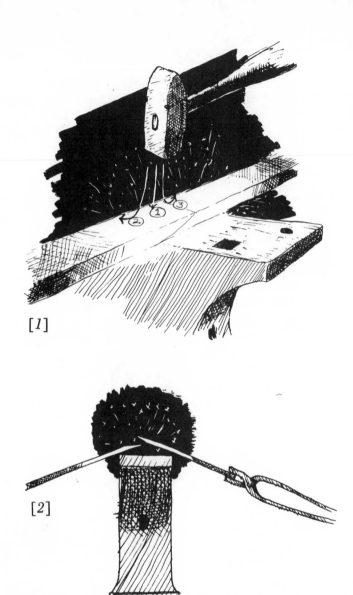

Welding: [1] *where to place blows for a lap weld,* [2] *how to hold iron on anvil before the first blow.*

the fire. If right-handed, he carefully places the iron held by his right hand on the anvil, places the other iron on top of the first piece, drops the tongs in his right hand, picks up the hammer, and beats the twain together. Dropping the tongs requires a quick eye and precise coordination, plus a good bit of experience. It also helps to have a blacksmith's helper mounted on the anvil block to steady the lower piece of iron.

Brazing was another method of joining practiced by the old-time blacksmith because it required the heat of his forge before the days of electric brazing.

Most brazing is used to join broken objects that are impossible or extremely difficult to weld, such as cast-iron objects or saw blades. It takes a master smith indeed to properly weld and retemper a crosscut saw that is split or broken.

To braze, the smith places the broken pieces in the forge and heats them until the broken edges are orange-red. Then, placing the edges together he applies flux and sprinkles spelter, no more than brass filings, between the two broken pieces. When the brass melts he gives the two pieces a sharp tap with his hammer, driving them closer together and evenly distributing the melted brass. The rejoined piece is left in the dying fire until it loses its red heat and the brass is solidified, whereupon the smith removes it from the forge, cools it, and files or chisels off any excess brass.

Tempering steel for cutting edges, the faces of hammers, springs, and other uses that require hardness or resiliency, is another skill that requires a discriminating eye and a great deal of experience. Contrary to popular opinion, the term "tempering" is not applied to hardening steel, but rather to controlled softening after the steel has already been hardened with heat and rapid quenching in a brine bath. Hardening, however, is the essential step before tempering.

Both hardening and tempering call for some degree of experimentation. When blister steel and cast steel were the only available metals for tools, weapons, and springs, each piece had a slightly different carbon content, enough to affect its hardening qualities. Even later, when modern methods for producing tool steel were developed, it was impossible to produce steel to absolute specifications from one smelting to the other. Accordingly, smiths approach hardening and tempering warily. Some tool steel hardens at a cherry-red color, and other steels require orange-red or even white heat before hardening. While the old-time smith did not have any chemical laboratory or elaborate testing equipment to determine the proper hardening heat, the conscientious smith did test whenever possible before tempering.

The test is simple, its effectiveness determined by the smith's eye and experience. A thin piece of the steel being worked is heated in the forge so that the end becomes white hot, with the color varying from this end toward the other end through orange-red, cherry red, sunrise red, dull red, and gray. The smith must keep in mind the places where these various colors appeared on the steel. After the end has become white hot the steel is quenched in brine and is laid across the anvil face, its end projecting ¼ inch over the edge. With a light hammer the smith breaks off the brittle end and examines the texture of the inside. Usually the end shows a very coarse texture when broken, indicating that the steel was burned somewhat by the white heat, and is therefore inferior at that point. Other chips are broken off and examined until the broken end shows very close texture, indicating proper hardening. Remembering which heat was shown at this particular point, the smith uses the same heat to harden the tool or weapon on which he is working.

Testing for the proper tempering heat is very similar to testing for hardening. The same test sliver of steel is hardened at the heat found suitable, then cleaned of all oxide with a file until it shines. Again one end of it is placed in the fire until it turns gray with oxide, and again it is quenched in brine. Upon examination the formerly shining metal will be seen to have been transformed by the heat into a rainbow of color between the gray scale and the still-shining end away from the fire. Next to the scale it is a deep irridescent purple, and, next to that, blue in varying shades, then brown, then yellow, until a very light yellow shows the extent to which the heat traveled up the hardened steel.

Proper tempering color is determined with a small file, somewhat worn. Of course, the shiny portion is still at maximum hardness, and this hardness is dissipated through the range of colors to the oxide, which will be soft and malleable, capable of being bent without breaking. As the file tests the various colors, the smith guages its degree of hardness. Coldchisel edges should have only a slight degree of hardness drawn from them. Saws and carving tools for soft wood should be tempered to a point that they are almost malleable, just hard enough to retain a good edge when honed. Razors and springs require a temper somewhere between the extremes of maximum hardness, and brittleness, and maximum softness. The smith determines the proper color for tempering whatever he is working on by how deeply the file bites when it is run across the metal. Only delicate senses trained by experience can make this determination with accuracy.

While each piece of steel tempers differently, there are some general rules that tell the relationship between color and proper temper for various classes of steel use.

Spon's Mechanics Own Book, an instructional trade book published in London around the turn of the century, provides a table based on color which is as accurate as any table, but which cannot substitute for the need to test each separate piece of steel being worked. Here is Mr. Spon's table:

COLOR	TEMPERATURE	TOOL
Very pale straw yellow	430°	*Lancets and metal cutting*
A shade of darker yellow	440°	*Razors*
Darker straw color	470°	*Pen knives*
Still darker straw yellow	490°	*Cold chisels, wood tools*
Brownish yellow	500°	*Hatchets, plane irons, pocket knives*
Yellow tinged with purple	520°	*Chipping chisels, saws*
Light purple	530°	*Swords, watch springs*
Dark purple	550°	*Tools for cutting sandstone*
Dark blue	570°	*Small saws*
Pale blue	600°	*Large saws, pit and hard saws*
Paler blue with tinge of green	630°	*Too soft for steel instruments*

There are other ingenious methods for tempering developed over the ages, methods that do not depend on a good eye for color. One tested way of tempering gun springs is to coat the spring after hardening with soot from a burning pine splinter. When covered, the spring is held over heat until the soot burns away, and at the instant the last vestige of soot disappears the spring is quenched in oil. Still another method of tempering springs is to sprinkle sawdust on the oil-quenched spring after it has been hardened. When the sawdust burns over the fire the spring is quenched again. The process is repeated twice more. After the third quenching the spring is properly tempered.

In recent times the proper hardening color may be realized by touching the steel with a small magnet as the heat rises. The magnet will stick until the metal reaches a red heat. At the exact moment that the magnet ceases to stick the steel should be quenched for maximum hardness.

Large pieces can be tempered on the forge, but only after

the fire is flattened into a bed. During forge tempering the bellows are generally immobile, the fire retaining enough heat without blowing for the time necessary to temper. Small pieces are usually tempered by laying the piece on a bar or plate which has been heated orange-red in the forge. Some smiths temper knives by holding a red-hot bar on the blunt back. By the time the bar heats the blunt back to a blue, the cutting edge has turned dark yellow, and at this point the knife blade is quenched. This gives it a hard edge and a springy blade.

Some technique is required even in quenching. The steel is immersed in the brine and is moved around in the liquid vigorously until cool, the purpose being to bring it continually into contact with cold brine and to avoid a concentration of air bubbles, which can cause uneven temper or hardness. Large, thin objects such as swords and scissors are never quenched by immersion from the point, but always by immersing them along the cutting edge. Otherwise the progressive cooling of the metal as it is thrust in the brine will sometimes warp the blade, requiring straightening before attempting to harden once more. Anvil faces are hardened under a stream of falling water, which quickly carries away the tremendous heat held by such a huge mass of metal. In some shops warm water that has been standing, and thereby has lost its oxygen content, is considered a better tempering bath than brine.

Often tool hardening and tempering may be done in one operation, though some old-time smiths frowned on this economy, saying that the results were uneven. Tools such as chisels are brought to hardening heat on the end, then the edge is quenched ½ inch in the brine until it has cooled. The chisel rests on the anvil while a section of the edge is quickly shined with a flat piece of sandstone or a small file. The heat remaining in the part that has not been quenched then spreads

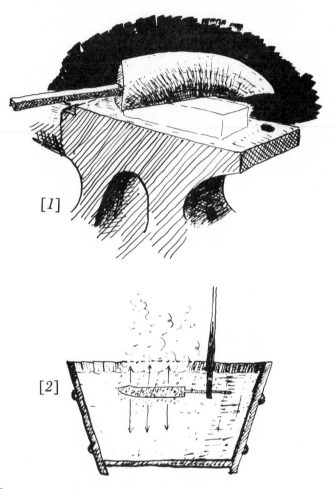

Tempering a knife blade: [1] *heating back,* [2] *immersion position.*

or runs down to the edge. When enough heat reaches the edge to give it the desired tempering color, the whole tool is immersed in the brine bath.

It should be reiterated that much of the fascination of the olden blacksmith's techniques lies in the fact that these techniques cannot be limited by number or description. Each smith, learning his art by word of mouth, observation, and experience, was continually adapting observed techniques to new uses, or else he developed new techniques for jobs outside his past experience. As a consequence, it is impossible to set down fully all the techniques used by all the smiths even in a limited area over a limited period of time. Each smith's techniques varied according to his experience, his equipment, his inherent intelligence, his powers of visualization and analysis, and his own personal characteristics.

The blacksmith was not a machine, he was a man meeting the challenges and glories of each new day in his own individual manner. Because of this, most smiths were happy men.

6.

THE TECHNIQUES OF
TOOL MAKING

Smithing has ever been a functional art. Back in the dim reaches of the prehistoric past, when the first forges were built, the world was a hard place in which to live. One never knew when to expect a band of strangers, queerly clothed and queerly armed, bent on stealing one's women, killing one's cattle, and trampling one's laboriously planted grain.

The elements, and man's hunger and his puny body, were enemies, too. Game was constantly hunted and killed for food and clothing. Shelter had to be built to protect against the snow and wind and rain. Man might have survived with his hands alone, but they were barely adequate. Tools gave him his place of mastery in the hostile world.

The blacksmith gave him the best tools he would have for many a thousand years, tools made especially for his peculiar needs, tools that gave his puny arms and hands titanic power.

The smith himself needed tools before he could purvey his art to his community. Unlike the other craftsmen, he made his own tools, as well as theirs, and in many cases his tools remained essentially unchanged, certainly in principle, from the very beginning of the art. For instance, the smith's tongs served the same purpose in A.D. 1900 as they had in 4000 B.C., and probably retained the same forms. Hammers serve the same function today as they did when man first used a *coup de poing* of hard stone, and have changed in form only by the use of iron and the adaptation of an inserted handle, and even this was found among the quite primitive societies of the earliest users of iron.

All hammers have the same basic form. Each consists of a bar of iron or steel with a hole in it to receive a handle. From that beginning it can be modified to many uses, both for the smith and for his fellow craftsmen such as carpenters, silversmiths, machinists, and others.

There is a cardinal rule with few exceptions that applies to making hammers as well as to other pierced tools. The hole is made first and all else is formed around the hole. Whenever possible the smith forms his hammer at the end of a bar long enough to hold in the hand, thus circumventing the need for tongs until the final stages of manufacture. The making of a simple cross-pein hammer is typical of the process.

Depending on the size of the hammer being made, an iron bar ¾-inch to 2-inches square is heated to a bright red, and the eye is punched, care being taken to see that the hole is exactly in the middle. The usual oval shape of the eye results from dressing the bulges caused by a round punch being driven through a square bar. The bulges are hammered at an even cherry red heat until flush with the sides of the bar. Next the hole is drifted out with an oval drift. Often the drift is left in the eye until the hammer is finished, to prevent a poorly aimed blow from ruining its symmetry.

If the hammer is to be made the old way, of iron with a steel face, the second step in manufacturing is to weld on the face. Generally the face is a flat piece of carbon steel about ½-inch thick. If a bar of steel is used the end is brought to welding heat before cutting it, while at the same time the iron bar with its punched hole is also brought to welding heat. When hot enough the two pieces are joined, and the thick bar for the head is butt-welded to the flat steel. Before the heat is

Punching hole in bar

lost the flat steel can be cut off from the iron with a hot chisel, and the smith can hammer the edges of the steel to fit the dimensions of the iron.

Sometimes a piece of steel slightly smaller than the intended face is used. The steel is first cut with a chisel once or twice on the corner of each of its four sides to form small teeth which are hammered out until they are perpendicular to the face. When cool the face is driven, teeth down, into the white-hot end of the hammer head. Thus the face is held in position while welding.

Next the fuller is used to dent the bar on each corner about an inch from the hole on either side. Then the corners on the face side of the hole are champfered, or beveled, from the dent to the face itself.

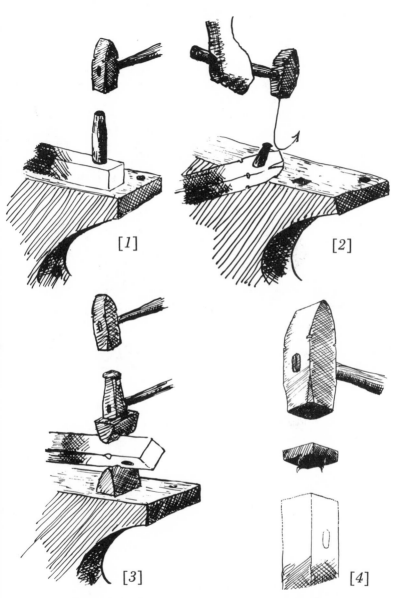

[1] *Using the drift.* [2] *Chamfering.* [3] *Using the fuller.* [4] *Preparing steel hammer faces for welding.*

At this time the drift is knocked out, the bar is heated to orange-red and cut off, either with chisel or hardie, about 1½ inches from the hole. For this the smith uses a special pair of hammer tongs, shaped to fit into the eye, to hold the short, blunt piece of iron steadily while the pein is shaped. This may be done in several ways. One is to reduce the thickness of the bar with the fuller, then smooth it with hammer and flatter. Another is to draw it out to its wedge shape over the horn of the anvil, turning the iron over every two or three blows to assure an even reduction on both sides. Following this, the smith can mold the pein with the cross pein of the hammer he is using, holding the red-hot iron across the anvil face in a position that allows his hammer to glance off the pein of the hammer he is making and yet miss the corner of the anvil.

When the pein is to be used for hard work, a thin piece of steel is bent and welded around its outside surface, or the edge of the pein is split and a small bar of steel welded in the split. After this the pein is dressed with a light hammer, and the eye is drifted for accuracy.

Tempering is simple. First the whole head is heated to about a cherry red and the face is quenched. Withdrawing it from the brine, the smith polishes a small spot on face and pein edge. When enough heat from the body of the hammer reaches face and pein to turn the spot a light straw yellow, then the whole head is dipped into the brine bath and the hammer is ready for use.

By following this general technique the smith can shape his hammers as he wishes for any special purpose. Handled set tools are made in essentially the same manner.

Whenever an old-time smith was called upon to make a heavy hammer and he found that he had no heavy iron bar in stock, he improvised his basic iron from what was available. For instance, a bar thick enough to make a 6-pound sledge

*Left: Shaping hammer pein. Right: Faggot-welding thin
iron to make a hammer.*

can be made by bending a 2-inch strip of wagon tire in an
accordion fold and welding the enfolded surfaces together.

For making small tack hammers out of ½-inch-square
stock, the smith may sometimes upset the bar or rod at the
point where the eye will be punched, to provide better support for the handle.

Ball-pein hammers are usually made from 1- to 1 ½-inch
round rods. The same basic technique is used as in making
other hammers, except that the fuller is used to draw out the
metal between the cylindrical face section and the eye and
between the eye and the pein. Then, with the drift still in
the eye, the sides surrounding the eye are flattened to extend
the vertical inside surface for better support for the handle.

Claw hammers were made by the smith for the carpenters
of his community since nails were first invented in prehistoric times. Until the beginning of the nineteenth century,
American and Western European carpenters had claw hammers almost identical to those of the Romans. Early in that
industrial century, in 1840, the adz-eye claw hammer was

161

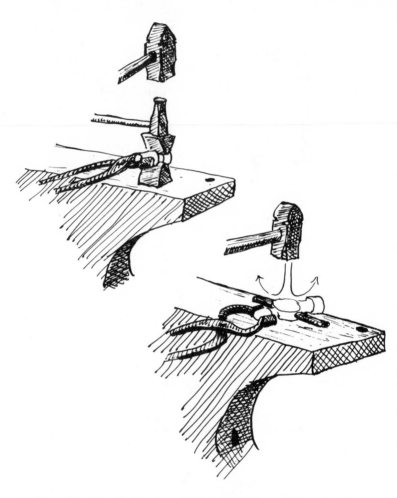

Top: Shaping behind a ball pein hammer face with a fuller. Bottom: Flattening the sides of a ball pein hammer.

invented by an American blacksmith, David Maydole, of Norwich, New York. Maydole found such demand for his new hammer that he started a hammer factory and mass produced them for an international market. Of course, the

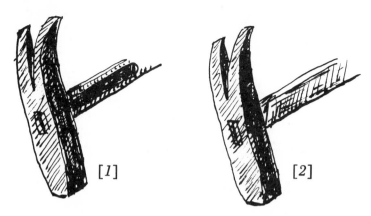

Hammers: [1] with strap, [2] without strap.

adz-eye hammer is so named because the eye, into which the handle is inserted, is formed as the long eye of a hand or foot adz.

The advantages of the adz eye on claw hammers are self-evident. The longer eye gives good support for the handle when drawing nails with the claw, and keeps the handle properly aligned for driving nails straight. Also it eliminates the need to weld to the hammerhead iron straps that extend down the handle, fastened to the wood with screws, to keep the head tightly in position. Not only do the straps require some rather delicate welding, but they also take the spring out of the handle, making it less efficient as a driving tool.

Adz-eye hammers, which generally have rectangular eyes, are made from a rectangular bar ¾ inch by 1½ inches, punched through the wider dimension with a ⅜-inch-by-¾-inch punch. After that the face end and claw end are drawn out and shaped. The claws are made by splitting the pein section down the center with a chisel and bending the claws around the anvil horn. With the drift still in the eye, the outside surface of the eye is drawn out to a sleeve to support the handle. Tempering, of course, is the last step. The face must be tempered to straw color, the claws to purple.

Top: The adz-eye hammer. Bottom left: Shaping claws. Bottom right: Drawing out eye socket.

In many early hammers, however, the boss for the adz-eye was formed by welding a piece to the square bar before punching.

Until the 1870s, before the advent of widespread mass production, each smith made his own tongs. While simple in shape and operation, it usually takes at least an hour to make a pair of tongs, and some complicated designs take longer. Tongs designed for a special purpose, however, could save many days' time and much frustration over the years.

Most smiths seem to prefer making tongs from four separate pieces of iron, instead of only two pieces as the uninitiated may conjecture. Generally the bits, or jaws, are made of two short pieces which can be handled easily in the forge. The handles, of smaller diameter than ½ inch, are made separately and are welded to the bits as the next-to-last step of manufacture, welding being easier and quicker than drawing out the original rod to a suitable thickness for handles.

Tong bits are made from ½ to ¾-inch iron bar about 6 inches long, sometimes longer, sometimes shorter, depending on the type desired. The bar is first offset for 1 to 3 inches on one end to form the jaw. Next the bar is again offset below the jaws on a plane perpendicular to the jaw, to form the pivot section. Below the pivot the bar is drawn out, rounded and scarfed in preparation for welding to the handle, or rein. After that a ½-inch hole is punched or drilled through the center for the rivet. Jaws may then be shaped appropriately for the intended use. Each part of a pair of tongs is made identical to the other.

Care should be taken to keep the pivot sections thick enough to hold up under years of use without having the hole wear through.

Forming the offset on tong jaws.

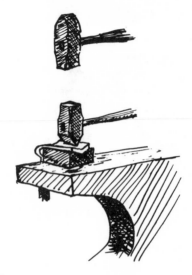

Forming square tong jaw with swage.

For arched jaws, however, which are found on many tongs, the metal is the same ¼-inch thickness from shoulder to tip, but is further drawn out to ½-inch width. Next a hole is punched for the rivet. The tips of the jaws are then bent at right angles to the long axis of the bit 1 inch from the end, and the jaws are curved almost round from the hole to the right-angle bend. A curve in the opposite direction is made below the hole to the handle butt. After that the handles are welded on and the joint is smoothed, either with a light hammer used as the joint is rotated back and forth on the anvil, or with a round swage.

Many tongs have special jaws or lips. One of the most common has lips shaped at a right angle on the long axis, a shape that will securely hold both square and round rods. With patience such lips can be shaped on the corner of the anvil. In a well-equipped shop, though, they should be shaped between a lower square swage, or swage block, and a cross- or straight-pein hammer may be used as the top

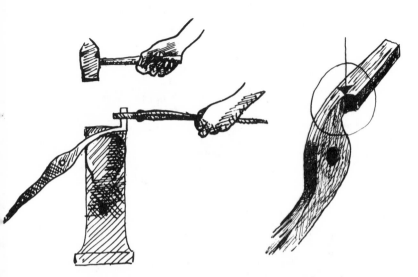

Curving tong jaws   *Scarfed shoulder of tong jaw.*

swage. Round-lipped tongs can be formed with the swage block, or lower round swage of appropriate size, and with a round rod of the proper dimension for the top swage.

One caution should be observed in forming tongs. The shoulder between the jaw and the pivot must always be scarfed, never squared. Because of strain when the tongs are closed, square shoulders tend to break after relatively little use.

Often a smith needs a punch of a size unavailable among his equipment. If he plans to punch only one or two holes he may use a handy rod of the correct size, even though it is of soft iron. Usually, though, he makes himself a set of punches of various sizes, all made as carefully as his chisels. Both punches and chisels require the same general technique, and both are tempered.

Set chisels and punches are started as hammers are started. The eye is punched, first of all, then the bit and butt are formed. For rodded tools, the tool is formed first and a groove is formed with the fuller around the body as the last operation before tempering. All of this is relatively simple for a good smith. The secret of making punches and chisels durable and effective, however, is packing. Some smiths know the secret; others never learn and as a consequence spend untold hours re-dressing chisels and punches after almost every job.

Before packing, the punch or chisel bit must be shaped under a cherry-red heat. Since packing spreads the edge of a chisel somewhat, initial shaping should take this into consideration, and vertical-side surfaces should be slightly beveled toward the edge.

Packing is exactly what its name implies. It is a technique whereby the fibers of the carbon steel are packed tightly with hammerblows to provide an extra degree of density to the chisel or punch point.

The color is important for packing (or tamping). It should be a sunrise red, barely discernible in regular light, neither too hot nor too cold. So important is the color that the wise smith checks it by thrusting the iron into a dark chamber, a small keg or box placed near the forge, so that the color can be judged more accurately. If the metal is too hot it will not pack. If too cold, it may crystallize and break.

Actual packing is done with a light hammer, usually ball pein, about 1½ pounds in weight. When the chisel edge attains sunrise red in the forge it is taken out and is laid across the horn, or on the anvil face next to its rounded corner. It is struck rapidly with the hammer at one point on the anvil, the smith turning it from one side to the other while he draws it toward him under the blows. This is continued until all red disappears and hammering is stopped. On chisels, the last three hammer blows are important. One should be placed on either side of the edge and the last placed in the middle of the edge at a slightly higher point. These last blows ar-

How to finish packing chisel bit—forming and packing

range the fibers so as to prevent the chisel edge from breaking in a crescent shape in later use.

Packing punches is only slightly different from packing chisels. Instead of turning a punch from side to side, it is rotated back and forth under the hammer on the anvil face. The last three blows on punches must be spaced equidistant around the circumference near the point.

After packing, chisels and punches are hardened and tempered to a straw yellow. The packing is not affected by high heats and can only be altered by heating to an orange-red and giving the piece a sharp tap on its blunt end.

Wood chisels are formed much like metal chisels, except that wood chisels have wooden handles. For this reason a wood chisel is either drawn out to a tang, formed next to a wide shoulder, or the butt end of the chisel is formed and welded into a conical socket in which a wooden handle is inserted. Wood chisels hold up better if packed.

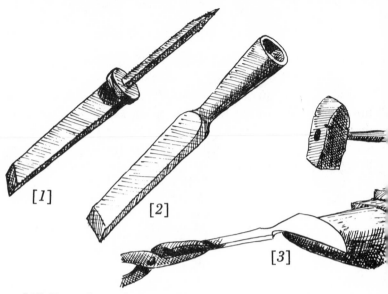

[1] *Tanged wood chisel.* [2] *Socketed wood chisel.* [3] *Forming socket.*

In making anvil tools the smith uses general techniques, his main problem being the drawing out and shaping of the square shank that fits into the hardie hole on the anvil. This is always shaped first, whether making a hardie, a beak, a leaf tool, or a larger swage. Of course, the fuller is used to draw out the shank and shoulders are dressed with the set hammer. After forming the shank, hardies are made exactly like any other chisel, including packing and tempering.

Swages are made of a square tool-steel bar. After the shank is drawn out to proper size for the hardie hole, the opposite end of the bar is brought almost to welding heat, the shank is placed in the hardie hole, and the hot end is upset with a heavy hammer. The partially formed swage is then taken from the hardie hole and its edges are dressed. Then using a rod, fuller, or square bar, the depression of the swage face is formed. The last steps are to level the face with a set hammer or flatter and to temper to a straw color. Often the face and shank of a swage are made separately, and the shank is butt-welded to the center of the bottom of the swage face.

One of the most useful tools for metalworkers down through the ages is the file. This instrument is mentioned in the First Book of Samuel. It is essential for smoothing and shaping iron into intricate forms. Files have long been made in every size and shape and degree of fineness, and until satisfactory file-cutting machines were perfected in Europe and America in the late nineteenth century, a truly infinite variety was available over the world.

Early in history file cutting became a specialty, requiring a steady hand, a good eye, and a delicate touch. Nevertheless, the production of files was often found within the province of the village blacksmith in isolated communities all over the world.

Since file teeth are cut into the blank with a chisel or

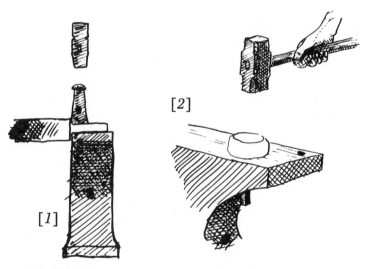

[1] *Shouldering swage tang with set hammer.* [2] *Upsetting swage face.*

punch in the days of hand manufacture, the file maker carefully anneals his blanks by heating them to cherry red, then burying them in ashes for at least twelve hours to assure maximum malleability before cutting.

Historically, and currently, files are made from smooth bars or blanks, of carbon steel or cast steel, the smoothing being done early in history with flatters, then by rolling after the seventeenth century, and after about 1800 sometimes by planing on a milling machine. Round, square, triangular, and half-round file blanks were formed with swages before the advent of rolling mills. Before the teeth are cut, a tang is forged at one end of the blank, and further smoothness is attained by grinding and filing with a fine file after annealing, to remove the oxide and level any minute rough spots.

The equipment needed for cutting the teeth is specialized but simple. First of all, there is a lead block with molded depressions fitted to various types and sizes of file blanks. This sits on the workbench, and the blank is held in the proper place with a leather strap at each end, which reaches through holes in the bench and is attached to a board. By pressing on this board with his foot the file maker holds the straps taut. The tang always points to the file cutter. Also, the blank is lightly oiled before being placed on the block.

Actual cutting of teeth is done with a short rigid chisel and a peculiarly shaped hammer with an oblique face and a crooked handle. For cutting rough files the smith employs a 7- or 8-pound hammer. Very fine files are cut with a hammer weighing only 1 or 2 ounces.

File making, as with any craft, had its own terminology. "Overcutting" describes forming the first row of diagonal ridges or teeth, while "upcutting" describes the second cut, which provides a crosshatched surface on mill files and small finishing files.

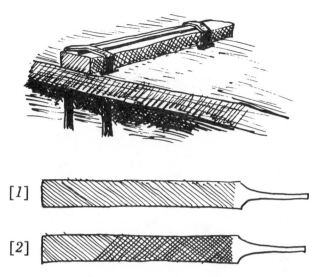

Top: Lead block and straps used in filemaking. Bottom:
[1] overcut, [2] upcut.

Cutting begins at the heel of the file. Holding the chisel at about a 60-degree angle to the blank, the cutter strikes the chisel a firm blow, which leaves a ragged diagonal ridge in the blank. Using this as a guide for the next blow, he continues his cutting down the blank to a point ¼ inch from the tang. His skill is reflected in the even angle of his cuts and the even force of each hammerblow. As the series of blows on one side of the blank will curve it slightly, the cutter must straighten his blank with a wooden or lead mallet on a lead anvil before turning it over to cut the reverse side.

Rasps, of course, are cut with a half-round punch instead of a chisel.

Perhaps the most delicate operation in file making is tempering the finished file without destroying the cutting edges of the teeth by oxidation. This is accomplished by using a paste made of yeast, or tallow, or other soft organic material such as bread dough.

173

Nearly every file maker in the old days had his own secret formula for this paste. After drawing the file through this mixture the sticky surface should be liberally sprinkled with salt or borax, or even clean sand, as a flux. Ancient file makers often mixed roasted and crushed animal hoofs in with the flux, thinking that the carbon in burnt hoofs would replace any carbon burned out in the tempering process.

Once thoroughly coated, the file is slowly heated to a cherry red, either on a flat fire in the forge or in a container of molten lead. It is then quenched in brine to harden. Residue of the paste is removed by scrubbing with diluted muriatic acid and sand. After this the file is soaked in limewater to help prevent rust. New files are tested on a prover, a small piece of hardened steel.

One of the first tools made by emerging mankind was the knife. The most primitive tribes throughout history all had some sort of knife, usually made of flaked stone, but sometimes devised of a razor-sharp splint of reed or bamboo. The blacksmiths of prehistoric times probably made more knives than any other tool, and knife making has been important all through history. Herbert Mitchum, a smith in the unincorporated community of Durand, Greene County, Georgia, continued the tradition by producing a number of heavy knives for soldiers from his area who fought in World War II.

This simple, basic tool, as important in the kitchen as it was in its many shop forms during the era of handicraftsmanship, is not quite so easy to make as it may seem on the surface. Of course, all knives—butcher knives, drawknives, pocketknives, and specialized forms such as plane irons— are made of .75 carbon steel. Some forms of knives are forged in one flat piece, the flat shank being punched so that wooden or bone or horn handles can be bradded on. Others may have a thin tang, such as a file's, forged to fit a solid handle with a hole bored through its length. Blades can be shaped any number of ways for various uses. The general technique for forging all knives, however, is similar.

When a tang is wanted, this is forged first, and for fancy carving knives a small button is then upset between the blade and the tang. Forming this button is a rather delicate operation done with a monkey tool or a bar with a hole through which the tang is pushed so that a flat shoulder will be formed during upsetting. The chamfered shoulder or the blade side of the button is formed with a fuller on the horn of the anvil. After that the blade is drawn out in rough form and cut diagonally to form a rough point. Next the width of the blade is curved over the horn, making the intended edge slightly concave. Rolling blows above the round corner of the anvil face both thin the edge and extend its length so that the concavity of the edge is straightened. As best he can, the smith shapes the point to fit his preconceived design, then smooths the blade with his flatter, again working over the rounded corner of the anvil face. The shape is finished with a file. In forging any thin piece such as a knife blade the smith must be careful to lay on his hammer-blows evenly. Otherwise the blade will warp when being tempered.

Heavy hunting knives sometimes require a blood gutter, or flute, down the length of the blade. Fluting is done with the top and bottom fullers in combination, the blade being placed on the bottom fuller and the top fuller being placed directly over the bottom before being struck by the helper.

A smith must be particularly careful in heating a knife during forging. The steel is forged at cherry-red heat, but once the edge is formed great caution must be met lest the paper-thin edge overheat and burn. Once this happens, always when the knife is nearly completed, the steel is ruined and the unfinished knife must be discarded.

Equal care must be taken in hardening knives, especially

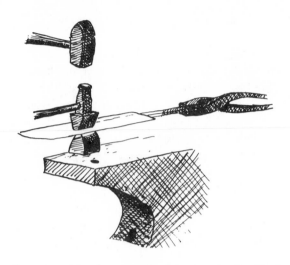

Forming blood gutter in hunting knife blade

for thin blades. After being heated to cherry red, the blade must be immersed in brine edge-down, with the blade exactly perpendicular to the surface of the brine. This prevents air bubbles from collecting on one side of the blade, making cooling uneven and causing the blade to warp. Tangs should be hardened with the blade. In drawing the temper the smith may employ either a heated flat bar of iron or a large soldering iron. The bar is brought to an orange-red. The hardened blade is laid upon it, its edge being off the edge of the bar. As the blunt back of the blade turns straw color, then yellow, then purple, the heat spreads slowly toward the edge. Quenching is done when the edge is straw yellow. Generally the back will be purple or blue at this point. When a heavy soldering iron is used, it is heated to a dull red and laid along the back of the blade until the heat runs through the blade as described above.

On knives with thin tangs the smith must be careful that the tang is soft. Unless the temper in this thin portion is drawn out at least to a purple, there is an excellent chance

176

that it will break off while the handle is being installed. The handle is secured by bradding the end of the tang over a punchplate the shape of the cross section of the handle.

For flat-shanked knives with two-piece handles, the handle may be bradded on with iron, brass, or copper brads.

Knife blades can be finished to a glossy surface with a file, preferably one somewhat worn, held across the blade by both hands and rubbed the length of the blade until all rough spots are cut smooth.

Hunting knives often require a handguard between the handle and the blade. This is no more than a thin bar of iron punched to fit the tang and placed in position before the handle is put on.

Knives are a pleasure to make. The smith can easily see the result of each of his hammerblows as he draws the hot steel toward him across the anvil face. When he gets to the point of thinning the edge, the blade curves gracefully, as if by magic and the smith feels himself a detached observer as he succumbs to the regular, hypnotic beat. Then, when forging is done and the blade is clamped in the bench vise, the file carves the final shape, sharpens the edge, forms the back and the point, and leaves a thing of graceful beauty.

Clasp knives are more difficult to make, having a number of separate parts which must be formed to fit and then assembled. The blade is forged as any other knife blade, except that it has no tang, only a butt which is drilled for a pivot pin and formed with a notch to hold the blade rigid. Max Segal, master smith from Philadelphia, states that the thumb nail groove for opening is made with a half-round file while the blade is bent. It then is straightened and tempered.

Frames for clasp knives can be of several designs. The simplest is merely two pieces of sheet iron, perhaps an ⅛-inch thick, shaped as desired to fit the hand. It is drilled with small holes in appropriate spots to pin the blade and spring

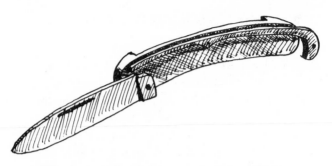

The iron and steel parts of a clasp knife

into position and to brad on a wooden or a bone handle. Some frames, the better ones for that matter, are forged from ¼-inch bar, drawn down from a boss, through which the blade pin is inserted, to ¹⁄₁₆-inch thickness, where the handle fits. This design gives much more strength to the pivot pin and, consequently, longevity to the knife.

Knife springs are shaped to fit inside the frame, to which they are riveted. For single-blade knives the spring must be curved to fit the butt end of the handle; for multiblade knives they fit only along the back of the handle. For any type of clasp knife, the spring must be riveted in at least two points.

From ancient time until about World War I, any farm or carpenter shop had a drawknife as a fundamental piece of equipment. After 1950 they were seldom even displayed in hardware stores, and they are unidentifiable to a majority of the population. Because of their many uses drawknives were one of the more common tools made by the blacksmith before factory-made hand tools became common.

In early days drawknives, as with many other cutting tools, were made of wrought iron with a thin strip of carbon steel welded onto the blade. After welding, the blade is thinned along its edge, as with any knife, and the resulting curve is straightened by drawing out the back to a steeper bevel. Tangs are then drawn out at either end, the tangs being

about 3-inches long. After that the blade is tempered, its edge
to a straw yellow and its back to purple or dark blue.

Now the tangs must be extended at right angles to the
blade so that handles can be applied. This is done by welding.
The tempered blade is wrapped in wet cloth to keep it cool,
and the tang and its intended extension are brought to welding heat after being scarfed on their ends. Usually the handle
extension is cross-welded to the tang, though it might be lap-
welded and later bent to its right-angle position.

Wooden handles, bored through their length, are driven
on the tangs, and the end of tang is either bradded through
washers or clinched over the wood.

There was another form of shaving knife supplied by the
olden blacksmith, the plane iron. Up until the beginning of
the twentieth century most carpenters, and all cabinet and
coach makers, sometimes required as many as a hundred
different planes for their work. Some were round and some
were hollow; some were flat and some were designed to cut
very elaborate moldings. All of them, before 1870, con-

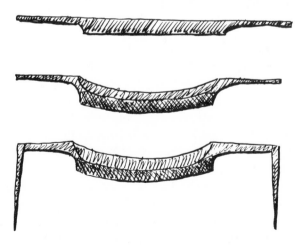

The steps in making a draw knife

sisted of a hard wooden stock into which the iron was wedged into position. Irons were ordered from the blacksmith.

A plane iron is no more than a flat strip of iron faced with steel with a beveled cutting edge ground to about a 60-degree angle. When designed to cut molding they were shaped on the cutting edge to fit the molding desired.

Though simple in design, plane irons were not easily made, especially before 1860, after which carbon steel was abundant and the plane iron could have been forged of solid steel. Before 1860 they were usually made of wrought iron with a thin steel strip welded to the iron. Because thin strips of carbon steel burn easily the smith must be extraordinarily careful to watch the steel as it is brought slowly to welding heat.

The steel must be slightly smaller and thicker than the iron back. Its edges will become coincident to the iron when hammered. Since small iron cools quickly when taken from the fire, hardly allowing time to put two pieces in position for hammering before welding heat is lost, it is well to clamp the wrought-iron bar and the steel together with tongs secured with a tong ring. They are placed in the fire with the steel uppermost to allow the iron to reach its higher welding heat at the same time the thin steel reaches its own welding heat. When brought to welding heat, the two are taken from the fire together and quickly joined. After welding, the iron is dressed into shape, packed as with a chisel, and tempered to a straw yellow. Sometimes the smith will feel it necessary to file his plane iron smooth after tempering.

Back in the days when 90 percent of Americans and almost as many Europeans were farmers, every farm needed axes and adzes. In America the frontier required that peculiarly American tool, the tomahawk, both for hunters and for the Indian trade. Each of these tools might be found in a variety of shapes for a number of different uses. All, however, were made using the same general techniques. Until 1870, usually the body of each was made of iron with a steel blade welded to the iron.

Tomahawks were made in different designs by English, French, Spanish, Belgian, and American smiths from the time America was colonized until the last of the free Indians around 1880. They generally maintained the form of the ancient Saxon ax and the Norse ax of prehistoric time, a form carried down through the ages with the eighteenth-century English and German felling ax and still seen in factory-made felling axes used in South America in the latter half of the twentieth century. In design they are quite simple, merely the result of wrapping a strip of iron around a rod to form an eye and welding the double strip together before finishing. The smiths who made them for the Indian trade up until 1880 undoubtedly duplicated the technique of long-dead smiths whose helpers trod upon the wineskin.

Usually the eye of a tomahawk is formed by bending an orange-red strip of iron some 1½-inches wide and ¼-inch

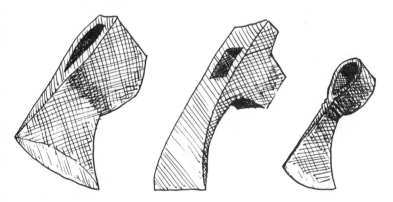

Left: Felling ax. Center: Foot adz. Right: Tomahawk.

thick around a 1-inch or a 1½-inch rod placed upright in the hardie hole of the anvil. If a perfectly round eye is desired the smith must first bend his iron at right angles in two places, the length between the two bends being equal to the circumference of the upright rod. This insures a tight seam where the strip meets after forming the eye. Next the iron is welded for about 2 inches from the eye, leaving ¼ inch on the end, which is not welded. The unwelded portion is then scarfed and, after scarfing, is separated with a hot chisel to receive the steel.

The easiest way of welding the steel bit to the iron head is to clamp the steel in position before bringing the two pieces to welding heat. This is done by scarfing the steel on its back edge, then cutting slightly with a hot set which is twisted be-

Left: Making a tomahawk. Right: Teeth formed in steel tomahawk bit before welding.

fore withdrawing, creating small, sharply pointed projections on either side of the scarf. The steel is allowed to cool, and the split end of the tomahawk body is brought up to a cherry heat. The iron is removed and the eye is placed over the end of the anvil horn so that the split section is upright. The scarfed steel is placed in the split and hammered in with a couple of good, firm blows, then the iron is removed from the horn and the red iron hammered down so that the steel points penetrate the iron, holding it in place. Brush both pieces with a stiff steel brush before the two are hammered together to remove any excess oxide scale which may be present.

Welding the steel and iron together is the next step. It must be remembered that the two metals reach welding heat at different temperatures, the iron requiring a higher temperature than the steel, and that steel burns and is ruined if heated beyond welding heat. When placed in the fire for welding, then the smith must place the iron portion nearer the hot center of the fire than the steel. Flux is liberally sprinkled along the edges of the joint when the metal reaches a cherry red.

The two pieces must be brought to welding heat gradually to minimize oxidation, and a close eye must be kept on the two pieces so that they can be moved if the steel seems to be heating too quickly. When both pieces become white hot the smith sprinkles more flux on the joint, using his spoon so that the flux can be applied without removing the pieces from the fire. When welding heat is reached the two pieces are removed and placed resting on the edge of the anvil face at a slight angle that prevents the hot iron from touching the cold anvil. Then it is hammered with quick, sure blows, starting at the end of the split in the iron and working toward the edge with glancing blows that mold the iron and steel together, making, generally, an invisible joint. The piece should be turned over quickly as soon as one side is hammered and quickly molded on the opposite side.

At this point, while the joined metal is still hot, the roughly shaped blade may be forged into nearly finished form by hammering edgewise over the horn and flat on the face until brought into proper shape. Often a decorative notch is put on the bottom of the blade using a small fuller or the wedge-shaped pein of a hammer. After that the eye is dressed or drifted to a round or oval or a diamond shape, and the top and bottom of the blade is dressed by forging or by trimming with a hot set.

The flatter is used to smooth up the cheeks of the blade. If no flatter is available, the cheeks can be slightly bulged in the center section to make final filing easier. After tempering to a pigeon blue, the tomahawk can be ground or filed to remove all oxide scale and to finish shaping.

Some smiths in the Indian era made a number of different forms of tomahawks; some, called pipe tomahawks, had a pipe bowl forged or brazed to the back of the eye. Techniques for these more elaborate tomahawks are described in an excellent book, *American Indian Tomahawks*, by Peterson, published by the Museum of the American Indian, New York.

There is virtually no difference in making a tomahawk and making a pre-eighteenth-century felling ax. The ax is just made of heavier stock. In the American colonies, however, where cutting trees was a necessity, the felling ax was refined and given a short blade and a poll behind the eye to provide balance. Sometimes the poll was preformed as a boss on a strip of iron which was then bent around a drift. Often, though, the polled ax was made of three pieces, two pieces of iron to make the sides and, of course, a steel blade.

For making axes most smiths kept wooden patterns for the heads of felling axes, broadaxes, hatchets, half-hatchets, and for any special design or weight his trade might want. To make an ax the smith must use a hot set roughly to trim two flat bars of iron to fit the pattern. These are welded together at the poll, with care taken not to carry the weld into the part that is intended for the eye. Now an elliptical drift is inserted between the two wings of welded iron and the eye is formed by hammering each wing tightly around the drift. After removing the drift the blade is welded, except for the front ¼ inch, which must receive the steel. As with

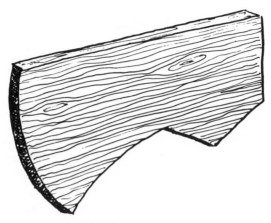

Wooden ax pattern

tomahawks the steel is roughed on its back side and driven into the split left from welding and welded in. Finishing is accomplished by drifting the eye, shaping and straightening the blade, and tempering and grinding to its final shape.

Some old-time smiths preferred to punch the eye to avoid too much welding, with its danger of burning the iron. This is often satisfactory with a long, narrow ax-eye if the finest-quality Swedish iron is used. Poorer iron, however, may split along its fibers. With punched-eye axes the slit into which the steel edge is welded must be cut with a hot set.

"Adz" is a word hardly heard of, even in isolated rural areas, after World War II except in a game of Scrabble. To eighteenth- and early-nineteenth-century carpenters, and to certain specialized workmen in the timber industries, however, the adz was an important tool. It is a form of ax or hatchet, differing from these fundamental tools in that the plane of its blade is perpendicular to its handle. Hand adzes were used to shape boards, to hollow out wooden troughs, and to smooth barrel staves. Foot adzes, which were used with both hands, were used to smooth squared logs in cabins, to shave down boards from half-logs, and, most recently, to shape railroad ties. They were widely used to carve ribs and smooth strakes in the shipbuilding industry. Of course, in the days before the mass production of all tools, adzes were made of iron with a steel blade welded in place. The manufacture, though, is quite different in that the square eye was always punched and drifted, rather than welded around a bar, as with axes.

Adzes are generally made from quite heavy iron bars, 1 inch by 1½ inches, or perhaps 1½-inches square. For ease in handling, the smith should try to start an adz on the end of a long bar, so that much of the work can be done by holding the iron barehanded instead of with tongs, which become more awkward the heavier the work being done.

While an adz blade is quite thin, the eye of the tool is a rectangular extended sleeve, designed to hold the handle without any play whatsoever, in order to insure accurate strokes while adzing. Despite the difficulties this creates in forming the tool, it is easier in the long-run to follow the general rule of thumb and punch the eye first through the wider dimension of the bar. A rectangular punch 1 inch by 1½ inches is used, the long axis of the punch running lengthwise along the tool. While the iron is white hot the hole, previously worked with a center punch, is punched three quarters through from the bottom, 2½ inches from its end. The iron is then turned and punched from the top and the plug driven out over the edge of the anvil. A slightly tapering rectangular drift is now used to stretch and dress the hole, the point of the taper being on the bottom.

If a long bar is available the blade is formed at the end. This is done by fullering the bar on one side, starting within ¾ inch of the eye. After fullering, the blade is smoothed and further drawn out with a hammer until it is about ½-inch thick at the eye, 3½-inches long, and it is spread 3-inches wide at the end. It should not be drawn to less than ¼-inch

Forming center ridge on adz blade

thickness on the end, which is then scarfed for welding to the
steel edge. The blade is beveled along its edges to ⅛ inch,
leaving a ½-inch ridge in the center section next to the eye
to provide strength and to insure that the blade will not bend
in use.

Unlike axes, the steel bit of adzes is lap-welded to the top
of the blade. The steel, slightly narrower than the iron and
¼-inch thick, must be scarfed on one edge. After welding to
the top of the iron blade, the bar is trimmed and the steel is
drawn out to a sharp edge. Since an adz is tempered rather
hard and relatively brittle, the edge cannot be forged to as
thin an edge as an ax.

Forming the poll is also done with the fuller, starting
close to the eye. The poll should be further drawn out with
a hammer until it is about 1-inch thick, its width being that of
the original bar. If the adz is being forged on the end of a

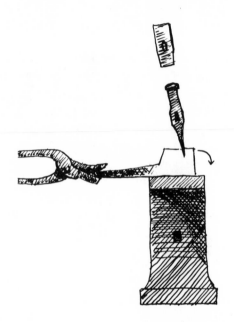

Cutting with chisel to form adz poll in mild steel

long bar, it can now be cut off 1 inch from the eye, and the face of the poll can be dressed flat.

The corners formed by the eye and both blade and poll should be dressed with the set hammer, or with a small fuller for a rounded corner. To draw out the eye, this part is heated to a white heat and the drift is inserted. The sides of the eye are then drawn out with glancing blows of the hammer, molding each of the four sides into a flat surface, which is beveled from the top of the adz to a thickness of only ⅛ inch at the bottom of the eye.

Curving the blade roughly to fit the arc formed when an adz is in use is done with a soft hammer over the big end of the horn. After curving, the bottom side of the blade may require some smoothing and chamfering with a light hammer.

Tempering is the last step before grinding and finishing with a file. Adz edges are tempered to a purple, almost as hard as a razor.

There is some variation in the manner of making an adz. One example of an old handmade adz demonstrates that its maker merely welded the eye—punched in a 1-inch-thick bar of iron some 3-inches long—to a long piece of steel that formed blade and poll. Undoubtedly he drifted the eye out after welding. In using mild steel after 1870, some smiths formed the poll by using a chisel to cut the heavy metal behind the eye to about ¾ inch from the top. This portion was then bent back and forged into shape. Such a method, of course, is unsuitable for iron, since the chisel would cut through the fibers and weaken the poll.

Making hand adzes required the same techniques on a smaller scale. Also hand adzes were curved to fit the needs of the customer. A carpenter with short arms might have required slightly more curve than one with long arms. Gouge blades, as in a small cooper's adz or a large gutter adz, were hollowed over the horn or in a bottom swage.

Augers, drill bits, and reamers, for wood and metal, were a product of local smithies until the 1860s and 1870s in Europe and America. Neither are particularly difficult to make. All were generally made of steel rather than a combination of steel and iron.

Drill bits and reamers for metal are no more than flattened rods with the end of the shank upset for about ¾ inch down, to form a tapered square portion that fits into the chuck of a brace or beam drill. Usually this is done by heating the end to a white heat, then cooling the first ¼ inch of the end in the slack tub before upsetting. By the time the upsetting has been accomplished, enough heat has run into the cooled portion so that it is again red and can be dressed in the same heat. Drill points are formed by flattening the end of a steel rod after upsetting the shank and filing it to a point which measures 30 degrees between the long axis and the perpendicular. Reamers, made of a rod flattened for from 1 to 6 inches, are filed to a 30-degree angle along the edges. Both

Welding wide drill blade to shank

reamers and drills are packed, as in making cold chisels, and both are tempered to a straw yellow. The old-fashioned drill bit was replaced generally in the 1870s by factory-made twist drills which are made on special milling machines.

Auger bits present more of a problem to manufacture to the smith than metal drills. Essentially a drill is a scraping instrument, while the auger bit cuts and must therefore have a cutting edge. A simple bit is formed from a steel rod, upset and square-tapered on one end to fit the chuck. Sometimes an added piece of steel is welded on to the opposite end to give it width, but if the rod is big enough the bit end can be drawn out flat, or a flat bar of steel can be drawn down into a shank that is then upset on the end. Forming the cutting blade is done with either chisel or file. The flat end is shaped to provide a pivot in the center, a scriber on one side that cuts a circle into the wood as the bit is rotated, and a triangular cutting blade perpendicular to the flat of the bit, slightly slanted across its width, that cuts out the wood outlined by the scriber.

Between the pivot point and the scriber the metal is cut or filed out with the top edge perpendicular to the axis of the bit. The cutting blade is formed by a diagonal edge from a spot at the base of the pivot point to the outside corner of the cutting side. This triangular section is then heated and bent to its perpendicular plane, which is even with the base of the pivot point and scriber.

A long, twisted auger bit can be formed from a long rod upset at one end, which is drawn out thin and to the width of the hole desired. If for cutting a large hole, it can be made from a flat bar of steel to which an iron or steel rod is welded at one end. Its cutting end is formed as with a simple auger bit. The twist is formed by heating the flat section evenly along its width to a cherry-red, holding one end in the vise and twisting the other end. The smith must be careful to twist in a clockwise direction so that the wings of the bit will extract chips of wood while the brace is being turned. Twisting is even as long as the heat is even, otherwise the hotter sections of the bit will twist more tightly than the cooler sections. The twist must be done in one heat.

After twisting, the bit can be straightened with a wooden mallet or a lead hammer, then tempered. Both simple bits and twist bits should have the temper drawn to a pigeon blue.

While a straight, well-tempered twist bit was important to an old-time carpenter who fed his brood by boring holes, making such a bit can be an artistic experience for the smith. If his eye is good enough to insure an even tone of cherry-red along the part to be twisted, the twisting itself demonstrates the satisfying qualities of hot iron as a working material. The smith must be somewhat careful in twisting, but so long as he turns evenly and does not drop his tongs accidentally in the debris of his shop floor, the iron twists quite naturally into a graceful, perfect spiral. What smith, on seeing it turn out right, can help having the slight feeling of being a demigod, a touch of the mythical magic of Hephaestus, a sense of well-being in his choice of a trade and pride in the craftsmanship resulting from his cumulative experience? Such control over a reluctant element brings a certain headiness which cannot be bought by all the wealth of the Indies.

There was another type of wood bit used during the days of handcrafts. It was called a spoon bit, and it was used more to enlarge holes than to bore them. Its shape resembled an elongated spoon bowl with the regular shank found on one end. To make it the smith starts as though with a twist bit, but forming a round end. Instead of twisting, however, he

Forming spoon bit on bick

hollows, using the fuller in the correctly-sized cavity of a
bottom swage or a swage block. He takes care to hollow the
two ends of the bit evenly and to see that the center axis of
the shank and the long edges of the bit lie on the same plane.
After tempering to a pigeon blue he sharpens the end and the
left-hand side to a razor edge.

Shovels are such pedestrian, commonplace ditchdigger's
tools, so taken for granted by gardeners and workmen alike,
that few speculate how they were made by hand before the
days of factories. Well, they were made by the local blacksmith, and it was not easy. The difficulties of making a shovel
stem from the fact that a large surface must be heated and
thin sheet iron must be welded. Shovels recovered from a ship
sunk at the Battle of Yorktown and those dug up from Civil
War battlefields are made in the same manner, indicating
that the mode of manufacture was well established in the
eighteenth century and was not improved in the next one
hundred years.

Sheet iron ⅛-inch thick and as wide as necessary is the

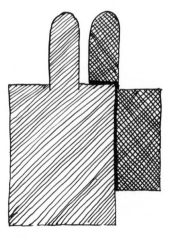

Shovel patterns—front and back

basic material used. Two sheets are required for a shovel, one shorter than the other by about 6 inches. These are cut with bench shears to fit a wooden pattern roughly resembling a shovel, with a 10-inch-square blade and a tang some 2½-inches wide and 10- to 12-inches long. After cutting to fit the pattern the tangs are heated to orange-red and three or four rivet holes are punched down the center axis of each. While still hot the tangs are roughly hollowed over the horn.

A special mandrel is needed to finish shaping the tangs and the hollow of the blade into which the handle fits. It is no more than a sharpened rod of the same diameter as the intended handle. Some mandrels are straight, but some are curved gracefully to shape the shovel for a curved handle. The mandrel is placed on the anvil face, and the sheets of iron heated to orange-red are hammered to fit it, top and bottom. Once shaped, the two pieces are welded together.

It is extremely difficult to fit two thin pieces of sheet iron precisely together and weld them before they lose welding heat. The solution is to fasten the two together with a couple of light rivets or by doubling the back edge of one over the other or by clamping with heavy tongs secured with a tong ring. This avoids the problem of precisely fitting the two

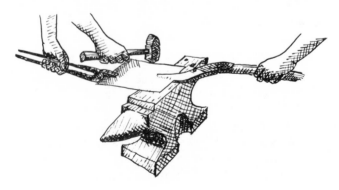

Forming handle socket with special mandrel

pieces very quickly. Also, the double thickness of iron holds the heat longer than a single thickness, giving more time for welding. Before fastening, though, both plates should be heated and sprinkled liberally with flux on the surfaces to be welded.

With such a large surface, welding must be done one half at a time. To avoid burning or excess oxidation of the thin sheet iron, the fire must be deep and the bellows must be pumped gently, to slowly bring the pieces to a semimolten state on one half. Once that state is reached the shovel is brought from the fire and hammered, starting at the back, following the edges, and then across the bottom of the shorter sheet. Hammering must be done quickly before the iron cools too much to join. The process is repeated on the other half. Final finishing consists of reinserting the mandrel to dress the tangs and the handle cavity in the blade, and to shape the blade to a curve or hollow if desired. Handles are riveted on.

Some old handmade shovels were riveted together instead of being welded. This method, however, must be considered an expedient, for a riveted shovel cannot be so durable as one that is welded. On occasion a meticulous smith might have welded a thin strip of steel to the digging edge of a shovel blade to make a more effective and durable tool. Most would have renovated an iron blade by welding on a new strip of iron when the original had worn down. Some riveted shovels were fitted over a wedge-shaped wooden core which gave them additional strength.

Any smith skillful enough to make a hammer, an ax, or an adz can make digging tools such as pickaxes and mattocks and hoes. Mattocks and pickaxes generally had steel points and edges, with more steel than an ax; they had to be re-dressed frequently and drawn out to a new point.

Since pickaxes and mattocks are still part of the equipment of building and utility companies, the shops of these businesses are about the last refuges in industry for forges. Some still maintain a small forge for redressing picks and mattocks and air drill bits, now that the general blacksmith and the specialist tool dresser are so diminished in number as to be almost nonexistent. There is a master tool dresser, however, still active in Atlanta. Mr. E. W. Horne, son and grandson of blacksmiths, makes a very good living dressing and tempering all manner of tools for a very large clientele.

A sometime product of the old local smith was the saw. Most saws, though, were made by specialists in a few centers of Europe until first made in America by Lindley, Johnson and Whitcroft, about 1840. A saw, in principle, is not difficult to make. It is nothing more than a thin sheet of steel with teeth filed into it, the teeth then being set at a slight angle, to widen the cut and avoid binding. Before rolling mills were developed, however, it must have taken a very careful worker to draw out steel to the evenness required by a saw blade, but it was done, for the saw is an ancient instrument. Thinning evenly was probably done with a flatter. The main difficulty in making a saw by hand from scratch would be tempering such thin stock without warping or breaking it. A special elongated fire and a special quenching tub are surely needed. Even with such special equipment, the problem of bringing the whole blade to a uniform cherry red, and later a pigeon blue, is immense.

In America, and probably in Europe, the local smith was sometimes called upon to repair a broken saw. Old John Whitley, a bearded smith of great reputation who lived in the upper settlement of Vinings, Cobb County, Georgia, between 1842 and his death in 1910, was said to have been able to weld a broken crosscut saw so skillfully that one could not tell it from a new one. His skill, however, has so overshadowed his methods that no record of how he tempered the repaired blade has been kept. Usually a saw that developed a split was repaired by brazing.

One of the more ingenious tools which has been discarded by modern craftsmen, for reasons unknown, is the holdfast. This simple device was merely a crooked rod jambed into a hole in the work bench or anvil to grip a piece of wood or metal being worked. In essence it serves as the upper jaw of a vertical vise, the bench or anvil acting as the lower jaw.

Although the function of a holdfast was stable, its form varied according to the taste and skill of the smith who made it. Some were made of round rod, and some of square. The square jambed better than the round, but it also disfigured the hole in the benchtop more quickly. In general form they resembled a misshapen "L," the long leg being the shank, which was jambed into the bench. The other leg was short and had a button upset on its end or on the flattened end. The bridge between was sometimes flattened vertically to provide strength.

Holdfasts can be made from ¾-inch rods or bars cut to

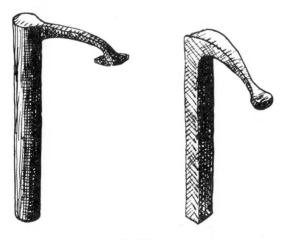

Holdfasts

12-inch length. As usual, if long stock is available it is much easier to forge and shape one end before cutting, to avoid the need for tongs. First of all, the end is upset into a button 1-inch or 1¼-inches wide, or merely flattened to a surface 1-inch square. The bridge portion, about 3-inches long, is drawn out with fuller and hammer to a dimension 1-inch wide by ½-inch thick, tapering to the buttoned end. This bridge portion is first shouldered where the flattening begins. After drawing out it is bent over the round corner of the anvil, on the side opposite the shoulder, to a 90-degree angle, and is then curved downward to the button. The end is curved back to make the bottom surface of the button, perpendicular to the shank.

Holdfasts with round shanks are made the same way, or they can be made of two pieces of iron. The shank, ½ inch to ¾ inch in diameter and 4-inches long, may have a tenon ¼ inch in diameter and ⅝-inch long formed on one end. A piece of flat iron ⅝-inch wide, ⅛-inch thick, and 5-inches long is wrapped around this tenon and welded to the shank, the extensions being welded together as with a tomahawk blade. After welding, this flat piece is tapered and a button

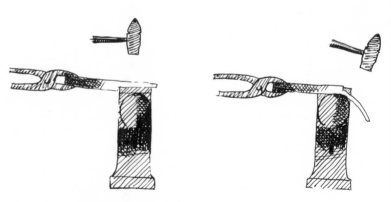

Shaping and bending arm on square bar

Welding arm on round bar with tenon

is upset and flattened on its end. The arm thus joined is curved gently for 2½ inches, then curved sharply to a 70-degree angle so that the flat bottom of the button is perpendicular to the shank.

Before 1790 nails were an important product of any smithy. Most smiths, as a consequence, had a variety of nailheaders, made in the smithy, to produce all of the dozen or more types of nails needed by craftsmen, from the millwright to the upholsterer. Nailheaders are easy to make from a bar of steel ¾-inch thick and from ¾-inch to 1-inch wide. First they are pierced ½ inch from the end with an acutely pointed four-sided punch. The size of the nail desired determines the depth to which the punch is driven. The hole where the punch protrudes should fit the base of the intended nail. Headers should be tempered to a straw color.

Next the bar is drawn down to a ⅜-inch thickness to form a boss surrounding the small end of the hole. For horseshoe nails, a depression the shape of the nailhead is swaged in the

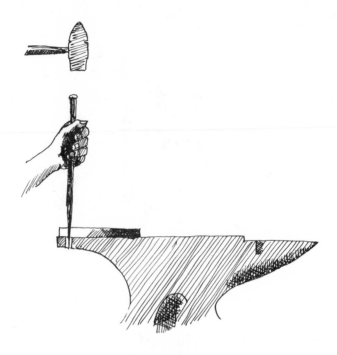

Punching nail header

small end of the hole. Many smiths made double-ended headers that would serve for making two different types of nails.

When machinery repair became an important part of the smith's trade, he developed some ingenious methods of forging these parts, methods requiring much visualization. For instance, the making of a valve handle demonstrated how a little thought can make a seemingly difficult job a simple task.

A valve handle usually is square, about 1 inch thick, with four cylindrical projections emanating from its corners. Welding seems in order, but there is a much easier way to make it.

In the center of a 1-inch-square bar 3-inches long, a square hole is punched to fit the valve stem. Both ends are drawn out to shoulders about ⅝-inch thick and 1½-inches

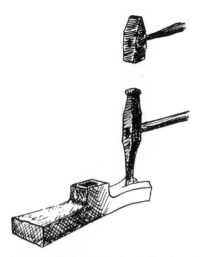

Cutting rough handles in valve handle

long, leaving a 1-inch-square boss surrounding the hole. The shoulders should be slightly thicker on the ends than next to the boss. Next each shoulder is split from the boss to the end.

These splits are widened until the two legs of each shoulder are spread into a 90-degree angle. Each leg is then forged smooth and round, and the base of the boss and the angle between the legs is finished with a large fuller.

Spanner wrenches are made generally of flat steel bars. The bars are drawn down in the center portion, reducing the width and leaving a boss at each end. Each boss is punched to create holes of the proper size. The smith should punch these holes slightly off-center to leave the metal thicker and stronger in that part directly opposite the opening of the jaw. Jaws are formed by using a chisel to cut out a section of the hole's circumference equal in width to the diameter of the hole. After filing smooth, the wrench is tempered to a brown color.

The tools used by mankind throughout history are legion. The blacksmith played a major part in making most of them.

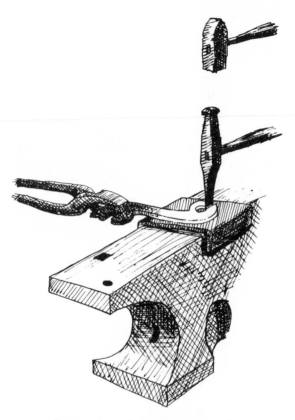

Cutting jaws in spanner wrench

To describe his technique in making every tool needed by burgeoning progress requires an encyclopedia, and even an encyclopedia could not possibly be complete, for each smith had his own problems and ideas, much as individual painters and musicians develop one of a thousand ways to create the illusions of form and sound. Aside from the basic tools of forging—hammer, anvil, bellows—the smith usually had the creative ability to design his own special tools needed for making the tools of his customers. Therein lies his strength; and therein lies the problem of describing all the techniques of tool making of all the thousands of smiths for all the thousands of years the individual blacksmith has served mankind.

If ever a modern man must make some special tool of iron or steel, let him consider the basic qualities of the material; let him use fire and air and weight to shape the metal. He will find that a little imagination applied to his problem will provide him with a strange and exciting alchemy. Through his science, combined with his art, he will find that he can transform the most reluctant metal into the most tractable, and literally shape it to his will.

Interestingly, the blacksmith is serving one of our most modern industries, jet aircraft maintenance, in at least one instance. The U.S. Air Force base at Warner Robins, Georgia, has a smith at the base who is frequently called on by mechanics to make special tools needed for maintenance, and unavailable from normal sources of tool supply. In effect old Hephaestus still lives to help furnish thunderbolts which are hurled through our contemporary skies.

7.

THE TECHNIQUES OF
MAKING HARDWARE

Modern mass-production methods of stamping out the hardware of houses and buildings is so taken for granted that one hardly gives a thought to it. Who notices the simple ingenuity of a hinge or a window latch? Who pauses to give thought to the thousands of nails used in even the simplest building? Who takes the time to count the myriad metal parts and separate screws of all the locks and latches that insure privacy and security to home and office? Indeed, who cares! All the separate items of hardware we see or use every day are as much a part of life as our clothes and transportation. These items came from the building supplier or the hardware store, and these establishments order them from the factories, and nothing is simpler.

Prior to 1870, however, most of this material came from the blacksmith, perhaps the village smith who made it all on order or, in larger areas, from a specialized forge that manufactured only one item, such as Thomas Jefferson's nail factory. This was hardly great industrial organization, for the personnel consisted of two young colored boys, each equipped with forge and anvil, hammer and hardie, and a supply of nail rods. Even the great demand for hinges for wagons, house doors, barns, and finely made cabinets was satisfied with handmade hinges until the 1870s. In St. Louis, the Hager Hinge Company, which started as a blacksmith and wheel-

204

wright's shop in 1849 and is now one of the three largest hinge manufacturers in the world, did not acquire its first hinge-making machine until 1873.

Nail-making machines were perfected just before the end of the eighteenth century, but because they made a limited variety of cut nails they did not entirely replace the smith as a nail maker until almost a hundred years after their invention. Much late-Victorian furniture, for instance, has its molding fastened with small handmade nails. Until modern times in some backwoods areas in America and Europe, and perhaps still in the backward regions of the world, nails were a product of the blacksmith.

Nails are ancient devices, and over the centuries were developed in many forms for many special uses. All, however, are made according to the same basic technique.

There were roseheaded nails, some with flat points, clasp nails for soft wood, and finishing nails with a T- or L-shaped head, as can be seen in the fine carpentry of the Governor's Palace in Williamsburg. There were Flemish tacks, wide-headed brads, cabinet brads, flooring brads, and tenterhooks, as well as clouts and clogs and scuppers. Then there were horseshoe nails.

Nails are made from nail rods, long slim rods usually about a ¼-inch square, which, from the seventeenth to the nineteenth centuries, were supplied by rolling mills and slitting mills and were delivered in bundles tied together with wire. Remnants of bundles of nail rods have been found on the site of Jefferson's nail factory. Before the time of slitting mills, nail rods were forged by hand, usually by an apprentice, who was given a pile of old horseshoes and other scrap from which he would draw out the rods. Indeed the transformation of scrap into nail rods was practiced in isolated smithies well into the nineteenth century, until cut nails were manufactured cheaply in volume beginning about 1830.

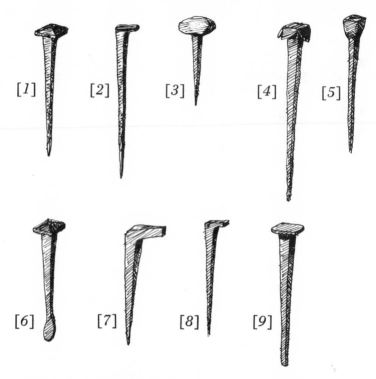

Types of handmade nails: [1] *rosehead,* [2] *flooring brad,* [3] *brad, or scupper,* [4] *diamond deck spike,* [5] *horseshoe,* [6] *flatpoint rose,* [7] *tenterhook,* [8] *fine cabinet brad,* [9] *common flathead.*

Henry Ison, a Negro smith of Spalding County, Georgia, made his own fence staples out of heavy wire well into the twentieth century, as his apprentice-grandson Otis Hall remembers.

Nails, once one gets the hang of it, are not difficult to make in volume. Several rods are kept in the fire, heated to an orange-red, taken out one at a time, and forged to a long square taper on the end. While still red, the rod is cut nearly through, about ⅛ inch beyond where the taper starts, usually a couple of inches from the point, either on the hardie or with the sharpened pein of a straight-pein hammer. The rod is inserted point-first in the nailheader placed above the hardie or pritchel hole. The rod is then twisted in two at the cut, and the head is formed with a good blow or two of the hammer. In the case of roseheaded nails, four hammerblows

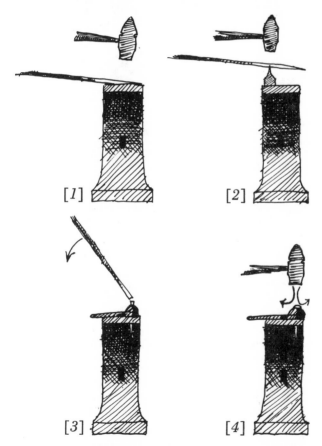

Making nails: [1] *pointing,* [2] *cutting,* [3] *breaking off (in nail header),* [4] *bradding head.*

Cross section of bradding head *Welding bolt head*

are given at a slight angle. Of course, nails with special heads have the heads swaged to shape in a depression in the header. After heading, the nail and header are quenched. The point of the nail, protruding through the bottom of the header, is then tapped on the anvil and driven out onto the floor to be collected later, or into a bucket set next to the anvil.

Staples are made in a similar manner, though no header is used. The wire is heated and cut off with the hardie at about a 10-degree angle. It is then bent double over the small end of the horn and cut off again on the hardie. Staples can be bent in a fork inserted in the hardie hole, but use of a fork requires a sharp-peined hammer for cutting.

Small tacks and nails are more difficult to make than large spikes, simply because the small rods used will not hold heat for a very long time. Despite this, however, an accomplished nail maker can manufacture a couple of thousand tacks a day.

In shops where nails were a big item of trade, or in the

rare specialized operations such as the factory at Monticello, special stake anvils were used instead of nailheaders. Some were even equipped with treadle-operated hammers, though the advantage of this device over hand hammers is hard to see.

Bolts were frequent products of the old-time general smithy, and the technique of welding the heads on to large bolts is useful to know, for it may be applied to many other items. To make a bolt head, the smith wraps a piece of carefully measured bar around a rod. The ends of the bar should not meet, but should have a space between equal to its thickness. When brought to welding heat the ends are drawn together with the hammer and butt welded. The stretching assures that bar and rod are also tightly welded.

Hinges are an essential part of any established society, and in the old days they were handmade in a number of forms, each with many variations. Doors in houses needed "L"- or "H-hinges"; small cabinets were fitted with finely forged "tulip" or "butterfly hinges," chests and boxes had hidden "butt hinges." Great churchdoors were often hung by huge decorative strap hinges, marvels of craftsmanship and design.

Butt hinges are the simplest to make. The smaller ones are no more than flat, thin sheets of iron, the middle of which is folded tightly around a rod to form the channel for the hinge pin. Two or three holes for screws are punched in the double thicknesses of the leaves, later to be countersunk with the brace and a countersink, or the point of a larger drill. With the rod still enclosed, the openings are cut so that the two leaves will fit together, held by the hinge pin. This is done by cutting the double leaf with a fine chisel, the cut being parallel to the rod and along the interior one third of the hinge on one and the outer two thirds on the other. The rod is then removed and the openings cut through with a hacksaw and filed smooth.

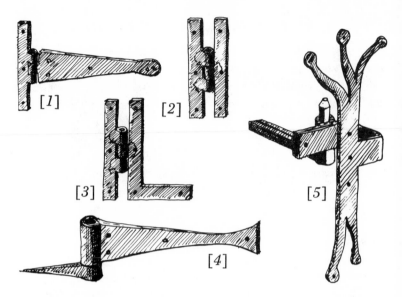

Hinges: [1] *"T"*, [2] *"H"*, [3] *"H-L"*, [4] *strap*, [5] *gate.*

After necessary filing the two leaves are then fitted together, pins are inserted, and the hinge is completed.

Butterfly and gunstock hinges are made similarly, but usually they are of single thickness. Only the edge of the sheet is folded around the rod for each leaf. Finishing follows the same procedure as with flat hinges. Shapes are cut with a cold chisel or with large shears after the pin channels are formed and fitted.

Lettered hinges, T-, L-, and H-hinges, require welding. A T-hinge, for instance, consists of two straps, perpendicular to each other. The horizontal strap is easy to make. It is bent round a rod at one end and welded, as with making tomahawks. Usually it is gracefully tapered with an acorn, a fleur-de-lis, or a ram's horn formed on the open end. Holes for nails or screws are punched and later countersunk if desired. The vertical jamb strap may be a straight bar or it may have deco-

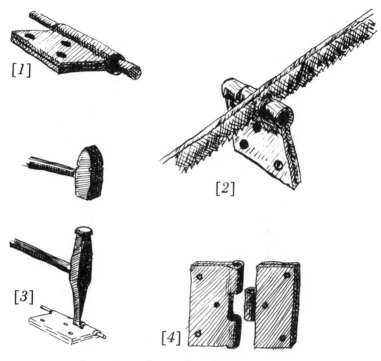

[1]

[2]

[3]

[4]

Steps in making a butt hinge

rative ends to match the door strap. Some, indeed, are bent into a semicircle to provide strength and decoration. To the basic strap, two smaller straps are welded on at right angles, far enough apart to receive the horizontal door strap. These are then bent around a rod and the ends welded. A pin, sometimes with an upset and decorative head, holds the two leaves together.

Both leaves of an H-hinge are made like the jamb strap of the T-hinge. L-hinges are no more than H-hinges with an additional strap welded at a right angle to the leg of the "H." Or the "L" can be cut from plate with a chisel.

Tulip hinges, which grace so many Colonial cabinet doors, require great delicacy of technique to make. On them, only the leaf on the jamb has a channel, usually no more than ³⁄₁₆ inch in diameter. This is formed, as with strap hinges, by wrapping around a rod and welding. The pin is a tenon at the butt of the stem of the other leaf, which at its other end is forged into a graceful tulip-shape, to give the hinge its name. Starting with a small bar, the smith flattens one end for the tulip bud. If he wishes to get quite fancy and provide tulip leaves also, he thins the iron below the tulip bud into a lozenge shape, then with a chisel makes two cuts that form the stem and at the same time divide the leaves from the stem. Below the leaves he draws down the base of the stem, rounding it to a ¼-inch diameter. This then has a ³⁄₁₆-inch tenon formed in the end with a small set hammer, or the flat end of a bar substituted for the set hammer. Tenon shoulders are dressed flat with the monkey tool, while the stem is held in the vise, bud down. In the absence of a monkey tool, a fairly thick bar through which a ³⁄₁₆-inch hole

Tulip hinge with leaf

has been drilled can be used to dress the tenon shoulders. Final shaping of the stem, a rather delicate job, is done while the iron is orange-red, either with a light hammer or a pair of pliers. Smoothing is done with a fine file, and sufficient holes are drilled in bud, leaves, and stem for small screws or nails.

Making large strap hinges, which were used for barndoors and, in a decorative form, for church and castle doors, followed inversely the technique used for tiny tulip hinges. The strap is formed as with a T-hinge by bending the end of the strap around a rod and welding it. There is no leaf on the jamb, only an upright pin with a sharp shank at right angles to the pin for driving into the jamb. This is made by doubling a narrow bar ½-inch wide and ¼-inch thick around a rod of proper size. The bar is welded to the rod and welded together where it extends. The extension is then drawn out to a sharp point which can be driven into the jamb. This is called a "pintle." The strap is fastened to the door with spikes long enough to penetrate the door and clinch on the other side.

Welding hinge pintle.

Decorative strap hinge

Decorative strap hinges require good power of visualization and considerable ingenuity to make. Suppose, for instance, one wishes to make a hinge with a fleur-de-lis terminal and two or three scrolls extending from the strap. First a bar 2-inches wide, ¼-inch thick, and 2-feet long is roughly shaped into a stepped-down taper with a spade end. The fleur-de-lis is formed by making two slanted cuts on the spade-shaped end. These are then bent into semicircles. Scrolls are formed in the same manner. The steps are split off with a chisel for 2 inches parallel to the axis of the strap. Each is then curved away from the strap. Holes are punched for spikes or screws and the edges are finished with a file.

There is hardly a limit to the elaboration that can be applied to a decorative hinge. Some may be punched in suitable places with holes of different shapes. Some may be split at certain points and the splits widened to any desired design. On occasion, some have extra extensions welded on, but those made from one piece seem to have more grace and strength to their curves.

Before the 1860s almost every house in any civilized land had shutters for each of its windows. Each shutter required a fastener to hold it open during daylight hours. Before 1790 shutter fasteners were hand-forged, a simple job for an experienced smith, and far more graceful in finished form than the patent fasteners made partially of cast iron after 1790.

Shutter fasteners consisted of two pieces, a tenoned spike

driven into the side of a house and a rotating fastener, traditionally S-shaped, through which the tenon was bradded. The spikes are made just as nails are made before heading. Instead of a head they have a tenon formed on the blunt end, using a small set hammer or a bar with a flat end, with shoulders formed by the monkey tool or a drilled bar. To make a fastener the smith takes a small, narrow bar 3-inches long by ½-inch wide and punches a hole to fit the tenon in its center. He then forms a boss on each end, but on opposite sides, the bar being drawn down to a taper from the hole to the base of the boss. The boss itself can be formed on the edge of the anvil or with a bottom fuller. The tapers can

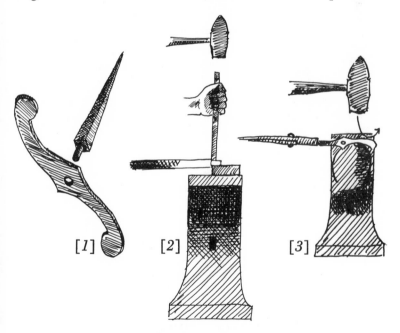

[1] *Parts of shutter fastener.* [2] *Forming tenon with end of bar.* [3] *Forming boss and taper of shutter fastener.*

be formed into a gentle curve over the horn, each end curving in a different direction toward its boss, to form an elongated "S." The fastener is then placed over the tenon, and the end of the tenon is upset to form a brad. (Incidentally, "bradding" means "broadening.") When the shutters are put in place, the fastener is driven into the clapboards or mortar of the house. Many old fasteners were forged to pointed ends, which were then curled into scrolls.

Some forms of door latches are now mass produced in the forms developed by olden smiths in the days of handmade hardware. There were beautiful latches, in the days of the smith, some simple and some ingenious in design, each a little different from others of the same type. They are worthy of copying, and a few manufacturers have become capable of imitating them.

Perhaps the simplest and easiest to make of all the door fasteners is a hook. One starts with a slender square bar, resembling the nail rods that might have been used in the old days. If no bar of proper dimension is available, the smith must resort to drawing down his own from an old horseshoe or whatever else can be adapted from the scrap pile.

The eye is formed by heating the end and bending it

Twisted hook

Welding hook eye

around a rod stuck upright in the pritchel hole of the anvil. It is easier to form the eye so that its center is through the center axis of the rod if a right-angle bend is made over the corner of the anvil before forming the circle.

Most hooks had unwelded eyes, but a few were butt-welded or lap-welded where the circles end. Welding, however, is a delicate operation in this case. As always with small stock, the iron must be brought to welding heat slowly, to prevent burning the iron. When brought to welding heat for a butt weld, the joint is made by gentle tapping with a light hammer of less than 1 pound in weight. Even with great care the smith may expect some distortion in the perfect circle of the eye. This can be corrected by drifting, using the rod the eye was originally formed around, and driving it through over the pritchel hole.

Lap welding is easier, though perhaps not quite so neat as butt welding. For this, the end of the rod must be drawn down into a long taper before the eye is formed. This is lapped over the stem of the hook and welded on the edge of the anvil with the eye hanging over the corner.

The hook is easily formed by first tapering or pointing the hook end and bending it to a right angle about 1 inch from the point. The hook is shaped around a rod in the pritchel hole. Instead of closing the circle, however, the end of the hook is left perpendicular to the stem. The end is gently curved outwardly over the horn. Many hooks can then be finished by providing a full twist in the middle of the stem.

Eyes that screwed into the door and jamb were seldom used in the old days. With each hook the smith provided two long staples, one to be nailed through the eye into the door and the other nailed in proper position on the jamb to receive the hook.

Hasps were quite plain and strictly utilitarian in the old days. They were found mostly on barn doors and the doors of other outbuildings, such as corn cribs, chickenhouses, smokehouses, and the like. They could be secured with a hook bradded to the hasp, with an iron pin attached to a small chain, with a wooden pin attached to a string or thong, or with a heavy padlock—all of which were inserted into a heavy staple.

A hasp is easily made from a small bar of iron, ¼-inch thick, 6-inches long, and 1-inch wide. While most are quite unrefined in appearance, an artistic smith forges a long taper on each end and rounds all corners. Then a ¼-inch hole is punched in one end and the other is split with a chisel, the split starting ½ inch from the end and continuing toward the center for 2 inches. Unless the highest-quality wrought iron or mild steel is used, the smith would be wise, however, to punch two holes marking the ends of the split and to cut

Handmade hasp

between them with the chisel. This prevents the iron from splitting out the end when it is spread. This split is then widened, after heating to a white heat, and a lozenge-shaped aperture is formed over the end of the horn. Hasps are attached to the door with a staple through the hole, while another staple is positioned in the jamb to fit into the aperture.

Sliding bolts are found on many interior and exterior doors in homes all over the world. Most are quite simple to make, though many have small decorative details that require time and artistry. For instance, most acceptable sliding bolts are made with a ball end. They are shaped by drawing down a flat or square bar of the proper length to a long taper with the end left slightly larger. This end is then upset to broaden it, and it is hammered spherical with a light hammer. A small hole is punched at about the center of the portion not drawn down. The end with the ball can be curved over the horn in any shape to fit the taste of the smith or his customer. To complete, the bolt is heated a dark, barely perceptible red around the punched hole, and a cold rod of the proper size is driven into the hole. Quenching shrinks the bolt tightly around the pin, which, when trimmed flush on the inside of the bolt and left projecting about ¼ inch on the outside, acts as a stop, to prevent the bolt from sliding out of its keepers.

Keepers are more difficult to make than one might imagine, because of the problems of four right-angle bends in each. They are made of strap iron ⅛-inch to ¼-inch thick and ½-inch wide. To determine the length needed to make a keeper the smith may make his pattern of thin sheet iron or lead sheet, or even wire. This is bent over the bolt with ½-inch tangs bent on both ends. Then the wire is straightened and used to measure the length of strap iron for the three keepers needed for a single bolt.

Some English smiths use a set of swages which form perfect keepers with one or two blows, but such tools are difficult

Sliding bolt and keepers.

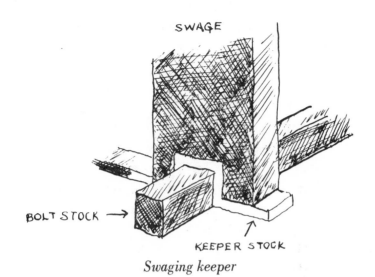

Swaging keeper

to find and time-consuming to make. There are two devices which are more easily made and fully as effective.

One may be made by first fullering, then filing a notch in the end of a heavy square bar. The notch should be as deep as the intended bolt plus one thickness of the keeper and as wide as the bolt plus two thicknesses of the keeper. To use, one places a piece of bolt stock on the anvil, puts the cherry red keeper over the bolt and forces it into shape by hammering down the hot iron with the simple, homemade top swage.

Another device is to make a deep "U" of bolt stock which has a tongue of the same stock drawn out to ½-inch thickness on one end, where it is riveted to the base of the "U," being somewhat springy where it is drawn out. Space between the sides of the tongue and the inside surfaces of the "U" should equal the thickness of the keeper iron when hot. When the keeper iron is heated to a cherry red, the hot part is inserted into the tool, tongue on one side of the iron, both legs of the "U" on the other side. Then tool and iron are put into the vise which is closed to force the iron into a perfect keeper.

A Norfolk latch is considerably more complicated to

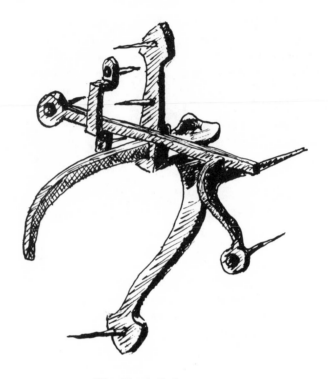

The Norfolk latch

make. It consists of five separate parts, each shaped differently, and assembled together to create a small door-opening machine using Archimedes' principle of leverage. Actually, it consists of a swinging bar with keeper, a thumb lever to raise the bar, and a handle for pulling the door open once it is unlatched.

The bar is nothing to make, even for an apprentice; it consists of a flat bar of iron drawn down to form a boss on one end through which a hole is punched for the pivot. Its action is restrained by a single keeper made exactly as the keepers on a sliding bolt. It fastens into the notch of a thin bar fastened to the doorjamb so that its notch protrudes beyond the jamb opposite the doorstop. It is slanted beyond the notch so that the swinging bar is cammed upward to fall into the notch automatically when the door is closed, and has two nail holes punched into the end away from the cam. The notch is easily punched with a rectangular punch or the end of a bar, using a swage block as a punching surface.

Complications arise in making the handle-thumb lever assembly. There are two methods of shaping the handle. One form can be shaped from a ½-inch-square bar 4-inches long, drawn down on opposite sides of a rectangular boss into ¼-inch-thick tangs, one 4-inches long, the other 2 inches. A rectangular hole ¼ inch by ½ inch is punched through the boss for the thumb lever, its direction being perpendicular to the plane of the tangs. The boss is then drilled through its sides for the pivot pin of the lever, the hole being ¼ inch.

After curving the long tang into a handle and bending a short tang at its bottom, both top and bottom tangs can be formed with round or acorn flat bosses, or into double curves, fleurs-de-lis, arrowheads, or any other device the smith wishes. This type of handle has no backstrap between

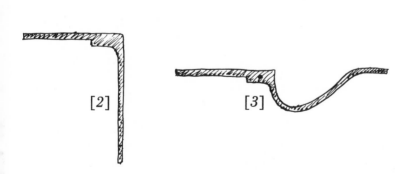

Forming boss and bending handle

handle and door, but is quite strong and easier to make than a handle with a backstrap.

In making the more complicated handle, handle piece and backstrap are shaped separately, the box-shaped boss being part of the handle. The handle is then welded to the backstrap at boss and lower tang, after which the boss is punched and drilled for the pivot pin.

Thumb levers are easily made from a flat bar long enough to protrude through the door after being drawn out to a long slim taper. The slightly curved, flat thumbing surface on one end is formed by heating the bar orange-red and battering it to a flat surface perpendicular to the width and about ¼-inch thick. The remainder of the bar is then drawn out to a long rod ¼-inch thick and ⅜-inch wide, ending in a long taper. Next the set hammer is used to form a raised spine in the center of the bottom of the thumbing surface, forming an extension of the drawn-out rod. Then the thumbing sur-

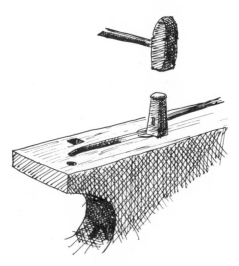

Forming bottom spine or thumbpiece with set hammer

face, now flattened to a ⅛-inch thickness, is slightly curved over the horn, and the long taper at the other end of the rod is curved away from the upper surface of the thumbpiece. A hole is drilled sideways through the rod a quarter inch behind the thumbpiece to receive the pivot pin.

In fastening to the door, bolt and keeper are on one side of the door and the handle on the other. Pushing the thumbpiece down lifts the bolt on the other side of the door. Lifting the curved end of the rod performs the same action.

Many blacksmiths, especially in smaller villages, became locksmiths of necessity. The heavy old locks which graced the doors of Colonial and federal houses and fastened strongboxes and the gates of European castles required forging and tempering. If the blacksmith did not make locks, then the locksmith needs must have been an accomplished blacksmith, with his equipment, in the shop.

So many books have been written on the subject of locks, and there are so many practicing locksmiths in today's society, that this volume will not duplicate their knowledge. All the forgings in a lock reflect the general techniques used in forging other small pieces, and lock springs are tempered in the same manner as gun springs and the springs on pipe tongs. The locksmith undoubtedly used more files than the general smith, for his work required a much finer tolerance and a tighter fit of its parts than most articles turned out by the general smith.

Other items of door hardware, though, were part and parcel of the trade handled by the general smith in every country of the civilized world. Doorknobs and knockers are practical items which perform their functions in a variety of designs.

Old doorknobs, for instance, were sometimes actual knobs, sometimes rings, and sometimes handles similar to umbrella handles. Most were used to operate some sort of mechanical latch as found on the doors of modern houses. Consequently the knobs were forged on the end of a square rod that fit a square hole in the tumbler of the latch, but often the knob on either side of the door was punched to fit the rod and fastened to it with a pin. Sometimes the rod was inserted in a square hole in a handle and bradded on. As with all handmade articles, the many nuances of design and assembly found in old knobs was determined by the taste and circumstances of the smith. There never was any dogma on forging methodology.

Wallace Nutting, in his *Furniture Treasury*, illustrates an unusual ring handle that served double duty as a knocker. It consists of the usual square bar, one end of which was bradded to the inside handle. The outside handle consists of a swinging, nicely-shaped ring that presumably was knocked against a bolthead secured in the door beneath the handle.

To make such a device the smith starts with the ½-inch-square pivot rod. This is upset at one end to form a boss slightly larger than the rod and pierced through with a ¼-inch punch. The ring is made from a piece of ½-inch rod or square bar. First the fuller is used to form a boss in the center of the rod. From this point the rod is drawn out on both sides to a taper which is just less than ¼-inch diameter on the ends. The taper can be forged square or octagonal, or rounded by first forging to an octagonal shape, then hammering the corners round by turning the rod back and forth while battering with a light hammer. Working at an orange heat, each point is bent to a right angle ¼ inch from the end; the inside of the bend is formed square on the corner of the anvil.

Next another right-angle bend in the opposite direction is made about 2 inches from the first bend on both sides of the boss. After this, the length between the bends is rounded on the horn of the anvil, care being taken to see that the boss is in the center of the curve. This knocker-handle is attached

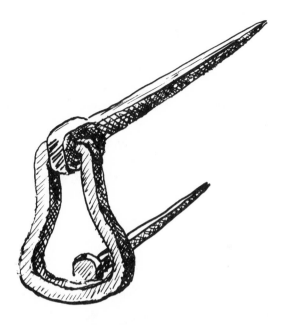

Simple knocker

to the pivot rod by heating the curved section to a cherry red, spreading far enough so that the upset end of the pivot rod passes between the right angles at either end; then, when ends and hole are in position, tapping the ends together with a light hammer so that they meet in the hole of the pivot bar.

L-shaped handles can be made from a ½-inch-square bar, drawn down to ⅜-inch thickness from a ½-inch boss on one end. This boss may be hammered octagonal or rounded while at a cherry red. A square hole is punched into the boss, either all the way through over the hardie hole if the pivot rod is to be bradded on, or partially through if the handle is to be secured by a pin. After punching the hole, the remaining portion of the handle is drawn down to a flat taper and formed into a gentle S-curve over the horn of the anvil. Some designs call for leaving a flat boss on the end, like shutter fasteners; others may have the pointed end scrolled, and still others may

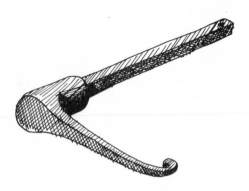

"L" door handle

have the end curved toward the door. Incidentally, it might take half a day to make either a ring handle or an L-shaped handle, including careful finishing with a file.

Wrought-iron knobs, very similar to modern knobs though somewhat smaller, can be made in several ways. A boss can be welded in the center of a ¾-inch-thick plate that has been roughly rounded before welding. Then the square hole for the pivot rod is punched and the knob is finished by forging and filing. If the knob is to be fastened to the rod with a pin, the pinhole is drilled rather than punched. A knob and boss can be forged from one piece of heavy bar or rod by drawing out the boss with a large fuller and shaping it with a set hammer or with the monkey tool, or by swaging it round or square on the side of the swage block. After shaping, the square hole is punched. The knob is forged smooth by heating to a white heat, reinserting the boss in the swage block, and upsetting the shape of the knob with a 4-pound hammer.

Doorknockers can also be made in a variety of shapes and sizes. Many, particularly in medieval and Renaissance times, were no more than large rings secured to the door with an eyebolt. To make this simple knocker the smith bends a ½-inch-square bar around a rod to form, the eye and welds the two ends together as with a hinge pin, but the pin is re-

Differently shaped knockers

moved. The shank is sharpened for driving through the door and clinching on the other side. A rod is then shaped into a ring of 3- or 4-inches diameter, with ends scarfed preparatory to welding, and this is inserted in the eye. After assembling the two pieces the ring is welded and smoothed on the horn of the anvil. The knocker set may be completed by furnishing a heavy brad or bolt to be driven through the door so that its head is battered when the ring is lifted and let fall.

The artistic smith may wish to shape his ring other than round. For instance, it may be heart-shaped, oval, or quatrefoil. It may have a boss formed on the ring where it meets the bolthead driven in the door.

Another type of knocker consists of ¼-inch-thick plate with two projections at its upper end between which an S-shaped bar is mounted with a stout pin. The plate itself may be cut with bench shears or chisel into some interesting shape such as a shield, a tulip, or an eagle. Holes are then punched in appropriate spots to nail it to the door. Generally it is easier to weld on the two projections that hold the knocker bar. First a bar ¾ inch by ½ inch is shaped into a square "U." This and the plate are brought to welding heat, the projections are quickly placed in position, and the two are welded together by inserting a bar with a flat end between the legs of the "U" and quickly hammering it with a light hammer. Some smiths may wish to fasten the two pieces together with a light brad before welding, particularly if the plate is light and subject to losing its welding heat quickly when placed on the cold anvil. A hole is drilled for the pin after welding. Welding may be avoided by using a forked spike, made by splitting and spreading the end of a sharpened bar which is driven through a punched hole in the plate through the door and clinched on the inside.

Bars for this type of doorknocker may be of simple or elaborate design. Some are no more than a modified "S," with the lower end upset to provide a larger battering surface and the upper curve drilled to receive the pin that fastens it to the plate. Sometimes this bar may be twisted, or curved at its upper end, or forged into a rough horse's-head, and finished by filing; the final design rests with the smith's artistic temperament and skill and with the taste of his customer.

Chain, that useful device which was developed far back in antiquity, was usually an important part of a blacksmith's trade even until modern times. The Boy Scouts of America offered a merit badge in blacksmithing until after World War II, and one of its requirements was making a chain of at least three links. Chains were used in a number of sizes for chandeliers, ships' uses, gate-closers, trace chains, padlocks, and, on occasion, as giant cables to close harbors or block rivers. History records the huge chain that closed the harbor of ancient Rhodes, stretching between the legs of the Colossus, and the heavy chain that stopped Norse longships from penetrating into France along the River Seine. Chain making was a large industry in nineteenth-century England. The London chainsmiths of that age became rich by hiring penniless victims of the Industrial Revolution at only a few pennies a day to slave over the forges making chains for fourteen hours a day.

Handmade chain differs somewhat from modern chain which is made wholly by machinery, the links being arc-welded together. Generally the modern links are more nearly circles than the links of old handmade chain which generally were long ovals in shape. It is easy to speculate that longer links meant less welding per foot of chain, thus effecting considerable labor-saving.

Trace chains have been in use from the time man first harnessed horses until the internal-combustion engine both displaced horses and brought about the demise of the blacksmith. To make a trace chain the smith cuts off 8-inch sections of ¼-inch rod. These sections are bent in the middle, scarfed on the ends and further bent to form an oval about 3 inches long, with the scarfed ends overlapping no more than ¼ inch.

Usually the smith will find that a rod stuck upright in the pritchel hole will provide a convenient mandrel for shaping the links. The horn may be used, but more uniform shaping can be done around an upright rod.

It is important to have the right sort of fire for welding chain. It must be deep and narrow, constructed so that the

Bending chain link around rod in pritchel hole

links being welded can be thrust into a jet of heated air from which the oxygen has been nearly consumed. For the first link the smith grasps the oval at its unscarfed end and fastens his tong handles with a ring, so he need not disengage the tongs while the iron is in the fire.

Since trace-chain links are made of relatively light rods, the smith must be careful not to blow his fire with too much gusto. To do so will make the fire itself burn out quickly, requiring early rebuilding, and it will also furnish more oxygen than the narrow fire can consume, thereby converting a large proportion of the iron into oxide, with consequent weakening of the chain.

Placing the ringed tongs, with link held tightly in the jaws, at the edge of the fire with the scarfed end of the link projecting into the jet of heat, the smith pumps the bellows slowly until the iron turns cherry red. The link is withdrawn and flux is sprinkled liberally on the scarfing, sand or salt for soft iron, borax or a patented compound for mild steel. It is then thrust back into the fire until the scarfing becomes white, and then an oily light yellow. Then it is taken from the fire and joined by quick blows from a light hammer. It is important first to join the side on which the thin end of the scarf is underneath, next to the cold anvil face, with the hammerblows progressing quickly to the other end of the scarf. Before the iron cools the smith may wish to dress the welded portion by rounding it over the small tip of the horn.

Usually a chainsmith will make his links up before welding so that as each link is welded he can insert a new link into the one last joined and speed up his work. If he has several pairs of lip tongs he may wish to keep several short lengths of chain in the fire at one time, joining them together as the terminal step in making whatever length of finished chain he desires.

After welding the first link, succeeding links are held by

Welding link—hammering over thin scarf next to anvil

the tongs so that the adjacent finished oval is fixed tightly, immobile against the side of the new link. This prevents finished links from falling in the fire. A hook formed on the end of a tong handle will hold finished chain out of the way.

A more easily made chain was made by the smith for hanging chandeliers, for connecting his bellows to the lever pole, and for decorative functions where strength was not too much of a factor. This type is made of rods from ⅛ inch to ¼ inch in diameter, cut in 6-inch lengths with an eye formed at each end. The links are fastened together by inserting one eye in another and tapping together without welding. The links are easily formed by curving the end of the rod, while at an orange heat, around the small end of the horn, having enough space at the end to insert the adjacent link. A right-angle bend should be made in the end before the circle is formed, to insure that the completed circle is centered on the shank of the link.

In those rare shops equipped with a floor mandrel, chain links are formed around the mandrel.

While the blacksmith is best remembered for his horse-shoeing, many forget the part he played in furnishing wagons

233

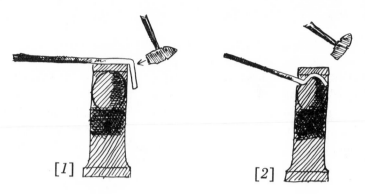

Forming eye in rod chain link: [1] *right-angle bend,* [2] *circle formed.*

and carts for horses to pull. The wheelwright was a separate occupation in England and Europe, requiring a blacksmith to furnish hardware for wagons and to weld the tires. In America the smith usually was the village wheelwright, also; he hired woodworkers as needed to make and assemble the felloes and spokes, axles and body of wagons. Almost every wagon maker displayed some peculiarity of design in his products, the difference being based on personality in America and on tradition, to some extent, in Europe and in England, where such traditional models as the graceful and sturdy Cotswold wagon were produced for a certain area generation after generation. Welded iron tires for the wheels, however, which were used from Roman times until Ford times, required the precise skill of a master blacksmith.

Tires must be shrunk on a wheel, which means that a 5-foot wheel, for instance, must have a tire measured and welded with no more than ⅟₁₆-inch tolerance between the circumferences of tire and wheel. The smith, using tools and techniques developed over the ages, arose to the occasion.

Measuring a wheel and cutting a strip of iron to an exact length before welding is fully as important in assuring a tight fit for a wagon tire as the bending and welding. Because of this, and because wood reacts to humidity, a good smith would not guarantee tires put on in wet weather and sometimes would refuse to tire a wagon that had forded a creek on the way to his shop.

To measure a wheel accurately the smith employs his traveler, a metal, or sometimes wooden, measuring wheel mounted in a handle. In the twilight years of smithing, travelers of quite fancy design were sold by most hardware wholesalers. They consisted of a flat iron wheel, its circumference marked with a stamped line every $\frac{1}{16}$ inch, and with a pointer mounted on the axle of the wheel which could be set to mark any part of the circumference. Of course, this wheel and pointer pivoted between two legs of a handle, just as the front wheel of a bicycle is mounted on the front fork. To measure the wheel, the smith marks an arbitrary starting point with pencil or chisel. The zero point of the traveler is placed on this mark, and the traveler is run around the wheel, the smith noting the number of full turns it makes. When the traveler again reaches the starting mark on the rim, the smith marks the traveler rim either with the pointer mounted on the traveler, a piece of chalk, or a soapstone pencil. The portion of the traveler thus marked plus the number of complete turns made is equal to the circumference of the wheel. Rather than ruin a piece of tire iron through overconfidence, the smith usually follows the ancient adage of all craftsmen: measure twice and cut once.

When the wheel itself is measured, the smith selects a tire iron of proper size and, laying it out on his bench or floor, measures it with the traveler to match the circumference of the wheel and marks the iron with a piece of soapstone or chalk.

Now comes the test of skill and experience. In tiring a new wheel the smith must take into consideration the spaces between the felloes (usually not more than $\frac{1}{16}$ inch between

each of the seven felloes) and subtract this aggregate measurement from the measured circumference of the tire iron.
He must also decide how much "dish" the wheel must have,
since dish, the drawing of the spokes outward at an angle to
the hub, provides torsion strength to the finished wheel.
Normal dish usually subtracts another ½ inch from the
circumference of a 4-foot tire, but for large wheels even more
must be subtracted. Because wood contracts and tires must be
shrunk on to fit tightly, an additional bit must be subtracted
from the measured circumference of the wheel to provide a
tight fit. This varies from ½ inch to ⅝ inch on tires 2-inches
wide, to ⁵⁄₁₆ inch to ⅜ inch on a narrow buggy-wheel tire
1-inch wide. These estimates are those of Sump Brown, who
proudly guaranteed every wheel he tired.

The subtractions noted above apply to new wagon wheels
in dry weather. In fitting together tolerant wood and intolerant
metal the smith, if successful as a wheelwright, has to note,
and to feel instinctively, the variables of weather and other
conditions. Of course, in re-tiring old wheels, which have no
space between the joints and already have a dish, all the
subtractions noted above may be foregone and only the last
applied, to shorten the iron after it is measured with the
traveler.

When the final measurement is determined and marked
carefully with a soapstone pencil, the tire is cut off with a
cold chisel. Some smiths scarf the ends before bending the
tire round, but this method was generally followed before
patent tire benders appeared around 1870. Before then,
tires were bent into a circle by one of several means. Some
smiths bent a tire by hand by holding one end with the helper
holding the other, and bending it around a post or a handy
tree. Wrought iron, which was the only type available before
the days of mild steel, bent easily in this manner. After
bending into a rough circle, the tire was made into a nearly

perfect circle by hammering over the horn or the end of a
log mounted horizontally. Only a soft hammer was used for
this to avoid battering the surface. There is some evidence to
indicate that a few smiths might have had special anvils
with the face concave on the long axis, to facilitate hammering the tire into a true circle. After about 1870 a number of
patent tire benders appeared on the market. These consisted
of a cast-iron form containing three or four rollers that were
turned simultaneously with a series of cogwheels actuated
with a handcrank. The rollers were easily adjusted to bend
a tire to any desired diameter after the end of the tire iron
had been inserted between two rollers and the crank turned
until the full length of the tire had passed through. So

Principle of tire bender

versatile were these simple bending machines that they could
be adjusted to bend the tire of a great 6-foot log-cart wheel,
or a hub band of only 6-inch diameter. Tire benders were
standard equipment for any shop in America and Europe
which worked on wagons. When so equipped, the smith
postponed scarfing the ends of a tire until after bending;
otherwise the ends would not pass between the rollers of the
bender.

Once bent, a tire was easily prepared for welding. In
England, and perhaps in other old-world smithies, the scarfed
ends were sometimes punched and bradded together with a

small nail to hold the ends in correct juxtaposition, but a tire was generally stiff enough to hold the ends in position without fastening, and most American smiths eliminated this step Instead they prepared about 1-inch overlap where the scarfs met, and before welding they reversed the positions of the ends so that the outside end rested on the inside surface. Thus the stiffness of the circled tire held the two ends tightly together without need of fastening. It is well also to chamfer the corners of the scarfs to prevent spreading when the ends are welded. The tire is placed on the forge with the ends in the fire and some 4 inches of additional coal is piled over the iron to hold in the heat. When a cherry red is reached, with slow blowing, flux is sprinkled on the scarfed surfaces, and the bellows are pumped slowly until welding heat is reached. At this stage the tire is removed and placed on the anvil where the ends are joined with a few quick blows with a 3- or 4-pound hammer. In welding a tire the smith must be careful not to hit so hard that the original thickness of the iron is made smaller, for this affects the inside circumference and causes a bad fit. It is better to weld it so that the joint is a mite thicker than the original iron, for then the joint can be drawn down to proper size. It is obviously impossible,

Holding tire ends in position by reversing ends

however, to upset a joint to proper thickness once it has been hammered too thin.

Shrinking the tire on the wheel is an operation done outside the shop. It requires some special tools and usually several men, although many a country smith with no helper had to do the job by himself.

First of all, a circular fire is built on the ground, large enough to lay the tire on it. Then small pieces of firewood are piled above the tire to insure that it heats evenly throughout. The purpose of this fire, of course, is to heat the iron so that it will expand, at which point it is placed on the wheel and cooled to shrink it tightly on the wheel. The smith watches his fire with care and from time to time rubs the heating iron with a small dry stick. When the tire is heated enough, before it becomes red, the stick suddenly acts as though its end is greased as it is rubbed on the iron, and a slight curl of smoke rises from its end, but there is no flame. This indicates that the tire is ready to be fitted.

Testing heat of tire with small stick

The tire is then lifted from the fire and carried to the wheel, which has been placed so that its rim rests on a circular platform of brick or stone, with a hole in the center into which the hub is inserted. At times, the platform may be an old millstone.

Placing the hot tire in position, the smith then prises it over the rim with a tiredog, or knocks it into place with a soft 6- or 8-pound sledge. As the tire is knocked into place the rim smokes and the joints of the wheel crack and groan. Once the tire is put on properly the tire is cooled quickly, either with water poured around its circumference or by placing the hub onto a special rack, set over a pit of water in which the hot tire is rotated until cool. The cooling brings forth more cracking and groaning from the constricted parts of the wheel, which are now literally bound together with a "hoop of steel."

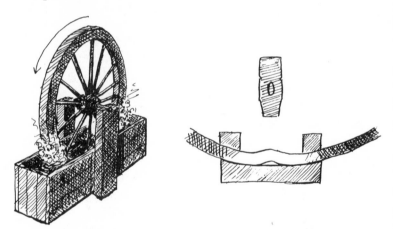

Left: Cooling tire on rack. Right: Shrinking tire.

If properly fitted on a dry wheel, a tire should last until worn through, which may take years. Sometimes, however, a tire is not measured properly and becomes loose in dry weather. Before 1870 this problem could only be solved by removing the tire, cutting it, and rewelding to a slightly smaller size. About 1870, though, some tool factories began making tire shrinkers, which found a wide market among smiths in America.

To shrink a tire without rewelding, the smith first heats

it to orange-red and hammers a dent in the outside of the tire. Then the tire is placed on the shrinker, which consists of a flat anvil and two heavy arms, which are levered tightly on the tire on either side of the dent. The inside bump caused by the outside dent is then hammered flat, the two arms of the shrinker holding the red-hot iron so tightly that the dent is upset into the thickness of the tire, rather than being merely flattened to its original dimension. Often upsetting makes the tire slightly wider where the dent had been. When this happens, the extra width is cut off with a cold chisel or hot set.

Hub bands are measured and welded as though they are miniature tires. Bands, however, are often shaped like the section of a cone, and are often bent around a floor mandrel. Also, bands often are punched in three or four places so that they can be nailed into place.

The decade of the 1870s was a period of transition in wagon design and manufacturing technique. During this time, wheels appeared with two steam-bent felloes per wheel, instead of the seven sawn or adzed felloes which had been used since ancient times. Also, wagons were beginning to be equipped with iron or steel axles mounted inside a wooden sleeve, following the design of Civil War cannon axles. This required a cast-iron box, actually a truncated cone, which the smith inserted into the hub as a bearing for the axle.

Before steel axles—until the 1930s on some makes of wagons in America and Europe—a wooden axle was used, usually a great oaken or hickory or elm beam shaped at each end into a cone. This axle was fitted with a small 8-inch iron bar nailed on the bottom side of each end as a bearing surface. The hub aperture, inside of the rings, was then fitted with two small bands ¼-inch thick and ½-inch wide, which served as hub bearings.

There were many other small pieces of wagon hardware made and fitted by the smith: hinges, rivets, linch pins,

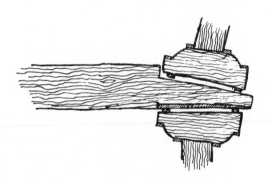

Cross section of wooden axle and hub, showing iron bearing surface on axle and inside hub bands.

braces, bearings, and bands. The smithing techniques used to form and fit such hardware items were generally the same as used for general hardware, and they need not be explained here. Experience teaches better than words.

In the latter years of the nineteenth century and the early years of the twentieth century, America and Europe had a number of carriage makers in settled areas. They were called buggy factories in the more democratic atmosphere of America, and those of any size employed smiths for welding the iron axles and special tire rims for rubber tires, which went into quality buggies and carriages.

Welding buggy axles is an exacting task, requiring that the two conical collared ends, which fit into the hubs, be welded to each end of the 1½-inch-square axlebar. First the separate pieces of steel, which, incidentally, are excellent for making various anvil tools and chisel bodies, are brought to welding heat and joined under a trip-hammer. It is *de rigueur* that the axle be welded totally in one heat, so that any axle that shows the slightest trace of the joint is discarded. Thus smiths, such as Herbert Mitchum of Durand, Georgia, who served their apprenticeships in buggy factories were generally expert welders with high standards.

Buggies were tired in the same way as wagons until the

day of rubber-tired buggies in the 1880s and 1890s. Rubber tires were fitted into a special channel-shaped steel rim which was supplied in 20-foot lengths by the steel mills of the day. Welding with a hammer necessarily destroyed the precise shape of the channel at the joint. Consequently buggy-tire channels were joined with a special set of swages that maintained the shape of the channel during joining.

During the decline of general blacksmithing, wholesale hardware houses sold most of the items for wagon hardware that, before 1870, had been made individually by the smith. Therefore the smith could order his parts as he ordered his tools and merely fit them on. Some smiths still alive, how-

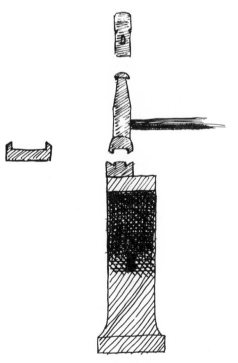

Swage for welding buggy channel tires

ever, still made many parts for older wagons during their careers, and a good smith was essential to farming communities until the internal-combustion engine replaced the horse on farms all over the world.

Without the smith, all the hardware found in our houses, stores, and offices displays a sameness that fails to arouse the interest found in an old handmade hinge or a specially designed knocker or a handmade nail. The contrast between the new and the old, however, increases the respect of modern ironware collectors for the skill and artistry of the old-time smith.

8.

THE TECHNIQUES OF
MAKING HOME UTENSILS

While the local blacksmith during his heyday was essential for making and designing the tools of war and industry, he was no less important in supplying the tools of domestic life. The stewards and chefs of noble castles and the housewives of humbler homes were quite as dependent on his skill as the warrior, the woodcutter, the farmer, and the craftsman. Not only was he necessary for kitchen utensils, but he was needed to provide hair curlers and gophering irons as well.

The home, regardless of its relative grandeur, centered around the kitchen fire, which, by the middle of the eighteenth century, had become quite sophisticated in its equipment. Basic among this equipment were firedogs, jacks, and andirons. "Andiron," of course, is derived from " 'end' iron," an adjunct to the firedogs needed to keep logs from the hearth floor so that a draft may be drawn beneath them to make the fire burn brighter.

Until casting iron became a practical art and industry in the sixteenth century, firedogs were produced exclusively by the smithy from heavy bars of wrought iron. Seldom were they made of stock less than 1-inch square, and seldom were they ornamented. From the time of their first use sometime in the Dark Ages, firedogs were purely functional, beautiful only in their simplicity and sturdiness.

Many rested on three legs, like the later combination of

245

andiron and dog. These are made by bending a 3-foot bar about 6 inches from one end to a right angle. The other end is split with a chisel for 6½ inches, the split is widened to form two legs, and the legs are then bent at a right angle. Another type is made by bending each end at right angles, but pointing in opposite directions. Two additional legs are welded to one of the bends to give support in the front, the original bend serving as a rudimentary andiron, which prevents heavy logs from rolling off the fire into the room. All bending on the heavy iron used for dogs can be done by inserting the bar in a fork inserted in the hardie hole while the iron is at an orange or even a white heat.

Andirons, which originally were made of iron, but which eventually were also made of brass, had a functional as well as a decorative purpose. They kept logs in the fire, but they also served to hold spits on which meat was cooked before the fire. Those used in fireplaces for living quarters and bedrooms were usually short, not more than 2-feet tall, with no brackets on which to rest spits; kitchen andirons, on the other hand, while often decorative, were quite tall, sometimes with several brackets welded or bradded at different heights for the spits.

One finds, with only desultory study, that the designs of andirons are as endless as a roll call of all the blacksmiths who made andirons during the development of Western

Fire dogs

civilization. Each pair reflects to some degree the individuality and personality of the smith who made them.

Perhaps the most common type found in Colonial and nineteenth-century America was made of a piece of strap iron with two legs fashioned at one end and decorated with a ring or scroll at the other end. Dogs were usually bradded to the andirons, but often were welded.

The material used for making these simple andirons was frequently scrap; the end cut from a wagon tire being used for the andirons and a worn-out wagon linch pin or the end of a house bolt being utilized for the dogs. To make an andiron the smith takes an 18-inch or 2-foot length of tire a couple of inches wide and ⅜-inch thick. This is heated to an orange-red at one end preparatory to forming the ring. In using mild steel, the hole in the end can be punched, and a shoulder can be formed with a fuller at the point where the ring meets the body of the andiron. Once formed in the rough, the ring may be dressed evenly all around by placing it on

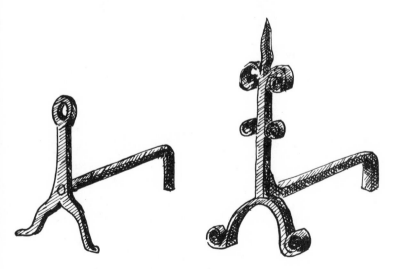

Kitchen and parlor andirons

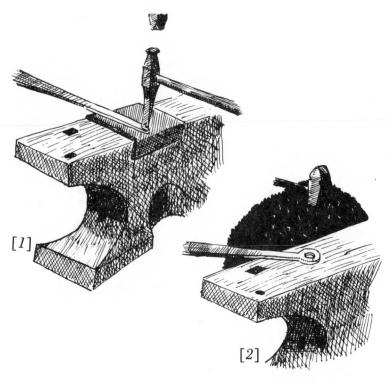

Making ring in wrought iron andiron staff: [1] *splitting*
[2] *welding*

the horn and forming with a light hammer. In using wrought
iron, a different technique is followed by the discriminating
smith to form the ring. To preserve the integrity of the fibers
in wrought iron, the smith draws out the end for about 3
inches, making a tang about 1-inch wide, the shoulders being
dressed with a fuller. This tang is punched with a ⅜-inch
hole at the point that designates the bottom of the ring and is
split from this hole to the end. The two legs of the split are
then each formed into a semicircle over the horn, with an
overlap of ¼ inch or so. After scarfing the ends, the smith
welds them to complete his ring. If he is making them for

newlyweds, he may form the ring into a heart-shape instead of a circle, or into any sort of shape that suits his fancy.

Legs of simple strap andirons are formed by punching the end opposite the ring some 4 ½ inches from the end of the strap and splitting from this hole to the end. These legs are spread and shaped to the smith's taste. Sometimes feet are either upset at the end of each leg, or formed by flattening the ends and bending them outward.

The most common method of joining andirons and dogs is to punch a hole in the andiron at a height matching the bend in the dog. The end of the dog is heated to a white heat and inserted in the hole, and the slightly protruding end is upset to brad it to the andiron. If welding is considered more finished work than bradding, then the end of the dog opposite the leg must be scarfed for about 4 inches and lap-welded onto the andiron just above the fork in its legs. After welding, the dog can be bent to a right angle to the andiron.

There is really no limit to the variety of design already found in handmade andirons or to the potential designs of an imaginative smith. A more graceful andiron than the simple country type made of a strap can be created with ¾-inch-square bar or rod. Here a bar 3-feet long is used to fashion the firedog and the body of the andiron from one piece by bending the dog leg, then bending the andiron body in the opposite direction. Next andiron legs of the same-size bar are welded to the body at the bend. If the andiron is to be decorative, the upright portion above the legs may be upset into a button on the end and then formed into a gooseneck. Others may be flattened on the end and a scroll curve formed; or drawn out into a corkscrew spiral formed around a rod held in the bench vise.

Some European smiths, in the best craft traditions of the Middle Ages, might have welded small petals of sheet iron to a button to form full-blown rose blossoms, or other types of flowers, on the ends of andirons. Such delicate welding must be done with great care and slow, careful action of the bellows. The button, of course, requires more time in the fire to be brought to welding heat than the petals. Each petal must be placed and welded very quickly before the thin stock loses its welding heat. One way of making the job easier is to form each petal by flattening the end of a rod and shaping the flat part into the shape of a rose petal. When sufficient petals have been made the ends may be wired around the button on the andiron, and the whole may be brought to welding heat and joined. Often the smith finds it easier, when working with wrought iron, to form his rose blossoms on a short bar, and then to weld this to the body of the andiron.

Some andirons are huge and heavy and intricately formed. These types may be made of a 2- or even 3-inch-square bar,

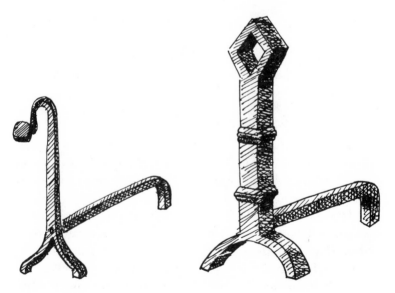

Left: Gooseneck andiron. Right: Heavy andiron with welded collars.

which is split to form legs, then molded into artistic shapes with hammer and fuller and swage. One method is to form a heavy base from which the legs curve, and to forge the body into a column decorated with molded collars and capped with a large ball or pineapple. When made of 3-inch bar, such shapes can be molded by carefully shaping the top and bottom surfaces of the collars with top and bottom fuller and drawing out the heavy iron between. The ball on the end is, of course, upset and shaped with a heavy hammer, then given a smooth surface with a light hammer. Final finish to all decorations may be done with a file, although a master smith will disdain the file for all but the finial ball.

Other fireplace equipment, such as pokers, shovels, and tongs may also be made in the smithy. Most are made of $3/8-1/2$ inch rod.

There are two ways to make a poker with a hook for turning logs. On heavier stock the end may be flattened for 3 or 4 inches and split, one leg of the split being shaped into the hook, the other being drawn out to a point. For a smaller, $3/8$-inch rod, however, it is far better to scarf the end and bend it back upon the rod to form a loop some 3 inches long. The scarfed end is welded to the shank of the incipient poker and the loop is cut through on the hardie. The welded leg so created becomes the hook, the other the point.

Handles for pokers may be formed in a number of different ways. Some merely have a ring for a handle, sometimes welded shut, sometimes not. Most are formed by flattening and shaping the end to a cigar-shape and forging some sort of scroll on the end. Others are upset to thicken the original rod to a comfortable diameter for the hand, then drawn down almost to a point, with a button upset on the point. To follow one of the most common forms of scroll decoration in Colonial times, the smith points the handle, then splits the point for $1\frac{1}{2}$ inches. Scrolls are formed on the end of each split, and the scrolls are then bent at right angles

Welding loop and splitting for hooked poker.

to the handle. They may be left this way, or they may be hammered at a yellow heat to flatten the top until all traces of the end of the split have disappeared. This leaves the scrolls tight against the sides of the handle.

Unlike large digging shovels, hearth shovels are made of one thickness—⅛ inch or thinner sheet iron. This is cut to fit a pattern the shape of a truncated triangle, 6-inches wide across the base, 6-inches high, and 4-inches wide at the truncation. One inch from each corner of the base the sheet is split 1-inch deep pointing toward the truncation. The end of this split will be the corner after the walls have been bent up and welded. Before shaping the shovel, however, the handle should be welded on. Three-eighths-inch rod, the same as used for the poker and of the same length, is used for the shank and handle. First the handle is formed, as was done with the poker. Next the end opposite the handle is upset for 1 inch or faggot-welded for the same length, to form a double thickness. This end is then split with a thin hot chisel for a depth of ½ inch, the split being opened to receive the blade. After heating the split to cherry red, the cold sheet is jambed into it, with care being taken to place the split in the center of the sheet and to hammer the lips tightly together to hold the sheet. Sometimes roughing the small section of the sheet, which will be placed in the handle, with the corner of a cold chisel will provide small teeth which help hold sheet and handle together during welding.

Because of the tendency of thin sheet to burn up, the area to be welded must be brought to welding heat slowly and the metal must be watched with care. If both sheet and handle are wrought iron, sand or borax may be used as a flux, being sprinkled into the joint when the metal is cherry red. If mild steel is used, then borax or a patented welding compound is

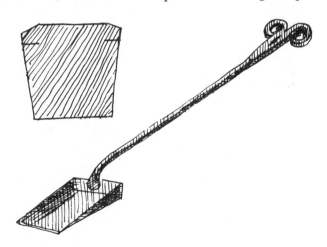

Left: Pattern for hearth shovel blade—split corners.
Right: Finished hearth shovel.

required. Once at welding heat, the shovel is removed and joined quickly with a light hammer. After this the blade of the shovel is heated to an orange-red and the back wall and sides are formed over the heel of the anvil. The two projections created by the splits into the base of the blade are bent to lie flat on the side wall. They are then welded to the side wall. Finishing is done by curving the handle where it is joined to the blade to make the bottom of the blade parallel to the handle, or at an angle the smith deems appropriate.

Some shovels had corners and handles that were bradded instead of. welded. If the handle is to be bradded on, the flat surface at its end should be 3-inches long, and it should be shaped to fit the back and bottom of the already completed shovel blade.

Tongs are more complicated to make than pokers or shovels, for they have two movable parts which must fit precisely. Made from the same size rod and of the same length as poker and shovel, tongs, as with shovels, have the handle forged first. Then $1\frac{1}{2}$ inches below the handle, the rod is bent at right angles to the handle and curved around the horn into a semicircle 2 inches in diameter, then bent again so that the stationary leg of the tongs will again follow the axis of the handle. One of two types of lips may be chosen. Often a smith merely flattens the rod for a lip, this being curved inward over the horn. Some, however, may upset the end of the rod into a flat button $\frac{3}{4}$ inch in diameter, and the rod is then curved so that the flat surface is parallel to the axis of the leg.

Next the shank between semicircle and handle is flattened to a thickness of $\frac{3}{16}$ inch, the flat surface extending $1\frac{1}{4}$ inches up the shank and the width of the shank extending into the rod forming the semicircle. This is to receive the shank of the movable leg of the tongs. Shoulders should be carefully formed with a set hammer, or if no set hammer is available, with the square end of a bar or on the corner of the anvil. A ¼-inch hole is then drilled, or possibly punched, in the center of this flat surface about ½ inch from its upper end.

In making the movable leg, first the button is upset on the end and the leg is curved to fit the already-formed stationary leg, with at least a 1½-inch shank protruding beyond the semicircle at the upper end. This shank is flattened, with the flat surface extending the width of the rod into the top of the semicircle. The flat shank is then cut so that it fits the flat shank of the stationary leg. At this point, it is brought to a yellow heat, quickly fitted to the stationary leg, and a ¼-inch hole is punched in it, using the hole in the stationary leg as a guide. Some smiths prefer to drill the holes in tongs to assure a tight fit when the two legs are bradded together.

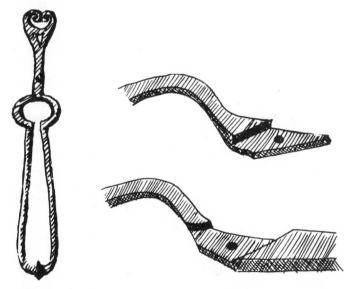

Left: Hearth tongs. Right: Shape of shoulders for pivot section.

The ¼-inch rod that holds the legs together may be bradded into large heads on both sides, the heads being dressed smoothly with a file and perhaps decorated with a center punch or a small cold chisel. A better method, though, is to drift out each hole with a tapered punch, punching from the outside so that the hole in either leg is larger on the outside than on the inside. When this is done, a short piece of ¼-inch rod, slightly longer than the combined width of both shanks, is brought to a white heat and inserted into the two tapered holes. This is pounded with a light hammer until the rod is upset at both ends to fit the tapered holes. The completed tongs are then quenched in the slack tub and the ends of the brad are filed flush with the shank on either side. When the brad cools it contracts sufficiently to allow a free pivot.

A smith may vary the details of hearth tools in many ways. He may use square rod instead of round, and give a most decorative twist to his handles if he likes. He may wish to square a section of a round rod and put a double twist in this section. At other times, he may flatten a section in the shank to create a long ellipse, and this may be decorated with center punch, or chisel, or special heart- and star-shaped punches.

Generally the European and Oriental smiths have followed the medieval traditions of exquisite craftsmanship and design of hearth tools more closely than the versatile, busy village smiths of the eighteenth and nineteenth centuries. Their work may be more appropriately placed in the category of decorative ironwork. The American smith, isolated as he was in the backwoods of the New World, was second to none in devising and making functional tools and implements. It must be said, however, that few Americans were able to import successfully the artistry and craftsmanship of the European— that infinite capacity for little things which is the mark of genius.

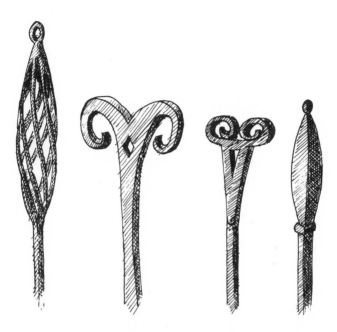

Handles for hearth tools

An essential bit of cooking equipment before 1800 was the fireplace crane, on which pots and kettles were hung over the fire. Many backwoods cabins in America and peasant cots in Europe had merely a bar of iron set across the back of the fireplace on which pothooks were hung, but on both continents a domestic establishment of any size had its cooking fire equipped with a crane. A crane is no more than a ¾-inch bar of iron, bent at right angles in some cases for small fireplaces, and mounted in two rings protruding from the hearth wall so that they may be swung in and out of the fire. Most kitchen fireplaces, though, were quite large—sizable enough in medieval castles to roast a whole ox in the kitchen! Those in the larger farmhouses of America and the manor houses of Europe were generally about 6-feet wide and about 3-feet deep. Cranes for these fireplaces had to be more elaborate than bent bars.

Larger cranes follow the principle of a bar bent at right angles, but with the refinements of pivot pins at both ends of the upright and a brace welded across the right angle to provide strength. To make one, the smith must acquire a bar 1½-inches square for his upright; he then forms 1-inch tenons 1½-inches long on each end, drawing the round tenons out of the bar with a set hammer, or if so equipped, with a large 1-inch round swage. The shoulders may be further squared with a small fuller or with a monkey tool. Sometimes a 1½-inch rod may be used instead of a bar for the upright, the ends being tenoned, as with the bar.

There are several ways for welding the horizontal arm to the pivot bar. Cross welding, or crossing the fibers of the iron, is not generally supposed to make as good a weld as lap welding, where the fibers in the joint coincide. It may be used in welding cooking cranes, however, because the diagonal brace provides extra strength to the whole. A better method is to split the upright about 2 or 3 inches from the top tenon. The horizontal bar, generally a bar ½ inch by 1½ or 2 inches, is then scarfed at one end on both sides and is inserted in this split, where it is welded. Still another method, per-

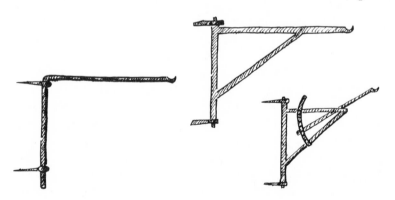

Types of hearth cranes

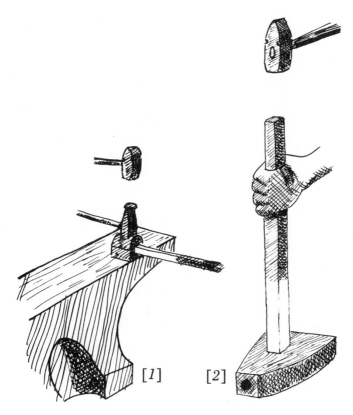

Forming tenon: [1] *with swage,* [2] *with monkey tool.*

haps the best of the three, is to elongate the top tenon so that its length is 1½ inches longer than the width of the horizontal bar. The horizontal bar is drawn down in thickness to ¼ inch on one end, the drawing down extending about 4 inches. After working a long scarf on the last 1½ inches, the bar is wrapped around the tenon, just as in making a hinge pin, and is welded. After welding, it may be dressed to the same size as the upright, its shoulders, where the lap weld occurs, being dressed with a set hammer or on the corner of the anvil.

Braces, made of a bar as large as the horizontal bar or perhaps a bit smaller, are prepared by scarfing both ends and lap welding the ends to horizontal and upright. In fancier households served by an artistic smith, the brace is sometimes decorated with scrolls, and variously shaped punched holes and designs are applied with center punch and chisel. Scrolls at the center and ends may be made of separate small bars welded to the brace and then scrolled; some can be made of a small split bar cross-welded at the butt to the brace, and scrolled; others may be formed by splitting a portion of the end for 3 or 4 inches and scrolling these appendages.

There is one other fairly common type of braced crane that has no upright, only a horizontal bar bent at one end to insert in a ring in the hearth wall, with a brace that has its end inserted into a bottom ring. These cranes are made either by welding the brace to the horizontal or by splitting the horizontal for 18 inches or so at one end and bending half the split down at a 45-degree angle to form the brace. Ends of

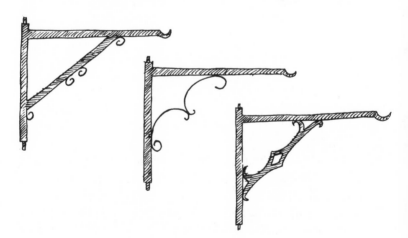

Decorated diagonal braces for hearth cranes

both horizontal and brace are tenoned and bent to a position perpendicular to the horizontal bar.

There are examples of quite complicated adjustable cranes, on which the height and angle of the horizontal bar and its length may be changed at will. Examples of such complicated devices are rare, mostly English in origin. The common kitchen attained the same results with a combination of pothooks and adjustable trammels.

Pothooks are probably the simplest of all fireplace cooking utensils. Otis Hall, who worked with his grandfather, Henry Ison, a Negro smith of Spalding County, Georgia, remembers making S-shaped pothooks as a boy helper in his grandfather's rural shop. He made them of ¼-inch rod bent to oppositely directed semicircles at either end.

Pot hook

Trammels, which were found in two main forms, were a bit more involved to make. Possibly the simplest form consisted of a flat bar from 12- to 15-inches long, ¼-inch thick, and ¾- to 1-inch wide. An old, worn horseshoe was easily converted to these dimensions when rolled bars were in short supply. To make a trammel, this bar is drawn out on the end to a ¼-inch-square tang 3- or 4-inches long. The body is then punched with a ¼-inch punch at intervals of 1 inch, starting with a hole centered only ⅜ inch from the flat end. The tang is bent into a hook on its end, and the flat end is bent to a right angle, opposite to the hook, at a point ¾ inch from its end. Now the second part is made from ¼-inch rod about

3 inches longer than the distance between the first and last holes punched in the flat bar. This rod is slightly flattened at one end for 1½ inches and is curved into a hook. The other end is bent to a right angle in the opposite direction and is inserted through the hole in the right-angle bend of the flat bar; then it is inserted in any of the other holes desired to hold a kettle the proper distance over the fire. Height is adjusted by reinserting the right-angle bend of the lower rod to any other hole in the upper bar.

A more easily adjusted trammel may be made from two ¼-inch bars from ¾-inch to 1½-inches wide and 9- or 10-inches long. Each is drawn down to a ¼-inch tang 4- or 5-inches long which extends up one side of the bar rather than in its center. One of these bars is then serrated with file or fuller to form notches, every inch or so, on the side of the bar opposite the tang. This will be the lower portion, with the tang being bent on its end to form a small hook on which a kettle bail can be hung. At the upper end of this bar the smith welds or brads a thin stationary keeper extending opposite the serrated edge far enough for the upper bar to slide easily inside it. Now the tang at the top of the unserrated half is formed into a hook by which the whole affair hangs from the crane. This portion requires a thin, pivoted keeper, bradded loosely to it near the bottom outside edge. Both keepers may be formed over the basic trammel stock of thin iron bar about ⅛ x ¼ inch in size. Bradding must be done after the upper bar is inserted through the keeper on the lower bar. The pivoted keeper, of course, fits into the notches on the lower part, thus making the lower hook adjustable in height from the crane. When assembled, both tangs should be on adjacent edges.

Trammels may be decorated with heart- or star-shaped holes, and designs may be applied with center punch and chisel.

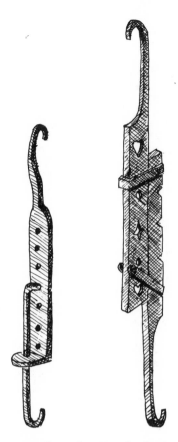

Left: Simple trammel. Right: Notched-type trammel with decorative punching.

Trivets and roasters, made by the local or the castle smith, were as essential to eighteenth-century cooks and their earlier counterparts as the grill in the oven is to modern cooks. Most were small simple grills mounted on three legs and made of heavy-enough iron to hold up under the heat of the fire for at least a generation. Trivets were stationary, while roasters often rotated on their stands to turn the roasting meat toward the blaze for even cooking.

A trivet, named because of its three legs, is essentially no more than a circle of iron to which three legs and a handle are welded or, in many cases, riveted. To make one the smith requires an iron bar ¼-inch thick and of any width up to 1 inch. He forges this into a ring over the horn of the anvil and, after scarfing the ends, welds them together. In early America, when swains were wont to take practical gifts to their intended, or were called upon to make the kitchen equipment for an approaching marriage, they made heart-shaped trivets to show their love. These may be made in two pieces, each formed into half a heart, which are lap-welded at the point and at the top.

Often the legs of trivets are bradded on, and the handle, when a handle is used, is frequently an extension of one of the legs. The better trivets, however, have the legs made of a small bar or rod welded to the ring. This is done with a cross weld on the two front legs. The rear leg and handle are formed together, the leg being bent at a right angle before the piece is cut to proper length. The handle portion is flattened to ¼-inch thickness and carefully shaped to fit the hand and is usually given a hook on the end for hanging up when not in use.

Common trivet plates consist of a plain ring; or a ring which has crossbars or interior, shaped, projections welded to it to support smaller pots. Some, though, are triangular, being made from small square or rectangular stock, the legs formed by doubling the stock and faggot welding it in three places to form a triangle, then bending the legs perpendicular to the plane of the triangle.

Roasters are made similarly to trivets, but in two parts, the ring, which rotates, and the three-legged stand. The ring, since it is designed to set a roast or ham upon it, always has a grill, and frequently a rather fancy grill. It is made of straight bars, an alternation of straight and serpentine

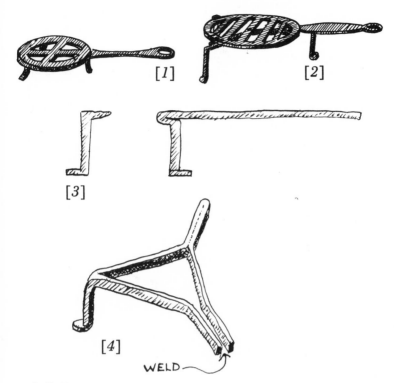

[1] *Trivet.* [2] *Roaster.* [3] *Profile of leg and handle for trivet.* [4] *Method of making triangular trivet.*

bars, two crossbars with scrolls, or a series of concentric rings fastened to the outer ring with crossbars. Roasters always have a flat surface in the center of the ring which is punched for the brad around which the ring rotates.

Roaster stands are made from a flat bar 1-inch wide, ⅛-inch to ¼-inch thick, and about 15-inches long, the length depending on the diameter of the rotating ring. The bar is first drawn down to a long point which extends 4 to 6 inches up the bar. This is split down the middle and spread so that the two sides form a 60-degree angle. The handle is shaped and fashioned with a hook or ring on its end. Next the ends of

265

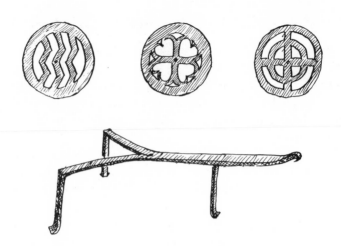

Top: Designs for roaster plates. Bottom: Roaster stand.

the split are bent into right angles to form legs at a distance
equal to the radius of the ring, and feet may be formed on
the legs if desired. The third leg is then formed and welded
or bradded to the base of the handle the same distance from
the fork as the right-angle bend in the legs. Of course, the
base of the third leg is scarfed before welding. A ¼-inch
hole is punched in the base of the handle with its center
½ inch from the fork of the two front legs. A brad joining
the ring and stand completes the roaster.

The practical smith soon discovers that the various dimensions of handcrafted wrought-iron items are always relative rather than standard. The diameter of a roaster ring, for
instance, would be determined by the size of the roasts generally prepared by the customer. The distance of the legs
from the center brad must always relate to the size of the
ring. Handles may be long or short depending on the depth
of the fireplace. Height of leg is related to the height of firedogs, the depth of coals used by a particular cook, and perhaps other factors peculiar to cook and fire. Thus each piece
of iron equipment is as individual in its shape and dimen-

266

sions as the person who uses it. The relative dimensions of each piece gives almost perfect proportions and functional beauty that cannot be matched by any utensil designed to be mass-produced on the basis of economical production, easy packing, and modish design, rather than efficient use by a specific person.

Perhaps the most interesting and beautiful kitchen utensils made by smiths in every area were the forks and spoons and spatulas which hung on kitchen walls and fireplaces of Williamsburg and old Augsburg, of Edinburgh and Stockholm. Many of these relatively small, generally graceful tools were doubtless made on a farm forge on a wintry day, but most, as with nearly all ironwork, were made by the village smith or his more artistic apprentices. Practically every technique used in ironworking is needed to turn out a set of hand utensils. They are a challenge and a pleasure to make. Because of their delicacy and the ill effects of flaws in the iron, only the best Swedish or Lancashire iron was used for these smaller pieces in the heyday of smithing.

Forks, often called toasting forks, are probably the most graceful and most interesting of these relics of fireplace

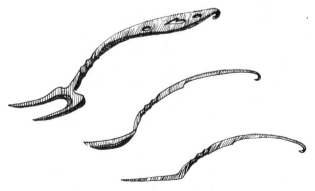

Toasting fork, iron spoon, and spatula

cookery. They may be made of ⅜-inch or ½-inch rod or bar from 12- to 18-inches long, depending on use and need.

When round or square bar rod is used the best method of making a fork is to weld one end of the rod into a loop some 2 inches long, as when making a hooked poker. The loop is then cut through. The resulting legs are spread and each is drawn out to a point. Usually the legs are spread to a 90° angle to allow them to be worked easily on the face of the anvil. After drawing out, the tines are shaped over the end of the anvil horn. The end of the rod opposite the tines may be welded into a ring or a heart, or if the rod is large enough, flattened to form a comfortable handle.

An attractive small cooking fork can be made from ⅜ x ½ inch bar. First the bar is fullered, either with ⅜-inch top and bottom fullers or with two lengths of ⅜-inch rod, which serves as a most effective expedient when fullers are unavailable. Below the fullering the bar is drawn to a point which is split to form the tines. Tines may be spread, worked and finally shaped exactly as those on a fork made from rod. Next the stock above the fullering is drawn out to shape the handle, the fullering giving graceful definition to the point where the handle spreads into the tines. When drawing out the handle the shank will become thicker. This thickness must be left to provide strength to the shank. Such a fork may be finished by drilling a hole in the end of the handle, shaping the end into a hook, or off-setting the last ½-inch to form a spur about ¾-inch long, the spur then being curved back on the plane of the handle to form a loop for hanging.

The last step in making a fork is to bend the tines downward and then in the opposite direction to form the graceful curve which makes the utensil both beautiful and efficient in form. Small forks should have slightly curved handles. Large ones may be finished with a straight handle.

Many old continental forks would have flat handles pierced with decorative punches.

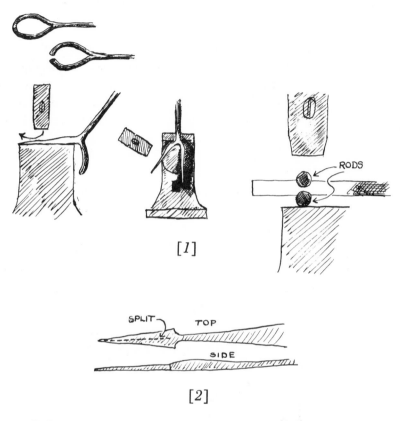

[1] *Steps in making a fork from rod.* [2] *Making a small fork from flat bar stock.*

It is important to shape tines only while the iron is quite hot. Better to reheat than to hammer cold and see one of the tines suddenly break off because of unnoticed strain in the fibers at the right-angle bend. Neither mild steel nor hot iron should be hammered at a blue heat.

A nice decoration for a fork of this sort is to put a twist in the shank about 2 inches above the tines. To do this the portion to be twisted is heated to an even orange-red or yellow. One end of the heated portion is quickly placed in the vise, and the twist is made by grasping the other end of the heated portion with tongs and giving either a half or a whole twist. All twisting must be finished in one heat, otherwise it will twist unevenly. If, as sometimes happens, twisting puts a crook in the shank, this can be straightened by pounding with a lead hammer, a wooden mallet or maul, or with a block of wood, while the shank rests on another block of wood placed on the anvil face.

There are other forms of forks, of course. Some have a flat shank on which are filed hearts or stars or circles or ovals. Handles are decorated with variously shaped punches or with designs applied with center punch or chisel.

Larger forks, the ones long enough to turn over meat in a frying pan without stooping, may have three tines instead of two. To make these, the smith may follow the procedure for making two-tined forks, except that he forges the end to be split at least ¾-inch wide at the base and splits it twice, bending the two outside portions and leaving the center straight. The center tine is cut off to match the length of the outside tines after they are bent. Some smiths used a hacksaw to split the tines, after this convenient tool was developed at the end of the eighteenth century, but splitting with a chisel is easier and somehow handsomer.

Often the smith may weld on the outside tines of a three-tined fork. Some may wish to weld a straight bar at right angles to the shank, then bend them to proper shape. A better way, however, is to lap-weld the ends of two straight bars to the shank and, after welding, shape these into the outside tines. A lap weld always provides more strength than a cross weld.

Among the relics exhibited at Old Brunswick, near Wilmington, North Carolina, are the two outside tines of a large cooking fork. It is obvious that these were cross-welded to the shank, but the smith got a "cold shut" instead of a good joint, and his fork became no more than a skewer.

The beauty of old hand-wrought cooking forks comes largely from the natural, graceful curves put into tines and shank as the last step of manufacture. Curving, of course, is done over the horn, generally with a light hammer. First the shank, just above the separation of the tines, is curved downward until the tines point to a 60-degree angle from the shank. Then the tines, just below the parting, are bent 60 degrees or so in the opposite direction so that their angle points 30 degrees above the shank. It is up to the smith to decide which portion of the horn will provide the proper arc to these curves to bring both beauty and functional efficiency to forks of various lengths.

Spoons and ladles and spatulas are made in a manner similar to forks, but usually in two pieces that are welded or bradded together. Handles and shanks are made exactly as are forks; only the triangular portion reserved for the tines is left off. Instead, the butt of the shank is slightly flattened for no more than ½ inch. This is then split on the same plane as the handle for ½ inch toward the shank.

Spoon and ladle bowls and spatula blades are roughly cut to shape from thin sheet iron before welding to the handle. Once cut to rough shape with hand shears or bench shears, they are jambed into the split, while the split is orange-red, and the lips of the split are hammered tightly around the base of the bowl or blade. Some smiths use a center punch or key chisel to rough up the part of bowl or blade that is inserted into the shank. This forms small teeth which help keep the two pieces in position while welding.

Welding must be done slowly, the bellows being worked with a delicate touch, to prevent the thin sheet iron from burning away where it is to join the thicker shank. While being brought to welding heat the spoon or spatula should be turned regularly to absorb heat evenly, and the small pointed poker should be used frequently to determine when the metal becomes tacky, or molten enough, to be joined. Very high-grade iron may not require a flux, but it is better to sprinkle borax, sand, or salt on the joint when it reaches cherry-red heat. As soon as proper heat is reached for welding, the iron is taken from the fire and is joined with a light hammer.

Shaping spoon and ladle bowls may be done in several ways. The easiest is to use a swage block that has the properly shaped depression for spoon or ladle. The orange-red sheet is placed over the depression and formed with the pein of a ball-pein hammer. Some smiths follow the techniques of the coppersmith and silversmith and have a special anvil stake with a rounded face, the other end of which fits into the hardie hole. The red-hot bowl piece is placed over this and shaped with glancing blows of the hammer, which forms the bowl without the wavy surface caused by a ball pein. The smith who has neither swage block nor stake can hollow the bowl

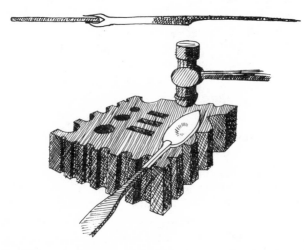

Top: Cross section showing cold bowl metal jambed into hot split of handle. Bottom: Shaping spoon bowl on swage block with ball pein hammer.

by hammering the hot metal on the anvil face with the pein of a ball-pein hammer.

Where a swage block is unavailable the spoon bowl may be easily shaped on a block of wood, the hammer and hot iron making its own very satisfactory depression. Also, a ball-pein hammer placed in the vise serves as an excellent substitute for a round-faced stake anvil.

After forming, the edges of the bowl are dressed with shears or file. Spatula blades need only be scarfed on the front edge. This is done on the rounded edge of the anvil face, or top of the horn.

After forming the bowl of spoons, ladles, and so on, the shank is heated orange-red and twisted to match the fork. Then the curves of shank and bowl are formed.

Colanders and other types of strainers are made exactly as are spoons and ladles except that small holes are punched in the bowl after it has been formed.

Often spoons and colanders, in Colonial days, had the bowls bradded to the shank. This is done by punching two brad holes in the shank and using these as a guide to punch matching holes in the bowl or spatula blade. When bradding is used, the smith generally forms each piece completely before bradding them together. Brads are always used to join iron handles and copper or brass spoon bowls. The smith who makes utensils of two different metals will find it sensible to have his brads of the softer metal. They are more easily replaced when wear makes the joint loose, and they do not enlarge the brad holes in either iron or softer material.

Among the more attractive and interesting items made for the kitchen by medieval and later smiths were meat skewers and skewer holders. The skewers, in simplest form, are only ¼-inch or ³⁄₁₆-inch rods or square bars 7- or 8-inches long and drawn out to a point on one end. The other end is generally formed into a 1-inch-diameter circle

Meat skewer

which is sometimes welded shut, but usually not. Since skewers were brought to the festive table stuck into the roast, however, the proud Colonial housewife or chatelaine liked to have a number of well-made decorative skewers with which to enhance her status as a hostess. Consequently, she usually had a collection of skewers decorated with punch marks and chisel marks and twisting. One beautiful skewer illustrated in Wallace Nutting's *Furniture Treasury* is decorated with a double twist. This may be put into a square skewer by heating the shank orange-red, placing it diagonally in the corner of the vise, so that the vise jaws cover no more than about ¼ inch of the shank, and quickly twisting each end in the same direction for half a twist. Again the smith must be careful to heat the entire shank evenly or his twists will be unevenly formed.

Concomitant with attractive skewers were attractive skewer holders. In humble kitchens they might have been hung on a peg or nail driven into the wall. In more affluent households, though, the kitchen was usually equipped with a wrought-iron skewer holder which hung on the wall near the hearth.

Normal skewer holders may be made of sheet iron ⅛-inch to ¼-inch thick. A favorite design is a heart-shape with two prongs extending to either side from the point of the heart. This design is first roughly cut with shears, bench shears, or cold chisel, with the body of the heart left somewhat thicker than its final intended shape. The sheet is then brought to an orange-red and the thickened sides of the heart are split ¼ inch from the edges to within ¼ inch of the point to form two prongs. These are bent down until they

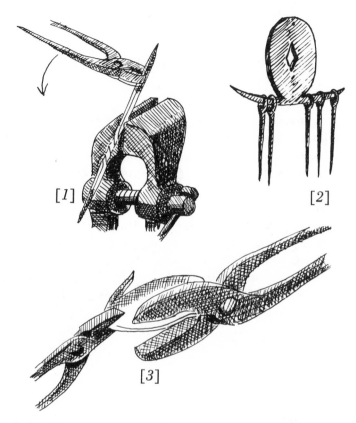

[1] *Double twisting.* [2] *Skewer holder.* [3] *Splitting prong with bench shears.*

are at right angles to the vertical axis of the heart, then curved forward slightly with an additional gentle curve upward on the ends. The heart itself is punched at the top for hanging on a nail, and perhaps decorated with center punch or chisel.

A tool essential to any well-run household in olden days, as in many modern households, was scissors. A woman, in the days when all domestic tools were handmade, was as proud of the quality of her favorite sewing scissors as her husband was of his favorite shotgun. To make a fine pair of scissors by hand indeed required as much skill and care as did the gun. The first steel, one may remember, was described as shear steel, doubtless because of the demand for good scissors and shears. Good scissors did not wear out. In Europe they were generally made in the specialized shops of cutlers, who made only shears, fine knives, swords, and the like. In America they were provided by the general blacksmith, some of whom, because of their skill, devoted more time to fine articles such as sewing scissors.

Sump Brown, the smith of Cobb County, Georgia, has a pair that belonged originally to his great-great-grandmother, a Cherokee woman who lived in Cobb County before the Removal Treaty of 1836. These are made of high-grade wrought iron with a thin piece of steel, only $\frac{1}{16}$-inch thick, welded to the blade for a cutting surface.

To make scissors of this sort the smith first welds his two metals together. This must be done with extreme care so as not to burn the thin steel. To make a pair of sewing scissors 4-inches long requires a bar of flat iron $\frac{1}{8}$-inch thick, $\frac{1}{4}$-inch wide, and $4\frac{1}{2}$-inches long. The steel used for this size scissors must be $\frac{1}{16}$-inch thick, $\frac{1}{2}$-inch wide, and 2- to 3-inches long. Unless the smith particularly wants the steel to extend beyond the blade into the handle, he must weld each blade separately. This is done by placing the narrower steel down the center of the iron and clamping the two pieces together with tongs held shut with a tong ring, the tongs holding no more than $\frac{1}{4}$ inch of the iron and steel. Of course, the length of the iron intended for the handle extends some 2 inches beyond the steel.

When the two pieces are clamped tightly they are placed high in the fire, the iron on the bottom, and the bellows are gently pumped. Flux is sprinkled liberally between and over the pieces when they reach cherry-red heat, after which they

Using ringed tongs to clamp steel to scissors blade for welding

are placed in the fire again, iron on the bottom, until welding heat is reached. As soon as the steel turns from white to the greasy, liquid yellow which denotes welding heat, the two pieces are quickly removed and joined. Though welding heat for iron is a higher temperature than for steel, the smith in joining the two metals generally follows the steel, particularly when very thin steel is welded.

Joining can be done with rapid blows from a light hammer, but often the smith will find it more satisfactory to join such thin stock by placing the set hammer on the pieces and giving it a good blow with a 6-pound sledge.

After welding, while the iron is still hot, the joined pieces are cut off on the hardie at the end of the weld adjacent to the end of the tongs.

Next the handle is shaped by drawing out the iron that projects beyond the steel into a long taper. The finger hole is formed around the tip of the horn and welded shut with a lap weld. The blade is then carefully drawn out to a point, taking care that the steel is not twisted into the iron. The blade is chamfered on the side intended for the cutting edge by holding it on the edge of the anvil and forming a shouldered chamfer with a set hammer. The blade must be carefully forged with even blows, otherwise it may warp when hardened. Then the handle shank is curved and the finger hole dressed to a circle or an oval or a pointed oval, depending on the smith's taste.

Holes for the brad, or in later times a screw, are drilled, countersunk, and, when necessary, threaded with a tap. When a screw is used, the hole to be threaded must be smaller than the other hole by twice the depth of the intended thread, and the screw is threaded only on its end to the thickness of the hole.

Scissors, especially small sewing scissors, are always finished carefully with a fine file. After the shape has been dressed up the metal is polished by rubbing the file sideways, or perpendicular to its long axis, over every surface. Final polishing is done with an emery cloth or a paste of emery powder and oil, rubbed on with a soft rag or a piece of leather. Before bradding or screwing together, the pair of scissors is heated to cherry red and quenched in oil or brine for hardening. Some smiths may temper to a brown or straw yellow after hardening, but this is not essential; the iron backing will prevent the hardened steel from chipping. After tempering, the scissors are again polished with emery.

Pipe tongs went out of use about the end of the eighteenth century. Before then, after tobacco had become part of everyday custom in every part of the Western world, pipe tongs graced many a fashionable hearth and were considered utensils; but because they held a prominent position in the sitting room, they were usually finely made and nicely decorated, giving them a position midway between utensils and decorative ironwork.

Most pipe tongs are from 18 to 20 inches in overall length and made of round or square section ¼-inch rod or bar. Unlike blacksmith's tongs, most pipe tongs do not cross at the pivot, but are designed to open when the handles are pressed together, and to close automatically with a spring when the handles are released. To make them, the smith selects two rods or bars, one some 25-inches long, the other 30 to 32 inches. Twenty inches from the end of each he welds a small boss which is no more than a section of the original stock. It is easier to form these by welding the end of a long section at the proper point for about ½ inch and by cutting the excess beyond the weld off on the hardie. One of these bosses is drawn down to a ¼-inch thickness, using a set hammer on the edge of the anvil face to form good shoulders. The other is split down to the original rod and the lips of the split are drawn out over a chisel edge, each to about ¹⁄₁₆ inch, to form two thin studs. The channel between these is widened and its bottom flattened by hammering the end of ¼-inch-by-1-inch flat bar into the channel while the iron is orange-red. The two lips are then hammered around the end of the bar to make them parallel. These two bosses, the single fitting into the double, will form the pivot for the tongs.

Next the portion of the short bar above the boss may be slightly flattened for one handle. Then at a point some 3 ½

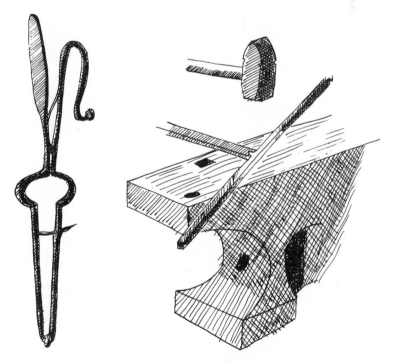

Left: Pipe tongs. Right: Shaping split boss on pipe tongs.

inches below the boss, a 1½-inch-diameter half-circle is formed in the rod on the same plane as the boss and on the opposite side of the shank. The straight extension of the shank below the half-circle should bend about 10 degrees in from the axis of the rod between half-circle and boss. Opposite the handle, the end of the shank is then either upset to form a button, which is flattened, or the rod is flattened to ½-inch width. The end of the rod is then curved inward.

Forming the other portion of the pipe tongs is identical to the first from the boss downward. Its handle, though, is quite different. This handle is first upset on its end to form a button, which may be flattened somewhat so that it is suitable to tamp tobacco in a pipe. Then the handle is bent in a curve to a 60-degree angle at the distance of the end of the handle on the other piece. It is then bent again in the opposite direction, some 4 inches from the first bend, to another 60-degree angle. Both bends must be in the same plane as the half-circle.

A flat tapered spring about 3-inches long and ¼-inch wide shaped like an elongated "S" is forged, and a ⅛-inch hole is drilled ⅜ inch from the thick end. This spring is hardened by heating to cherry red and quenching in oil or brine and the temper drawn to a pigeon blue; or the correct temper may be attained by covering the hardened spring with the soot from a burning splinter of pine, then laying on a red-hot bar. The moment the soot is burned off the spring is quenched in oil, which gives it proper temper. A ⅛-inch hole is then drilled in either handle, its direction parallel to the boss, and the spring is bradded to one handle so that it presses the other outward.

Most pipe tongs also had a built-in pick for cleaning pipe bowls which also served to keep the lips of the tongs in alignment. Resembling a long nail, this pick is a piece of iron ¼-inch wide, ⅛-inch thick, and 3-inches long, drawn out to

a fine point. Its butt end has a ⅛-inch tenon formed on it for
⅜ inch, which is inserted in a ⅛-inch hole drilled in either
leg of the tongs halfway between the pivot and the half-circle.
The other leg has a hole, large enough to allow the pick to
slide easily into it, punched in the opposite leg, in alignment
with the drilled hole. The tenon of the pick is inserted in the
drilled hole and bradded tightly, and the pick is curved in
the proper arc to allow it to slide easily in the punched hole
when the tongs are opened and closed.

A properly made pair of pipe tongs could have been
turned out in the old days only by a smith who knew his business. Because they were special, luxury items, the smith
seldom turned them over to his customer until they had been
dressed to perfection, filed smooth, and polished with emery.
Often these interesting items are decorated with punch marks
or chasing with a small graver.

There are several additional forms of pipe tongs. Some of
them are miniature versions of fire tongs, and some consist
of two simply made legs joined by an almost circular spring
welded to the butt of the legs. These are no problem to make,
once a smith has mastered the design and manufacture of the
classic type described above.

The housewives and cooks of all ages have used a far
greater variety of cooking and household utensils than have
been treated in this chapter. Indeed, no aspect of ironworking
is more interesting than the making of the commonplace, day-
by-day hand appliances of a simpler day. It is probable that
the smith invented many of these utensils, and the sense of
design of certain individual smiths, most of them totally unknown to history, provided a grace and satisfaction to kitchen
utensils that is almost entirely lost in this day of total mass-
manufacturing.

9.

IRON AMENITIES,
PLAIN AND FANCY

From the beginning of the Iron Age, man has depended on the blacksmith for his necessities of civilized life, his tools and utensils and transportation. When life became a little easier because of iron, man turned to his local smith for what may be termed the material amenities of living. These include the comfort and convenience of lighting appliances and the durable security of iron window grills, sturdy gates, and unassailable fences. Working within this field the smith evolved from mere craftsman to fine artist, meeting the challenge of iron in delicate and exquisite, and at times quite incredible, sculptured designs which provided aesthetic satisfaction as well as functional value.

An artist-smith can only be the product of general affluence combined with a feeling of individuality among the affluent classes. Thus the unbelievably intricate and beautiful wrought ironwork which has come down from the prosperous Renaissance of Italy, the gold-filled colonial period of Spain, the profitable medieval trade of the Hanseatic cities, the long imperial years of Britain, and the leisurely and relatively simple affluence of Colonial America.

Such artistic ironwork as was produced in these various periods was not really a new development in smithing, but a reflection of the standards set by ancient Hephaestus, the legendary prototype of all the smiths who followed him.

282

Hephaestus, crippled and ugly as he was, would never have been granted divinity had he concentrated his skill only on tools and utensils. His status came to him because he was capable of making four golden handmaidens to help him at his forge. Such a feat was art, not trade, and art which was never duplicated in all the thousands of years which followed his legend. The closest subsequent blacksmiths came to emulating the God of Craftsmen was in creating a wrought-iron blacksmith that struck a miniature anvil to mark the hours for the town clock of a late-medieval German town.

The smith of medieval Wales would never have been accorded a place equal to that of the priest and the poet in the Prince's court had his work been confined to horseshoes and billhooks. It was the armor, the finely decorated weapons, the elaborate and tasteful wrought-iron sconces and gates he made that earned his status. Without the technical skill and artistic imagination of the smith, the Prince himself could not have enjoyed the recognition that the ownership of unique ironwork conferred upon him.

Creative art, however, was undoubtedly the result of working iron, not the cause. Most successful smiths throughout the long and progressive age of hand-forged iron were, it may be presumed, thoughtful men of vision and foresight, men several intellectual cuts above the craftsmen in other fields who worked mainly by rote, however skillfully. The smith, even for the simplest job, never smote his iron twice with exactly the same blow, and his material, heating in the forge to a plastic state and cooling on the anvil, was never constant for a second as it was being worked under the hammer. These very qualities of obduracy, inconstancy, and plasticity of iron are fascinating to the ironworker, the smiter, the smith. The inconstant hot iron provides a constant challenge. Once forming a simple item is well-learned, the challenge to do a little more becomes almost an obsession to the smith who is intellectually equipped to become a master and an artist. The challenge of the smith, however, is somewhat different from that of artists in most other mediums. Other artists must work with their material as it is, shaping wood or marble or applying paint in an imaginative manner. The smith, on the other hand, may change the basic shape and, as with springs, the quality of his material as required, provided he has the skill and judgment needed. Other artists are somewhat limited in the tools they use, but the blacksmith can make new tools to create the effect he envisions. The challenge he accepted so eagerly has happily resulted in the often remarkable examples of decorative ironwork found in lamps and chandeliers, gates and fences, all over the Western world.

Lighting appliances as a group are the best examples of small pieces of decorative ironwork, though in England and America their forms did not often assume the Baroque elaboration of items found in Spain and Italy. The simplest of all lighting equipment was probably the rushlight used in lower-income homes on the American frontier and in the unassuming cots and farmhouses of England, Scotland, Ireland, and the Continent. Few rushlights could ever be classed as decorative; they were purely functional, but they may be classed an amenity. They serve as a good starting point for describing the techniques of making more elaborate lighting appliances.

Actually the rushlight is no more than a small pair of pliers or tongs, modified so that one handle is attached to a standard of wood or iron, and the other is curved and weighted to automatically close the jaws to hold a rushwick. For wooden standards, the upright shank is tapered to a point on its end so that it can be stuck into a block of wood. The shank of the other jaw may be curved outward to supply leverage to keep the jaws closed, or, if more weight is needed, its end may be doubled back and welded or upset into a ball or teardrop.

Some rushlights may be designed for double duty. Instead of having a weight formed on the end of the shank, they may have a candleholder. This may be formed by two methods. The rod of which the shank is made may be drawn out to a thin wedge-shaped plate which is formed on an anvil bick into a long cone, and its edges may be welded together. If the rod is too small for flattening, a wedge shape may be cut from thin sheet iron, which is then formed into a cone shape on the bick. This cone is jambed at its point onto the handle and is welded, first at the point and then along the edges of the sheet. Since the thin sheet will not hold welding heat too long, usually it is necessary to weld the point of the cone to the shank with one heat, and to bring the piece to a second welding heat to join the seam.

The two sections of a rushlamp are held together with a brad, exactly as the jaws of tongs are joined.

Left: Rush light. Right: Welding candle socket on anvil bick.

Iron candleholders may be made in a variety of forms, including standing candlesticks, candlestands, sconces, chandeliers, and various types of holders designed to hook on shelves or the backs of chairs. Candlesticks in simplest forms may be made by welding a socket on the end of a ¼-inch rod, as on the shank of a rushlight, with the pointed end of the stick to be inserted in a wooden standard. Fancier standards are made by welding two or three additional short pieces of bar to the end, flattening and scrolling the ends of each, and spreading them to provide a secure standard.

Tripod standards may be formed and welded from the same piece of stock from which the candlestick is made, thus avoiding the need for jump welding. This is done by measuring the intended length of the candlestick above the standard and marking the point with a centerpunch. Below this mark the stock is cut to provide a length three times that of the legs. The leg portion is then bent at a point equal to the length of one leg and doubled back once more so that the end of the rod reaches the first bend. Welding, of course, is done at the centerpunch. After welding the first bend is cut, forming three equal lengths which are formed into the tripod standard. Ends of the legs may be flattened, scrolled or made into dragon's feet.

There are a number of modern artists in iron who produce beautiful candlesticks of contemporary design. Many of these are made of heavy 1-inch or larger stock. Most have heavy drip pans, usually electric-welded to the upright and with a point instead of a socket for the candle. Standards may be formed from the basic stock, by perhaps splitting and forming, or may be formed with a forge butt weld or an electric or acetylene weld; later dressed carefully with hammer and file. Such modern candlesticks may have the basic design enhanced by forging certain forms, by fullering, by glass inlays and by inlaying with silver, copper or brass wire, or even gold wire.

Decorating with hammer, trip-hammer or fuller can easily be accomplished by a smith who has a sense of design and proportion, a feel for red-hot iron and familiarity with his tools. Inlaying, however, with glass or metal or enameling, requires experience. Written directions can only direct, not demonstrate.

Iron a ½-inch or more thick, so as to be inflexible, is required for glass inlaying. It may be punched or split to receive the glass, which may be small pieces of broken bottles, either clear or colored.

Glass should be inlayed over a smooth iron plate, working with an acetylene or propane torch. First the iron, with small chips of glass placed in the opening, is laid on the plate and brought to a bright red with the torch. At this time it begins to become plastic with heat from the torch. As the glass becomes molten it is packed into the opening with the pein of a ball-pein hammer or a short thick rod which has been rounded on

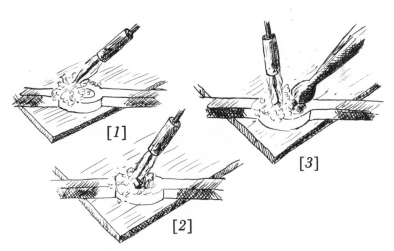

[1] *Heating iron for glass inlaying.* [2] *Melting glass in opening.* [3] *Packing melted glass.*

its end by forging or grinding. When the glass has been packed into one side the iron is turned over and the glass packed on the other side. When packing is finished the piece is laid close to the forge fire for slow cooling. Small flakes of glass around the edge of the opening usually pop off, but this does not affect the beauty of the inlay. Sometimes, with care, it is possible to mold the glass into a convex surface which extends above the flat surface of the iron. Such molding provides a jewellike effect that is well worth the extra effort.

Inlaying with wire follows the practice of ancient peoples, particularly the Vikings, who made battle-axes beautiful in this manner. The process essentially consists of chiseling a "V"-shaped channel, cutting keys into the sides of the channel and then hammering wire of softer metal into the keyed channel.

Chisels may be made from various-sized punches or carbon steel rods. They are ground or swaged to a "V" shape with the end ground to about a 45° angle. Cutting chisels are tempered to a straw color and then further ground on the bottom of the cutting angle to a slight curve. It is important, too, to very delicately grind the point to a small, undeterminable curve. Channels are cut by striking the chisel with a hammer of appropriate weight, the cut being guided by the hand. Keys are made by undercutting the sides of the channel with the same chisel, or by using a flat chisel driven squarely into the sides.

Enameling iron, which provides colorful highlights to flower petals, leaves or grooves, follows exactly the technique of enameling copper. Heat may be provided with a torch or kiln.

Sconces of wrought iron are a feature of lighting appliances found in every type of house from castles to cots from medieval times to mid-nineteenth century in all parts of the Western world. They evolved from the medieval brackets and

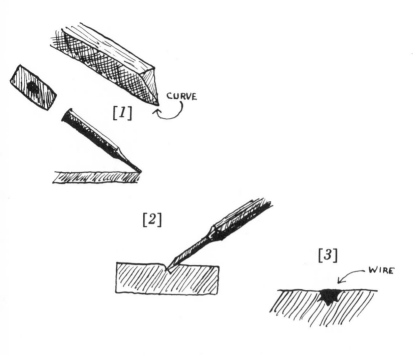

[1] Shape of "V" chisel. [2] Cutting keys in channel.
[3] Wire keyed in channel.

iron baskets which were attached to stone walls to hold
torches and pine knots. Brackets are basically no more than
iron rings, 3 or 4 inches in diameter, welded at a 45-degree
angle to a short bar which attaches to the wall. Baskets are no
more than iron containers made of thin flat iron, usually
bradded together and attached, as with a bracket, to a plate
fastened to the wall. Baskets may also be mounted with a long
rod welded to the bottom and bent at a right angle to insert into
the mortar of the wall, or when sharpened, to be driven directly into the heavy wooden frame of a manor house. Often
brackets and baskets are welded or bradded to an extension of

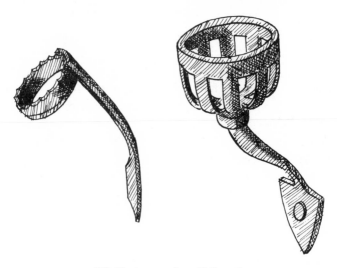

Wall ring and wall bracket

the wall plate, which is bent at a 45-degree angle. No special instruction is needed to make such an appliance in its simplest form.

Experience and time, more than instruction, are needed to duplicate some of the quite remarkable brackets and lighting baskets of the Italian Renaissance. These consist of a number of elaborate pieces joined together by welding or riveting and decorated with truly sculptured dragons, griffons, and eagles. No two highly decorative items were ever alike, but many shared various decorative devices such as dragons' heads, animal heads, snakes, incised rings, and twisted rods.

Decorated rings must have the decoration applied before the ring is welded together. Many of them may have scalloped edges on top and bottom. Scallops are formed with a fuller while the iron is at an orange or white heat, the position of each scallop having been drawn on the iron before heating with a soapstone pencil, and the points of impact for the fuller marked with a light chisel cut or a center punch.

As fullering one edge will extend the length of the iron, curving it, as when a knife blade is drawn out, the iron, as with a knife, must be curved over the horn so that the edge to be fullered is concave when only one edge is to be scalloped. This compensating curve is formed, of course, after the design has been marked on the iron.

When both edges are to be scalloped, no compensating curve is necessary; fullering both edges is compensation enough. Problems, however, arise in scalloping the second edge without battering the first into a shapeless mass. A set of top and bottom matching fullers is needed. When the iron is brought to white heat, the smith quenches only the edge that has been previously scalloped in the slack tub, holding it in the water to a depth that reaches only slightly above the bottom curves of the scallop. Then, working quickly, he

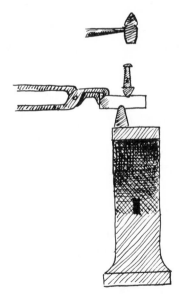

Using top and bottom fuller to form double scallop

places the iron so that the bottom fuller fits into a finished scallop and forms the top scallop in the hot half of the iron with a top fuller. If, by chance, a bottom fuller is unavailable, the horn of the anvil can be substituted, provided it fits the top fuller adequately. After scallops have been formed the curved edges may be dressed with a light hammer to remove any thickening of the iron at the bottoms of the scallops. Flat decoration, zigzag, straight, or serpentine indentations, punching, or dotting are applied with small fullers, chisels, or punches.

Next, the ring is scarfed for welding and formed. To protect the decoration, the iron should be heated to an even white heat and bent into circular shape by using a fork placed in the hardie hole. Normally forks are made of square stock. To avoid mutilating the surface of the ring, however, the smith should round the inside corners of the fork before bending the ring. Bending is simply accomplished by inserting one scarfed end of the iron into the fork and carefully bending around with tongs until the scarfs on both ends meet. Rings may be formed over the horn, but the smith must use a copper hammer or even a heavy wooden mallet to avoid marking the decorated surface.

After forming, the scarfs are brought to welding heat and the ends joined over the horn of the anvil. Instead of using a hammer to join the ends, the meticulous smith will use the square end of a large iron bar, ½-inch thick and as wide as the ring. The end of the bar is placed quickly on the scarfs after they are brought to the sparkling incandescence of welding heat, and the bar is hit once or twice with a 4-pound hammer to join the ends of the ring. The last step is to continue the design over the weld while the ring is held on the horn.

Often torch brackets and knot baskets are fastened to decorated rings on a stone pillar, instead of to a wall plate.

These rings are made and decorated exactly as are bracket rings except for the welding, which is impossible when the ring encircles a stone pillar. Instead of scarfing the ends, each end is punched for a rivet hole, then each is bent at right angles for about 1 inch. Then the ring is formed around the pillar and the ends are riveted together. Riveting is done by inserting a red-hot rivet in the holes of the ring, holding an 8-pound sledge against the head of the rivet and upsetting the other end with a 2-pound hammer.

The heads of animals, birds, reptiles, and mythical creatures may be formed to decorate the ends of rods and bars which serve as supports and braces of baskets, brackets, sconces, chandeliers, and other decorative iron pieces. Such iron sculpture is not so difficult to accomplish as may be imagined. Take, for example, a dragon's head formed on the end of a ½-inch-square bar. Roughly described, such a head will consist of the neck, formed by the original bar, cranium, long jaws, ears, and perhaps even a forked, waving tongue. First a boss is formed on the neck to serve as a foundation for the cranium. This is most easily done by doubling the bar ¾ inch from the end and welding it to the original neck. The snout is shaped by drawing down the boss from about ⅜ inch from the doubled-back end, using a set hammer or the corner of the anvil to draw out this portion of the boss to a rectangular section ⅜-inch thick and the same width as the original bar. At this stage the head and snout are molded with careful blows from a light hammer. Next the snout is split crosswise with a thin chisel to form the mouth, which is opened to a 30-degree angle, the bottom jaw being bent downward to form the angle. Teeth may be indicated by marking the upper and lower jaws with a small chisel or punch, or if the smith wishes to take the trouble, he may make a small thin chisel or gouge with which to cut projections to form more natural-looking teeth in the unnatural dragon. Eyes and

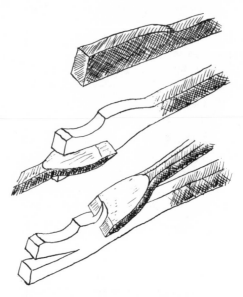

Steps in forming a dragon's head

nostrils are generally indicated with a small punch, which, for the eyes, may be forged into an oval shape.

Tongues may be welded or shrunk into the open mouth, a delicate, but not impossible, task because of the thin iron involved. When a wickedly curved tongue, perhaps forked, is desired, the mouth must be split longer for shrinking or welding. To shrink, the cold tongue, with a barb on its end, is jambed into the hot mouth as far as possible, this being most easily done while the head is held in the vise. It is then lowered and the vise tightened in order to clamp the tongue in place. To weld, the head is thrust into the fire and the bellows are pumped slowly, so as not to bring it to welding heat too quickly or allow too much oxygen, which will damage the thin tongue. While the dragon's head is being heated the

294

smith must watch it with great care to make certain that welding heat is only at the base of the jaw and farther back, not extending to the nose and the tip of the tongue. Once welding heat is reached, the last ¼ inch of the jaws is welded shut around the base of the tongue. This is more easily done by resting the head upside down on the anvil and hammering only the base of the jaw. To avoid excess hammering, the split jaw may be joined by placing the end of a ¼-inch-thick bar at the base of the split and smiting it with a 1½-pound hammer. When the welding is done, the portion of the jaws not welded may be opened and the position of the tongue, as well as any curves desired, may be adjusted with needle-nosed pliers while the iron is at an orange heat.

Ears may be formed by welding a thin strip or rod to the sides of the head and forming these into ears. An easier, and perhaps more effective method, however, is to cut the ears with a thin chisel, the same way teeth were cut. The head should be brought to a yellow heat and the neck part of the iron clamped in the vise so that the hot head extends out of the vise. A quite thin chisel is then driven at an angle toward the mouth, cutting a pointed sliver which is bent upward. The cutting should be carefully planned and done quickly so that possibly both ears can be formed in the same heat.

Wings, horns, and other appendages may be welded on by following the same general techniques used in welding tongues and ears. The heads of eagles, dogs, horses, and other creatures are shaped basically in the same manner as a dragon's head.

During the 1960s, in the Inverness region of Scotland, there lived an unknown smith who turned out exquisite decorative firepokers and other small household items, some decorated with animal heads. One poker, made so carefully that it might have been turned out of a rolling mill, except for the ram's head which formed its finial, demonstrates a most interesting technique which requires no welding.

Unlike the dragon's head described above, this particular ram's head is made with the end of the bar forming the back of the head. First the bar is tapered for ½ inch and shaped to a point. This point is split down its center for the length of the taper, to provide stock for the horns. Each horn is split for ¼ inch at its base on the outside to form an ear on each side. The horns are then heated to an orange-red and twisted to simulate the twists of a real ram's horns.

Below the horn and ears, the cranium and face of the ram is molded with careful hammering and with a small fuller, and the snout is drawn out to half the width of the forehead. Eyes are indicated with a small punch, and nostrils are stamped about ¾ inch from the base of the horns. Then the nose and lower jaw are formed by doubling the rod back under the head at a point under the nostrils, bending being done with a fork in the hardie hole. At the base of the horns, the rod is doubled back once more and curved downward into

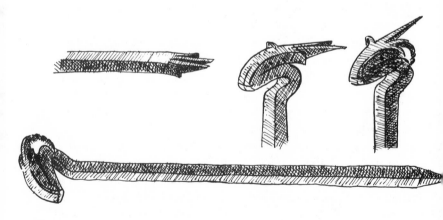

Steps in forming a ram's head poker

the shank of the poker. Finishing touches are given by indicating the line of the mouth with a thin chisel, adjusting the ears and curving the twisted horns downward into a spiral with small pliers. The shank of the poker may be decorated with chisel and punch marks.

A human head and face for a finial is more easily molded from iron than the uninitiated may think. First the end of a bar or rod is either doubled back and welded together or is upset to provide a ball the shape of a human head. This basic form is smoothed with a light hammer at a cherry-red heat until all contours are rounded. The basic features are formed with a small fuller. Midway between the top of the head and the chin, a groove is fullered across the face to form the brows and eye sockets. Midway between brow and chin, another groove is fullered which forms the bottom of the nose and the upper lip. Next the nose is formed by fullering two grooves from the middle of the brow at about a 25-degree angle halfway between the nose and the chin. This forms the nose and cheeks. A mouth is made with a small, thin chisel between the two diagonal dents; eyes are made with a punch. Ears may be welded on, but this is most difficult, and it is much easier to mark the ears with a chisel. Just a few marks with small fuller, chisel, and punch will clearly simulate a human likeness. A discriminating smith, however, will wish to go further than this. He will either carve with a cold chisel, which makes him a true sculptor, or he will make special small swages and fullers to stamp natural contours into the hot iron.

Perhaps the most difficult sculptured creations of the smith are represented by the large wrought-iron eagles, griffons, and winged dragons made by the ironworkers of the Italian Renaissance to hold candlesticks and brackets in their outstretched claws. These were almost certainly made in several pieces which were welded together, and the making

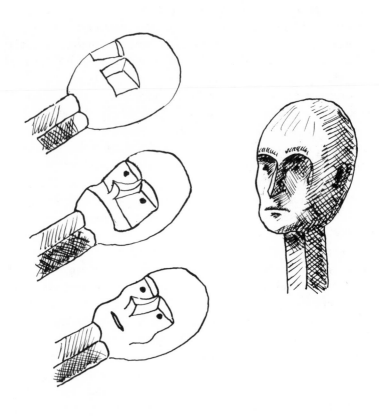

Steps in forming human face

of any one would require a large forge, cranes to move the heavy iron pieces from forge to anvil, and the combined efforts of several men. Apparently some of these creatures were forged from bars and others from sheet iron. Details were probably roughed in forging and refined with chisels.

Making such an elaborate sconce from a solid bar is a matter of carefully sculpturing the features of the piece with special hammers, fullers, punches, and chisels. It may be assumed that initially the head, body, and tail will be forged. Wings and legs are forged separately and welded to the body, much in the manner that eighteenth-century iron anchors were formed and assembled by welding in the large industrial smithies of France. Diderot's *Encyclopedia* provides some excellent illustrations of forging huge anchors. In the case of eagles and griffons and dragons forged from solid stock, however, it is quite impracticable to furnish step-by-step instructions. The tradition of handicraft dictated that each smith's design be somewhat different from any other. How a smith renders his design will depend largely on his shop, his tools, his experience, and the number and skill of his helpers. Welding several heavy pieces together will be somewhat easier than may be imagined. Heavy iron holds welding heat a relatively long time, allowing relative leisure in fitting and forming the pieces, once welding heat has been achieved. Suffice it to say that quick, good judgment, artistic imagination, and familiarity with the basic tools and techniques, heretofore described, will make the seemingly arduous and impossible task easier than may be anticipated.

There were other much simpler, but no less graceful and less beautiful, lighting appliances made in many a local smith in America, England, and Europe during the seventeenth, the eighteenth, and the early nineteenth centuries. These included wrought-iron hanging chandeliers, small wall sconces, often formed in the shape of lilies or roses, and table chandeliers decorated with leaves and flowers.

One of the most graceful hanging chandeliers is an eighteenth-century design made of ¼-inch iron rod, with four, six, or eight arms. For a four-armed chandelier, the material required is a ¼-inch rod, 18-inches long, and three rods of the same diameter, but only 9-inches long. The long rod is heated to an orange-red on one end and a ring of ¾-inch in-

Hanging chandelier

side diameter is formed around a rod inserted in the hardie hole of the anvil. Next the opposite end is upset to ⅜ inch, this being done at a white heat using a 1½-pound hammer for upsetting, while the rod is held across the face of the anvil, or by dropping rapidly, hot end down, on an upsetting plate at the base of the anvil block. Each short rod is upset in the same manner, or since these rods are short, upsetting may be done by placing the white-hot end on the anvil face and tapping the cold end with a hammer.

Candle sockets are formed separately and welded to the upset ends of the rods. Sockets are made of triangles, 2 inches through the axis of the point and 2¼ inches across the base. Edges leading to the point are scarfed, the sockets are formed into small cones on an anvil bick, and the edges are welded, leaving the point open to slip over the rod and rest against the upset end of the rod, where they are hammered tightly. Rod and socket are then placed into the fire and brought to welding heat, the joint being made with a light hammer while the rod is rotated back and forth across the face of the anvil.

It is a good idea on a hanging chandelier to supplement each candle socket with a circular drip pan to catch excess wax. Drip pans are made by cutting a 2-inch circle from ¹⁄₁₆-inch-thick sheet iron. When cut out, the pan is heated to orange-red, placed with its center over the pritchel hole of the anvil, and punched with a sharp tapered punch. A light hammer must be used to drive the punch in order to control the depth. The punch should be driven in until the resulting hole is about ⁵⁄₁₆ inch. Using a pointed punch for this operation offsets the edge of the hole where the punch protrudes and provides a wider and steadier base for welding to the base of the socket. When punched, the drip pan is returned to the fire and brought to white heat. The socket is placed on the anvil bick, and the pan is slid up the rod, offset portion away from the socket, and jambed tightly around the base of the socket. This operation can be facilitated by holding a pair of tongs loosely around the rod below the pan and tapping the jaws of the tongs with a light hammer while they are rotated.

Welding drip pan

Socket, pan, and rod are brought to welding heat once again. When ready for joining, the assembly is taken from the fire, the socket is placed on the anvil bick, and the weld is made with a small handled-fuller which is used as a hammer, joining the offset edge of the hole with the socket base. When welded, the assembly may be removed from the anvil bick and the pan held, top surface downward, over the edge of the anvil face and dressed flat with a small hammer or the flatter.

After completing socket and drip-pan assembly on each arm, all four arms are welded together. The ends of the short rods opposite the candle sockets are scarfed and tapered. Some careful smiths will round the inside surface of the scarf by placing the rod on a round bottom swage and forming a concave channel on the inside surface with a small fuller. After this preparation, the three short rods are placed in position around the long rod at a point where all four candle sockets are on the same plane. The scarfed ends are wired tightly to the long rod and the assembly is put into the fire and brought to welding heat. Joining is done with a medium-weight hammer. The joint is dressed in the same heat by hammering with a light hammer as the joint is rotated back and forth on the face of the anvil.

These simple hanging chandeliers are finished by curving the four arms gracefully, so that the candle sockets point upward. Curving may be done over the horn of the anvil if the smith has a good eye. They may also be curved with a scroll wrench while the arm is held in a scroll fork inserted in the hardie hole. All curves should be checked with a wooden or thin sheet-metal pattern to insure that each arm is identical. Perhaps the best way to curve all four arms alike is to use a hoop of the right size, if available, as a form around which the arms are curved while at an orange heat. Lacking a hoop, the smith can make his own form from a strap ¼-inch thick

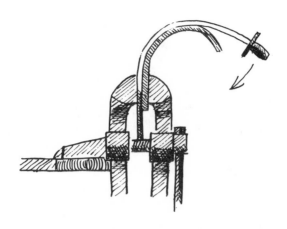

Bending chandelier arms on form held in vise

and 1-inch wide. This is shaped over the horn to the desired curvature. To use it, the smith places it and the chandelier in the vise, the two positioned so that one arm will have the same axis as that of the strap-iron form. The chandelier arm is then bent around the form with a light hammer or with round-nosed pliers. This is repeated until all arms are bent.

Other types of table chandeliers and wall candle sconces found in seventeenth- and eighteenth-century homes are often decorated with combinations of leaves and flowers. To make these exquisite creations, the smith must be equipped with a number of special tools, and he must be familiar with techniques far more delicate than those used by the general smith. Making an iron rose is sculpture at its best, demanding infinite patience and instinctive knowledge of iron.

The tools of the decorative ironworker include "double-faced hammers," sometimes referred to as leaf hammers, of a variety of sizes and forms. The most commonly used has a flat, square face on one end and a curved face on the other. "Round-faced hammers" are also needed to shape certain forms in true decorative ironwork. In addition to hammers, the decorative smith requires "scroll wrenches" of various

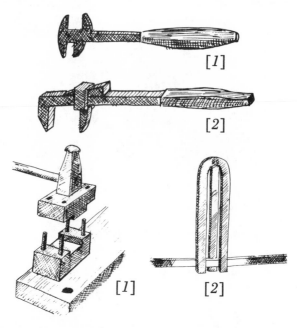

Top: Scroll wrenches, [1] usual type, [2] adjustable type. Bottom: Offset tools, [1] swage type, [2] vise type.

sizes and "scroll forks," which fit into the hardie hole. There are "offset tools" in various forms. Also there are a number of anvil tools besides the scroll forks: devices such as a "wedge-shaped stake iron," "leaf tools, "cup tools" in several shapes, "scroll starters," and the "halfpenny snub-nosed scroll." In addition there is a "combination stake tool," sometimes used in the vise as well as the anvil, which consists of a 1-inch rod some 6-or 7-inches long which is welded to the side of a shaper, a serpentine wedge with a sharp edge, both rod and shaper being perpendicular to the stake, which fits in the hardie hole or vise. Many smiths who work on decorative items also have a "snarling iron," a special type of stake anvil with a large semisphere formed on one arm and a straight,

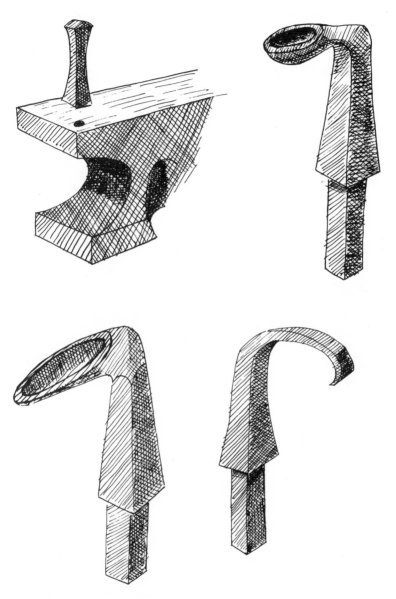

Top left: Stake iron. Top right: Cup tool. Bottom left:
Leaf tool. Bottom right: Scroll starter.

narrow, chisel-edged anvil on another arm, both attached to a pointed stake of iron that is driven into a large log. To dish leaves and flower petals he must have large blocks of lead and lead-filled cups. For some work, he requires special swages, such as a "rope swage" or a "curved-dish swage."

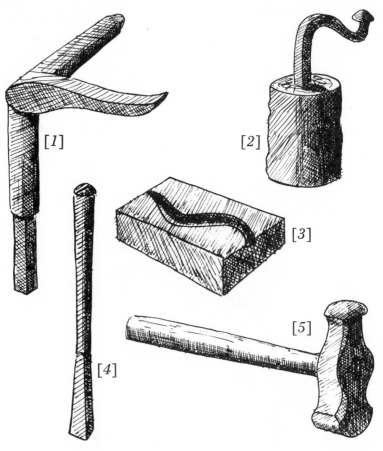

[1] *Combination stake tool.* [2] *Snarling tool.* [3] *Dish swage.* [4] *Veiner.* [5] *Cheese fuller.*

There are also special chisels curved to various forms on the edges, and tools such as the "veiner," which is used to form the veins of leaves. There is also a special fuller called a "cheese fuller." To achieve additional effects he often creates his own special tools.

With such tools, all of which he can make himself, the smith may confidently turn out beautiful artistic creations, limited only by his experience and imagination.

A simple, relatively easy-to-make decorative item is a semi-circular seventeenth-century Italian table chandelier, which consists of a welded frame made of ¼-inch rods, with four legs and four candle sockets. It is decorated with simple rose leaves made from ¼-inch rod and lap-welded to the frame. The frame consists of three parallel ¼-inch rods, two of them 12-inches long, and the upper 16-inches long.

Wrought-iron table candelabra

The upper rod is bent at a right angle 2 inches from each end, and the ends are scarfed, later to be bent to act as standards. The two short rods are cross-welded to the bent portions so that they are parallel to the upper rod and spaced ¾ inch apart. This framework forms the skeleton of the chandelier.

Four candle sockets are made exactly as for a hanging chandelier, but two of them are on 2-inch rods ¼ inch in diameter, the other two are on 2½-inch rods. It is easier to make them on both ends of 4- and 5-inch rods which are cut apart in the middle on the hardie after the sockets are welded. These are then cross-welded to the frame, the shorter ones adjacent to the end of the frame so that the socket is ½ inch higher than the upper rod; the longer ones 4 inches from each end of the frame, with ½ inch protruding from the bottom of the frame to serve as additional standards.

Decoration for this chandelier consists of eighteen leaves that are welded to the frame, six between each pair of standards. Leaves are made from 2-inch sections of ¼-inch rod. They may be formed one at a time on the end of a long rod and cut off the rod as they are finished. Forming is done by flattening the rod up to ½ inch from the end and shaping it to resemble a rose leaf. Veins are simulated with a chisel or a very small fuller. After forming the leaves the short stem is scarfed on the end preparatory to welding to the frame. Leaves are wired to the frame with the stems parallel to the frame rods. Three leaves, one on each rod of the frame, may be brought to welding heat simultaneously. This process is repeated until two leaves are welded to each rod of the frame between each pair of standards, eighteen leaves in all. The chandelier is finished by bending the leaves and stems into interesting angles that disguise the straight lines of frame and standards, and by curving the frame into a semicircle. The final touch is to bend the flattened ends of the standards to a right angle to serve as feet.

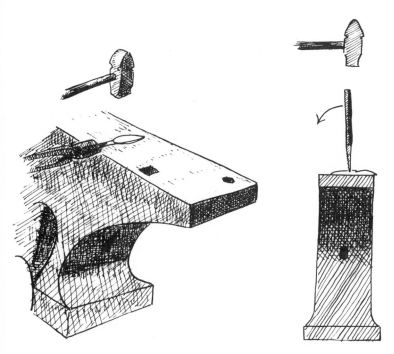

Left: Making leaves. Right: Using veiner to shape veins.

Making a table chandelier decorated with leaves is child's play, however, compared to creating a wall sconce to hold three candles and decorated with roses or lilies and the leaves appropriate to these delicate blossoms. First of all, the basic chandelier is constructed following techniques used in making a hanging chandelier. Three rods of ¼-inch diameter serve as arms for candle sockets and drip pans. These are then fastened to an oval plate of ⅛-inch sheet iron with a ring that is welded to the three rods and bradded to the plate. Ring and rods are assembled and welded in the same manner as a hinge pin, with a tang left on the ring. This is inserted in a hole in the middle of the plate and bradded. Roses or lilies are made separately and either bradded separately in artistic positions on the plate, or fastened within the same ring as the candle arms.

Wall sconce with roses

Both roses and lilies are made of several parts which are later welded together. The blossoms of both are shaped by a similar technique, but the leaves of each flower, being quite dissimilar, are made in different ways.

A rose branch with leaves alone, but no blossom, may be made from ¼ -inch rods. For a stem with five leaves, a rod 12-inches long is scarfed in two places: one 2 ½ and one 5 ½ inches from the end of the rod. Between these flattened spots the rod is slightly drawn out with a light hammer. Two rods 5-inches long are then scarfed in the middle and cross-welded to the long rod to form a sort of cross of Lorraine. Leaves are formed by drawing out the ends of the rods, except for the long portion of the main stem, to a $\frac{1}{16}$-inch thickness about ½ -inch wide. These thin plates are then cut to the shape of rose leaves with shears or chisel. Veins are indicated with a very small fuller. The characteristic waviness of rose leaves is accomplished by hammering the edges of the leaves while cold with a round-faced hammer on a lead block.

310

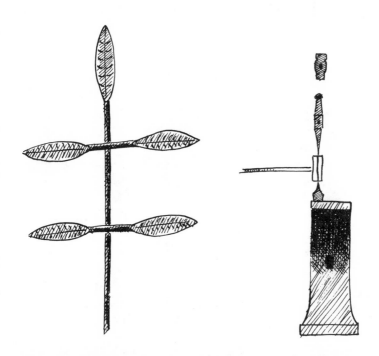

Left: Wrought rose branch with leaves. Right: Splitting upset to form rose leaves.

Rose blossoms are also made from ¼ -inch rod, but require a very delicate touch and a careful eye, as the blossom may be easily ruined by lack of care after most of the work has been done.

The rod is drawn out slightly along its length for about 4 inches starting at a point 3 inches from the end. The rod at the point above the drawn portion is brought to a white heat, then ½ inch of the end is quenched in the slack tub, the rod is placed in a hinged boltheader held in the vise, and the white-hot portion is upset until it cools to a cherry red. It is then removed and reheated to white heat. This is repeated until the upset is 2 inches in diameter and about ⅜-inch thick. At this point the upset portion is again heated to white, and the upset is split laterally into three layers, the split reaching all around to within ⅜ inch from the core of the head. Splitting requires the use of a helper to hammer a hot set while the head is held on top of a hot hardie. Positioning of the chisels is controlled by carefully marking with center punch or chisel where the splitting is to be. When the head is split into three layers, it is again brought to a white heat, is inverted on the anvil face, and is drawn out until each layer is no more than ¹⁄₁₆-inch thick and the head is 2½ to 3 inches in diameter. Petals are now cut out of all three layers at the same time, using a chisel while the head is orange-red. There are four petals surrounding the stem.

To shape the petals the smith heats the head to orange and lifts up one petal of the top layer to about an 80-degree angle. This is dished by shaping it over the cup tool with a ball pein. If a cup tool is not available, petals may be heated to a sunrise red and dished over a cylinder filled with lead, the smith being careful not to hold the hot metal on the lead long enough to melt the lead. When the top layer of petals has been formed, they are bent almost to a 90-degree angle from the plane of the head, the petals on the second layer are then raised, and the process of dishing is repeated. The same process is followed on shaping the lowest layer of petals. After shaping petals, the whole blossom is brought to a yellow heat, and each layer is twisted an eighth of a turn, so that each layer of petals will cover the division of petals in the layer above or below.

The rose is assembled by lap-welding the end of the leaf stem to the blossom stem and bradding the assembly to the oval plate in such a way that the ring holding the candle arms will be hidden.

Lilies are easier to make than roses. They are started exactly the same way as roses, by upsetting the end of a ¼-inch rod. The head thus formed, however, is not split, but is drawn out to about a $\frac{1}{16}$-inch thickness, with the metal around the edges being paper-thin. Also, for the lily blossom the initial upset is swaged or hammered into a semi-egg-shape at the base of the head, to resemble more the base of a lily blossom and to provide metal for forming the calyx.

After flattening the head sufficiently the pattern of the petals is scribed on the iron and the petal shapes are cut out with shears. A simple trick makes this task much easier. At the bottom of the division between each of the four petals, the smith drills a $\frac{1}{4}$-inch to $\frac{3}{8}$-inch hole. This allows him to avoid cutting a sharp angle with his shears at the base of each pair of petals. After cutting out the petals he drills a $\frac{1}{8}$-inch hole in the center of the blossom to a depth of $\frac{1}{4}$ inch and threads this with a tap.

Next the petals are heated one by one, bent upward into a natural position, and dished on an anvil bick and cupping tool until they are natural looking. Stamens are made of five small nails. The head of each nail is forged into a spherical button and the five are welded together at the point, which is

Left: Pattern for lily blossom, showing where holes are drilled to facilitate cutting. Right: Stamens made of nails welded together.

then drawn out to $\frac{3}{16}$ inch, threaded with a die, and screwed into the base of the blossom. Some smiths prefer to shrink the blossom around the stamens, but screwing is a little more secure.

Lily leaves are quite easily made, being no more than a $\frac{1}{4}$ -inch rod, 6-inches long, which is drawn out to form the leaves. Final shape may be cut from this thinned portion with shears. Most lily leaves have roughly parallel veins running from base to tip. These may be made with a small fuller, but there is an easier method, which probably harks back to the late eighteenth century.

When several lily leaves are to be made, the smith may save himself much arduous labor by making a leaf die. This is made in a block, or even a strap of iron a couple of inches wide and at least $\frac{1}{2}$-inch thick. The shape of a leaf is marked in the iron with a center punch and the iron is brought to orange-red heat in the forge. While hot, the smith fullers in the veins within the leaf shape, using a small $\frac{1}{16}$-inch fuller. When finished, this die is laid on the anvil, and leaves, heated to orange-red, are laid upon it and hammered to fill the fullered veins. Such a die saves many hours of work if a number of leaves are to be produced. Leaves are finished by

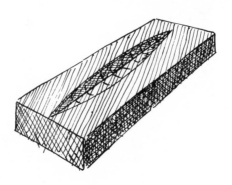

Leaf die

hammering cold with a round-faced wooden mallet over a lead block to furnish a wavy edge to the leaves. Leaves are then welded to the base of the lily stem, and all components are curved and positioned to a natural shape.

The smith may be tempted to curve and shape his metal in the finished lily without heating, but he takes a great chance of breaking stem or petal or leaf, especially if his material is mild steel. It is far safer to heat on top of the fire until a cherry red before final shaping.

German smiths for several generations have made quite interesting wrought-iron doorbell mechanisms based on a human figure, often a knight in armor, which, when a chain is pulled, rings a small bell. Such a creation is mounted on an iron frame attached to the side of the house next to the front door. Usually the bell is mounted on a movable bar with an elbow that pivots in an overhead bar. The overhead bar protrudes perpendicularly from the frame and is often finished with a snarling dragon's head. Beneath stands the knight. His body is a fork which extends downward to form legs and feet and has a crossbar welded to it near the neck to act as shoulders. His head is shrunk or screwed to the tang of the fork. Over this iron skeleton is placed a hauberk of sheet metal, no more than a thin sheet cut as the dress of a paper doll to fold over the shoulders and around the body, covering the crotch and legs almost to the knees. The head is covered with a helm. The hauberk is bradded in one or two places on each side beneath the arms.

One arm is straight and bradded tightly onto one end of the crossbar which serves as shoulders; the other is pivoted on the other end of the crossbar and is formed so that the elbow is bent and the hand is curved; to clamp tightly around the chain. The chain, of course, is attached to the end of the pivoted elbow bar on which the bell is mounted and falls downward through the hand of the knight's pivoted arm.

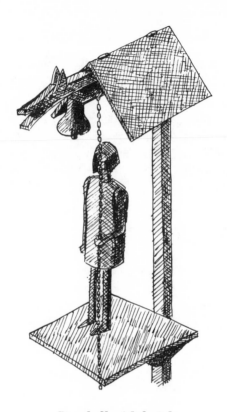

Doorbell with knight

When the chain is pulled, the arm is actuated as well as the bell, giving the rather doubtful illusion that the knight himself is ringing the bell.

Many hours of careful work go into the forming and assembly of such a mechanism. It demonstrates, however, that a smith can use his skill for more than horseshoes, and that he can at least attempt a creation approaching the golden handmaidens of Hephaestus.

The most common, and the most memorable, examples of decorative wrought ironwork are found in the lacy strength of balcony railings, grills, fences, and gates of old towns such as London, Toledo, Lima, Florence, Savannah, Charleston, and New Orleans. Much of the ornamental iron of American towns is not wrought, but cast-iron replacements for earlier wrought-iron items that were destroyed by fires around the middle of the nineteenth century.

Cast-iron decorations are often fancier than those made at the forge, for they include intricately molded leaves and vines, bunches of grapes, a variety of flowers and cherubs, birds and animals. They somehow lack, however, the feeling of strength and grace conveyed by well-designed scrolls and quatrefoils and wrought lotus leaves. Cast-iron fences and gates and window grills also lack the fierce spikes and naturally graceful curves of pure, soft iron shaped with hammer and anvil. After all, the cast-iron fence or gate is relatively a late-comer to the field of architectural iron; its function is mainly decoration, whereas wrought iron was developed in a rougher age, when security and protection was its first function, and decoration purely a secondary consideration.

Grills, balcony rails, gates, and fences all generally follow the same construction techniques. They consist essentially of iron rods and bars shaped in scrolls, quatrefoils, foliage, and additional designs without limit, held together by collars, brads, and welded joints. Since they required strength, these items seldom were made of any iron less than ½-inch thick. Often they were made of massive bars large enough to resist an army of chisels or the heaviest battering ram.

Most are contained within sections of heavy framework. Where security alone is desired without expensive decoration, a common way to make a fence, balcony rail, or gate is to punch two heavy horizontal bars of iron with a series of holes no more than 4 inches apart, and to insert in these holes parallel-vertical rods or square bars. Sometimes these vertical bars may extend 4 to 6 inches above and below the top and bottom horizontal bars. Vertical bars may then be clamped in place by hammering the sides of the horizontal bars with a sledge at the points at which they are intersected by vertical bars.

In some simple fences the vertical bars extend through the top horizontal bar only and may be mortised and bradded into the bottom horizontal. This requires making a tenon on each vertical ¼ inch longer than the thickness of the horizontal, which is punched with holes from ¼ to ½ inch smaller than the thickness of the vertical bar, depending on the size stock being used. Tenons, as described previously, are made by drawing down the end of the vertical bar, forming rough shoulders with a set hammer, and dressing with a monkey tool.

A simple fence or gate of this sort affords far more se-

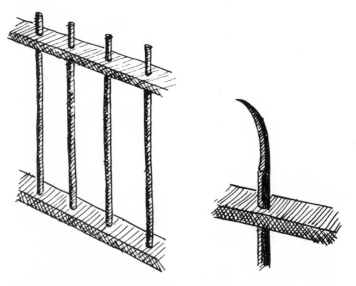

Left: Simple fence of rods and punched bars. Right: Spike at top of vertical bar.

curity when the extensions of the vertical bars at the top are sharpened into a spike 6-inches long or more. These spikes may be curved outward a bit to make it more difficult for even the most agile burglar or attacker to surmount the fence.

The easiest way to decorate a fence or gate of this sort is to form the spikes into a wavy line, called a "flame" in ironworkers' parlance. It is quite simple to form a flame. First of all, the rod is tapered into either a two-sided taper, as with a chisel, or a long spike from 6- to 9-inches long. The flame may be formed in one of three ways while at an orange heat—by curving into opposite quarter-circles over the horn; by forming the quarter-circles with a 1½-inch round-bottom swage or swage block recess and a 1-inch fuller; and by using scroll fork and scroll wrench. Of course, the pointed end is always left straight on the same axis as the

Left: Flame. Right: Forming flame.

rod below the flame. Using anvil horn or scroll wrench and scroll fork are the easiest, most flexible methods, for they allow the smith to make his quarter-circles smaller as the flame is shaped toward the point, thus providing a little more grace to the form. When the horn is used, the smith can control the uniformity of his quarter-circles on succeeding rods by marking the point or points of diminishing circumferences on the horn with a soapstone pencil. Undoubtedly the surest way to control uniformity, however, is to have a full-size drawing of the flame to which the finished iron may be compared. Also much trouble can be avoided if the smith makes a model of his design in heavy wire or a thin bar of lead before he makes his first flame. This will show him exactly how many quarter-circles of varying sizes he can put in his flames and still leave a straight spike long enough to be graceful. A little experience will teach the smith to start with the lower quarter-circle on each flame he makes. Straightening the flame so that axis of point and rod coincide is most easily done with a scroll fork and scroll wrench.

Flames may be made more ornamental by welding scrolls or leaves to the base to create a fleur-de-lis, or even more elaborate blossoms, depending on the number of leaves added. Such decoration should be welded on before the flame is formed. When this is done, it is almost essential that the flame be formed with scroll fork and scroll wrench, as the leaves encumber curving the flame over horn or swage.

Scrolls or leaves can be welded most easily by scarfing the base of either to fit rod or square bar, wiring them into place, and joining them with a regular lap weld. After the weld is made, the joint should be smoothed with either a round or square swage of proper dimension. If exact length is required, and it usually is on ornamental work, the smith must calculate how much length will be added to the rod after welding and smoothing, as the smoothing operation will draw out the rod to some extent.

Top left: Flame with scrolls. Top right: Flame with leaves. Bottom: Two ways to weld leaves and flame together.

Drawing out can be controlled somewhat better if a different technique is employed to join scrolls to the base of the flame. For instance, some smiths may roughly form the leaves out of one piece of strap iron scarfed in the middle

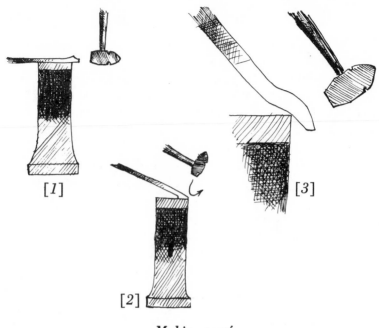

Making scarf

and doubled over the base of another separate piece intended
for the flame. These pieces are welded together and the stem
is drawn out to about 3 inches below the leaves. Both stem
and rod are then carefully scarfed so that the profiles of both
resemble the pointed section of a short curved teardrop.
Scarfs are overlapped so that the concave section of one fits
into the convex curve of the other. Such scarfs are formed by
upsetting the end of the stem and the rod about ¼ inch from
the end and hammering so that the upset protrudes only from
one surface of the rod. Then the portion between upset and the
end of the rod is drawn out into a short taper. This is curved
by bending slightly in each direction over the corner of
the anvil. When both scarfs are formed, the two pieces are
overlapped and hammered lightly to make them fit closely
together.

322

To weld, both ends are brought to welding heat slowly and with a minimum blast; then they are taken out and tack-welded together. As soon as the tack weld is joined, the iron is immediately put back into the fire and brought to welding heat once more and joined solidly. In the same heat, the joint may be smoothed between swages.

Sometimes, when decoration is more important than security, the finial of a rod consists of two drooping laurel leaves minus spike or flame. Usually one leaf will be made slightly larger than the other to simulate naturalness. The two leaves may be formed one on the end of the rod and the other lap-welded in position, or by forming leaves on both ends of an 18-inch rod of the same diameter as the upright, doubling 1 or 2 inches from the middle, and welding to the upright as with the leaves of a fleur-de-lis.

Laurel leaves are a most decorative design in themselves and are easily made. Both ends of a ½-inch rod, 18-inches long, are drawn out, one end for 6 inches, the other for 8 inches, until the drawn part is about ³⁄₁₆-inch thick. These rudimentary leaves are then rounded on the ends with the hammer to resemble natural leaves.

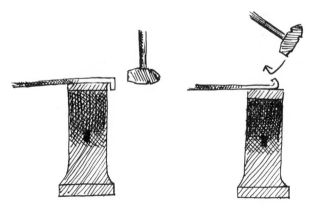

Starting scroll end with hammer on anvil face

Veins are formed with the veiner and a curved chisel. First the center vein is outlined with center-punch marks. After the leaf is brought to an orange-red, the lines indicated are then depressed with the veiner, its acute edge toward the center of the leaf. Care must be taken to see that each mark made by the veiner is correctly aligned with the last, and that the obtuse edge of the veiner is not depressed to the point that it marks the blade of the leaf.

A smooth vein and blade will result if this technique is followed: the outline of the vein is made by holding the veiner perpendicular to the leaf and tapping lightly with a 1 ½ -pound hammer. As the veiner is tapped, it is rotated slightly away from the center of the leaf toward the obtuse angle of its end. Rotation is stopped just before the obtuse angle comes in contact with the blade. This operation is repeated until both sides of the vein are depressed.

Side veins are simply made by marking with a curved

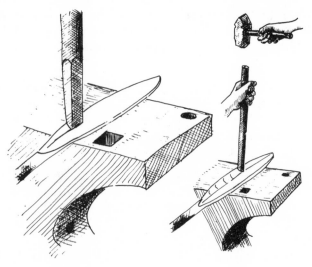

Forming veins with veiner and round chisel

chisel when the leaf is orange-red. Usually one solid tap with a 1½-pound hammer on the butt of the chisel will suffice to mark the side veins. As with lily leaves, the smith may also form laurel leaves with a die.

The two stems should be faggot-welded for ½ inch at their base before being scarfed and welded to the upright. A round or square swage may be used to dress the joint.

Further decoration of fences, gates, and grills may be achieved by attaching numerous scrolls between uprights to form pleasing designs. Scrolls, or curves, are no more than flat bars that are coiled on one or both ends. Double-ended scrolls are sometimes coiled in opposite directions on the ends, or sometimes in the same direction. Scrolls are easily made with some experience; the main difficulty is to achieve a graceful curve on the end of the bar that serves as the center of the coil and to maintain an absolutely even distance between each rotation of the scroll.

Two anvil tools, both of which can be made by the smith, are used to form the tip of the scroll. The first is that marvelously named tool, the halfpenny snub-end scroll; the other is simply called a scroll starter.

A halfpenny snub-end scroll is no more than a block of tool steel 1½-inches square and 2-inches deep, with a square shank that fits tightly into the hardie hole. The top of the block is slightly rounded, and one side has a concave impression, presumably the diameter of a halfpenny coin, adjacent to the rounded top. A scroll starter is no more than a flattened anvil bick with a perpendicular stake which fits into the hardie hole. The top surface is drawn out to a chisel-shape and bent on its end to the proper curvature for the beginning of a scroll, which is generally from ¼ to ½ inch in diameter.

Scrolls are started by drawing out the end of the flat bar to a sharp chisel edge. When the halfpenny snub-end scroll is used, the end of the bar is brought to orange-red and is laid across the rounded top of the tool so that the tip protrudes only enough to fit into half the cavity. Then the tip is formed into the halfpenny cavity with the rounded face of a double-headed hammer. When a double curve is wanted for the tip, the iron is extended farther across the top of the tool so that it will curve convexly around the edge of the top and follow the full circumference of the concave depression.

Starting technique is somewhat different when using the scroll starter. Here the tapered end is bent around the curved tip of the tool and held there with a pair of round-nosed pliers. Then the body of the orange-red iron strap is merely molded around the tip and curved face of the scroll starter, being bent by hand if the iron is light enough, or with a light hammer if the stock is heavy.

Many scroll tips are given some solidity by welding a section of rod crosswise within the curved tip. To do this, the smith cuts a rod almost through at a point equaling the width of the bar, around which the end of the bar is clamped. This is then welded and the bar twisted off at the cut.

Forming single and double scroll ends and snub end on the halfpenny snub end scroll tool.

Left: Using the scroll starter. Center: Welding rod to end of scroll. Right: Scroll form.

Scrolls are finished either with a scroll form, which fits into the hardie hole or is held by the vise, or by using a scroll wrench and scroll fork. Though the use of fork and wrench is somewhat easier and quicker, it requires an excellent eye and considerable experience. As a consequence, many modern smiths prefer to use the form, despite the limitations it imposes on variety and size.

To bend with fork and wrench, the smith places his orange-red iron between the rounded tines of the fork, places his wrench so that one jaw is on each side of the hot iron, with the lower jaw on the side opposite his position, and gently bends the iron to a desired curvature by pulling the handle of the wrench toward him. Control of the degree of curvature is controlled by the distance between tines of the fork and jaws of the wrench. A specialist in ornamental iron will find it necessary to have a variety of sizes of both tools. Indeed, most scroll wrenches are double-faced, one wrench being formed with two different sets of jaws of dif-

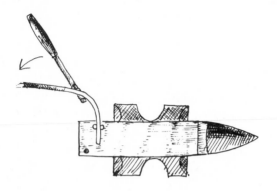

Bending with scroll wrench and fork, top view

ferent widths. Ernst Schwarzkopf, in his fine little book on ornamental ironwork published in 1916, illustrates an adjustable scroll wrench in which the lower jaw slides up and down the shank of the wrench and is secured in place with a small metal wedge. Although no example is known, it is quite conceivable that an imaginative smith could also design an adjustable scroll fork.

While the scroll is being formed, it is frequently measured against a pattern when it is removed for reheating, to assure that the curving is even and that the distance between each complete curve is equal.

A scroll form may be made by the smith in much the same way that a scroll itself is made. The form, however, is made of much heavier iron. For instance, an iron strap ⅜-inch thick and 1-inch wide and long enough to contain the desired scrolls it must form, plus an additional 6 inches for a shank, is drawn out to a long taper from the point where the shank will begin to its end. This is finished with a chisel point. Drawing out must be done with hammer and flatter, not the fuller, for the iron must be widened slightly as it is thinned, the chisel end being the widest point of the form. The shank is formed by doubling the end and faggot-welding together. This section is then drawn out to a square section of a size that fits snugly in the hardie hole. Next the shank is bent at right angles to the width of the scroll section. The form itself is shaped with fork and wrench to the proper curvature. After shaping, the whole form is brought to an orange-red, the shank is inserted in the hardie hole, and the form is lightly hammered so that the bottom edge is flattened to the same plane on all diameters. This, of course, forces the widened center, or end of the form, to protrude from the coil almost 1 inch, this protrusion decreasing in height as the coil continues to its base, which is at its original width. Some modern smiths make their scroll forms as described above, but they weld the form with an oxyacetylene torch to a flat plate to which the shank is welded to the underside.

To use this form the smith heats his iron to an orange-red along the whole length of the intended scroll. He then bends the tip so that it will hook around the center point of the scroll form and holds the tip in position with round-nosed pliers while he bends the remainder of the strap around the protruding edges of the form. As the iron is bent, it is pushed downward against the anvil face. All bending should be done quickly before the iron cools.

Double and triple scrolls are made by lap- or faggot-

Multiple scrolls

welding two or three straps together before coiling. Proper
length should be determined before welding by bending ⅛-
inch wire to the pattern, then uncoiling to measure accurately
the length of strap needed for each of the multiple scrolls.

Assembly of scrolls within the frame of a fence, gate,
or grill is done by bradding and with collars. Usually the
scrolls are fastened to the outside frame with brads, and to
each other with collars.

How collars are used to join scrolls to frame

Most collars are no more than short sections of strap iron,
⅛-inch thick and from ¼- to ½-inch wide. Length is pre-
determined by fitting wire or a lead strap around the parts of
the fence to be assembled, then removing and straightening to
show accurately the required length of iron strap. Each collar
is partially formed before assembly. First the strap is curved
double over the tip of the horn or around a rod of suitable
size which is inserted in the hardie hole. Next a square or
flat bar of a width the same as the diameter of the rod is
inserted into the doubled strap, which has been brought to
an orange-red or a little hotter. Both are tightly clamped together in the vise so that the rounded portion of the collar
protrudes above the top of the vise. This is hammered flat

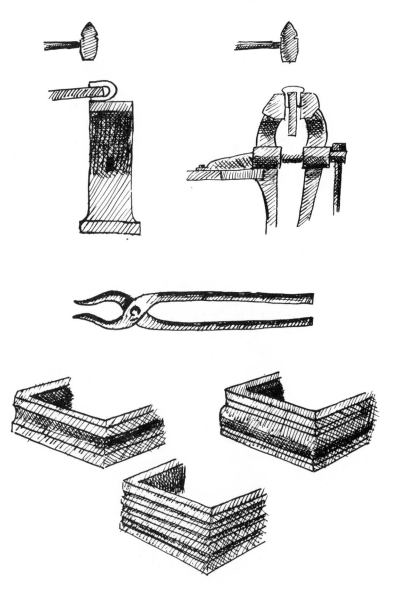

Top: Forming collar. Center: Bow pliers. Bottom: Molded collars.

against the end of the flat bar to form a flat end and, at the same time, to upset the corners of the collar.

When scrolls are fastened together, the partially finished collar is again brought to an orange-red and placed over the scrolls to be joined, and the straight ends are bent around the scrolls with bow pliers. Then, before the iron cools, the ends are hammered together.

Some collars are molded with small fuller or a top round or oval swage of suitable size. When such collars are partially formed, upsetting of the corners in the vise and dressing of the completed collars on the fence must be done with fuller or top swage, rather than by straight hammering.

Often in scrollwork a right angle is desired to provide some contrast to the basic design of curves and circles. Such corners, if they are to resist breaking, especially when made in fibrous wrought iron, require more technique than mere bending. To avoid breaking the fibers, the inside angle must be bent over the rounded corner of the anvil face, and this leaves an unsightly round outside corner. There are several ways to correct this.

One is to heat the area of the corner to an orange-red before bending and to upset the portion of strap where the corner is intended. After upsetting, the right angle is formed and the upset portion is forged to a true sharp corner. Another method is first to bend the right angle, then to hold the strap on the anvil face so that the corner protrudes over its edge. Each corner surface is hammered with a light hammer until the outside is upset to form a sharp right angle. Still another technique is required for heavy iron strap or bar. Any iron ¾ -inch thick or more should be cut halfway through with chisel or hardie at the point where the corner is to be. Then the iron is bent on the uncut surface, which leaves a right-angle cavity where the sharp outside corner is intended. This is filled and the corner is made whole by welding in the

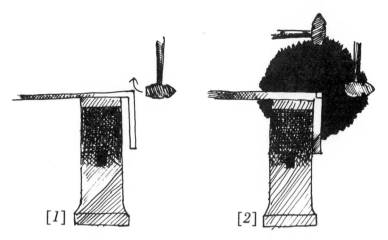

Forming sharp corner on a right-angle bend: [1] by upsetting, [2] by welding.

cavity a short square length of iron. After welding, the corner is dressed with a light hammer.

Incidentally, gates and fence sections are most easily assembled on a table 30-inches high, which is sheathed with ½–1-inch sheet iron. At least two men are generally needed to assemble large areas of ornamental iron.

Scrolled designs for wrought iron are the equivalent of pen-and-ink drawing in art; they present the design on the thin edge of strap iron, giving a laciness and delicacy that seems to belie the solid structural strength of the material. Most of the wrought iron of the Renaissance and the eighteenth century, periods of intellectual and artistic achievement, was composed to a large degree of scrolls in one form or another.

There is another type of wrought-iron design that offers a heavier silhouette. Much of this shares the delicacy of scrolling, but it departs from the beauty of thin lines and provides more dimension and sometimes more interest. Perhaps the most typical example of the heavy silhouette is the widely

333

used quatrefoil, a form found in stone- and brick- and wood-work, as well as in ironwork. Sometimes it consists of a grill of crossed bars, each with projections between the interstices of the bars which, four of them together, form a quatrefoil. At other times it consists of a number of quatrefoils, some plain and some elaborate, each made separately and joined together with collars.

How to modify a plain grill of crossed flat bars to a pattern of quatrefoils is described in admirable detail in a publication of Britain's Rural Industries Bureau, *Decorative Iron Work*. As a consequence, it will be touched on lightly here.

The first step is to offset bars of iron, usually ¼-inch thick and 1-inch wide, at the points where they will eventually cross and be mortised together to form a pattern of squares. A ¼-inch hole is punched in the center of each offset.

Offsetting sections of decorative grillwork is no different in principle from offsetting keepers for door bolts, as described in the chapter of this book devoted to hardware. Tools used are exactly the same as those used to form keepers. In offsetting the pieces of decorative grills, however, a number

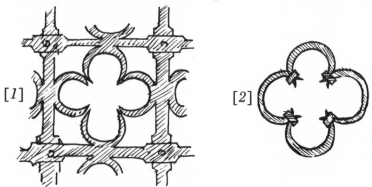

Quatrefoils: [1] on grill, [2] with collars.

of offsets must be made in a number of pieces, all of them fitting together precisely. This is quite a different and far more exacting task than making two or three individual keepers, particularly when the various bars used in the grill have been worked hot with the chance that the working has altered the lengths of the bars. The problem is multiplied if the design calls for offsets that are not equidistant from each other.

Possibly the best way to insure accuracy is to place the bars of iron to be used in place on a large assembly table, perhaps lying over a full-size pattern of the intended grill. Positions of the offsets should then be carefully marked with a soap stone pencil or chalk. These marks should be duplicated with a centerpunch or chisel mark on the side of the bar which will be hidden after assembly. After this careful preparation the iron may be heated and offset with confidence.

It is recommended, however, that the smith inexperienced in such assembly take time to experiment on a piece of scrap stock before making offsets for the finished design. Then he will know beforehand if the length of his stock will be affected by working.

One quarter of a quatrefoil is formed between each offset on each edge of the flat iron. Using a corner chisel with a rounded corner, the edge of the iron is cut through ½ inch from the offset. One leg of this cut is extended with a straight hot set to within ½ inch of the center between two offsets. Then each of the split portions is curved over the horn, or with a special form which is held in the hardie hole, until the two splits form a crescent attached to the iron by the unsplit portion between each horn. The crescent may be forged to a ridge down the center of each of its horns with a double-faced hammer, or it may be rounded or left flat, according to the smith's taste. Of course, the quatrefoils are formed when the bars are crossed and bradded together at

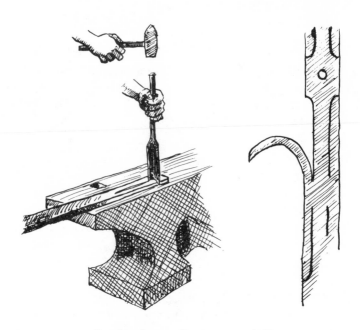

Cutting bar to form quatrefoils

the interstices. At this point, the four crescents in each square will touch at the points, if they were carefully forged to fit on a marked spot on the horn or with a proper curved form.

Quatrefoils may be made more elaborate by splitting the points of the crescent horns and curving one split one way, while the other is curved in the opposite direction, or by forming a small crescent inside a larger crescent.

The quatrefoil design is subject to almost limitless variation when composed of separate quatrefoil units which are fastened together with collars, as found so frequently in the beautiful ironwork of most European countries during the fifteenth, the sixteenth, and the early seventeenth centuries. A basic quatrefoil is formed by forging four separate crescents, with pointed horns and with round, diamond-shaped, square, or triangular sections. These crescents are joined at their

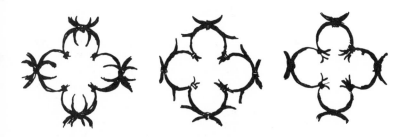

Variations of quatrefoil designs

points either by welding or by small collars. Welding is the better method of joining. As with all decorative ironwork, the smith who uses a form for shaping the separate pieces of the quatrefoil will have a far more even design.

There are many ways to vary the quatrefoil. An arrow may be welded or collared between each crescent. Each quarter may consist of two crescents welded together at the widest parts and then assembled with three other double crescents, the inner ones forming a quatrefoil, the outer ones a four-pointed star. There is hardly a limit to the variations which may be applied to the classic and ancient quatrefoil form.

Much of the most beautiful wrought ironwork ever was created in the neoclassical form in Italy in the seventeenth and eighteenth centuries. The variety found on the gates and grills of great *palazzi* in Rome, Milan, Florence, and Naples defies proper cataloging. Each is an individual work of art created by one smith, or perhaps designed by a sculptor or painter and rendered by a master smith into a veritable masterpiece of ironwork. Each of these includes its own unique elements, its peculiar applications of fundamental wrought-iron design, every element reflecting the qualities of iron and the mastery of the metal's seemingly immutable character under the influence of heat and hammer and imagination.

Most of the work of the neoclassical type is designed on

337

the basis of mass rather than delicacy. Its silhouette indicates strength and confidence more than charm and illusion. Yet, for all its weight, the neoclassical work is true art, emphasizing the skill of man more than the emulation of nature. The massiveness typical of the form is attained through upsetting, faggotting with collar or weld, and twisting to present the broad side of flat iron instead of its thin side. An encyclopedia would hardly suffice to describe all the techniques of forming all the individual design forms of neoclassical decorative ironwork. Only principles of technique will be offered here.

In forming a unique shape in multiples, the smith must remember always that he is master of his own tools; he can make any special die or swage he may need to reproduce a certain form which may be repeated in a wrought-iron design.

For making mass from lightness he must imaginatively apply the basic techniques of welding or merging several

Neo-classical joining of bars for effect of mass

bars of iron together to create one desired weight from many. The feeling of strength he creates in neoclassical design must be based on genuine strength. It must not be forgotten that iron is a most functional metal, regardless of how a master smith may transform it into sculptural material. Gates and fences and balcony railings have functional objectives, the integrity of which must be maintained. While the smith within his own wee universe of forge and fire and anvil and hammer is a minor divinity, he must recognize the limitations integral to this universe. Functional quality must be attained within the capacity of iron and his equipment, particularly in devising means to join together the many separate design elements of a large gate or fence. For instance, regardless of the fact that welding is stronger than using rings to join various elements, the smith must realize when he starts his design that no practicable forge is large enough to place a huge gate upon it, so that no two pieces of iron in the center of the gate can be brought to welding heat and joined with hammer and anvil. Collaring is the answer, and the gate must be designed for maximum strength with collars.

Also it is important in making elaborate decorative iron-work that the smith recognize the limitations of his own individual capacity. He should, when possible, avoid the slavish copying of some long-dead smith's creation and should create his own designs, suitable to his shop, his skill, his available time, and his experience. One of the most commendable statements in the little British book *Decorative Iron Work* is the suggestion that the smith apply the techniques described in the book to designs of his own. He will find that his original work is not only more interesting than his copying, but that the challenge of rendering an original design is far more interesting, more stimulating, more inspiring than copying.

Many of the problems of assembling decorative iron have

been practically eliminated in modern ornamental ironwork because of the availability of oxyacetylene or electric-welding apparatus. With such modern equipment the worker, in effect, is able to bring his forge to his iron. Modern welding, however, somehow lacks the feeling of strength and solidity of forge welding, a feeling that is an important aspect of the design.

The modern decorative smith, though (may his number prosper), often is forced to use modern technology as a stringent economic requirement. Electric welding is so much quicker than forge welding that it must be used at times in order to make a decent living. And it is permissible artistically if the smith dresses his welds carefully with hammer and grind-wheel, and uses the new welding technique only when necessary.

10.

THE INGENIOUS MEANS
OF MAKING WEAPONS

Whether or not tools were developed from weapons, or weapons from tools, in the evolution of man, no one can say for certain. The archaeological evidence is too limited, the story too misted by the centuries, to offer more than a hypothesis on the subject. We know, however, that weapons have been with us since the beginning of mankind, and perhaps were bequeathed to man by a club-carrying ape, if certain modern theories of anthropology prove to have merit.

Weapons have not really changed in the concept of their design since they were first invented. Bullets are no more than greatly accelerated spearheads, shrapnel a myriad of slashing swords, and a tank merely the ultimate in shields. This unchanging quality of lethal devices is apparent throughout their long history. Stone spearheads served the same function as a wooden point hardened in the fire or a bone point. New materials were adapted and modified to old uses as man learned to work stone, then copper, then bronze, and lastly iron. The blacksmith applied his special techniques and his special material to furnish improvements on the products of the bronzeworker. In many cases, he adopted and modified the tools and techniques of the bronzeworker to his own creations, particularly in making helmets, armor, and shields.

Probably the first weapons made by the blacksmith were

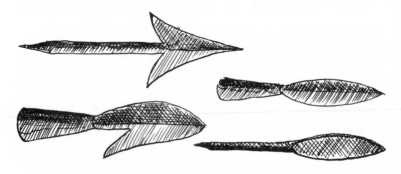

Types of arrowheads

spearheads and arrowheads of iron. Both of these items were made in two basic forms, one with a socket and one with a tang, both following the forms of earlier bronze types. Tanged points are rather easily made. A flat bar of iron, its width suitable to the point needed, is drawn down into a tang which is shouldered in a hole punched in a flat bar. The iron should be white hot for this operation. After the tang is formed the blade is drawn out to a point and beveled.

Many early spear- and arrowheads were lozenge-shaped, which eliminated the need for a shoulder and only required beveling each edge by molding the orange-red iron with glancing blows of the hammer while holding the blade along the edge of the anvil face or on top of the horn, as with packing a knife blade before tempering.

One does not know, incidentally, whether the earliest anvils of prehistoric times had horns, but surely the ancient smith was required to have as much if not more ingenuity than his descendants, and we may assume that an ancient

Primitive iron spear from the Cameroons

spear maker was able to devise and make a proper tool for beveling spearheads in a professional manner.

Some spear- and arrowheads were equipped with barbs, so that they would not fall out of wounded game and could not easily be extracted from a stricken enemy. Barbs may be formed with a chisel after the tang is formed. The smith makes two chisel cuts into the base of the lozenge-shaped blade, both parallel to the tang and divided by the width of the tang. The two split portions are then prised outward to form the barbs. Some arrowheads and most harpoons had several barbs on either one or both sides of the blade. These are formed by making additional chisel cuts along the edge

Forming barbs

of the blade at about a 30-degree angle to the axis of the blade. After cutting, the split portions are prised outward.

Socketed spear- and arrowheads may be made in much the same manner as socketed wood chisels, described in an earlier chapter. A flat bar of iron is drawn out for several inches on one end for a spearhead, not more than 1 inch for an arrowhead, until this end is thin and fan-shaped. The edges are scarfed and the socket is formed at orange-red heat on an anvil bick or small stake bick. After forming, the edges of the socket are welded together, a particularly delicate task with a small arrowhead since its very thin iron may burn if left in the fire too long, and it will lose its welding heat quickly if not joined immediately. When welding arrowhead sockets, then, it is necessary that the bick be close to the forge. One method of prolonging welding heat is to heat the bick itself to a cherry red and place it in the anvil just before the socket is to be welded. This prevents a cold bick from cooling the thin socket metal when socket is placed on bick for welding.

After welding the socket, the head is formed from the unforged portion of the original bar in the same manner as with tanged points.

Later, when steel became relatively plentiful, arrowheads were made of steel welded to an iron socket. First the socket is cut out of sheet iron in the shape of an isosceles triangle.

Socket pattern for steel point

Then the apex of the triangle is split down its center for ¼ inch. Next the socket is formed and a steel triangle is inserted in the point of the socket. Socket and base of the steel triangle are then brought to welding heat and are welded with a few strong taps with a light hammer. Before the metal has cooled, it is put back in the fire, and the socket is again brought to welding heat and joined at the edges. Lastly the steel point is tempered, blue, as for a knife, in regular points to be used against footmen, but light yellow if to be used for piercing the plate armor of mounted knights.

The technique described for making sockets is basically the same for spearheads made in African villages in the 1960s and for almost the last of socketed weapons, the boarding pikes used by civilized navies of the world until about the year 1880. Many boarding pikes were made of worn-out rasps. After the socket was formed and welded, the square-sectioned blade was forged. To provide strength, most boarding pikes had a 1-foot-long strap of iron ⅛-inch thick and ⅜-inch wide lap-welded to the rim of the socket so that the straps extended down the shaft, to which they were riveted.

In later centuries, the sometimes ornate pikes, spontoons, boar-spears, glaives and partisans used by soldier and officer were made in much the same manner. Many of these had elaborate designs punched in the blades. Most had a rather short socket, sometimes square, and long iron bands extending a couple of feet down the shaft. These bands, in the days when the pikeman was the king of the battlefield, not only gave extra strength to the union of pikehead and shaft, but they protected the shaft against slashing swords which would have

Boarding pike

effectively disarmed a pikeman by severing pikehead from shaft.

Boar spears and spontoons were badges of social and military rank from the Middle Ages until about the middle of the eighteenth century. As a consequence, many of these weapons are finished far more elaborately than workaday spear- and arrowheads. Many have square-shaped sockets with molded edges, the molding being applied with special swages. Between socket and base of blade there is often a button formed with a special set of swages or with fullers if the smith is skillful. In the old days, the forged points often were turned over to an ironchiseler, or "eisenhower" in Germanic countries, who would actually carve the metal with bas-relief boars' heads, the faces and figures of mythical characters, or flowers and birds. After this, the blade was tempered and decorated with etching. It is still possible to duplicate these real works of art, but the smith who attempts the task must have deep experience in a number of artistic fields besides blacksmithing.

A very simple defensive weapon, which was used particularly against horsemen from ancient times until the demise of horses as a military factor, was the caltrop, a four-pointed device resembling a children's jack, which could be scattered on cavalry approaches. Its effective design allowed the weapon to have one sharp point sticking up no matter how indiscriminately caltrops were scattered about. American gangsters of the 1930s used to scatter carpet tacks on roads to puncture police-car tires. The caltrop effected the same result on horses' hooves.

The smith may choose one of several methods in making caltrops, depending on the size of iron available and whether or not the smith welds easily. One way is to cut 2½-inch lengths from a piece of iron which is ½-inch thick and 1-inch wide. These pieces are then drawn out to a point on both

Caltrop

ends, making the iron about 3½-inches long. Each point is split, on the hardie or with a hot set, for 1¼ inches from the point, and the splits are spread so that they form 90-degree angles to each other. So far the procedure is fundamentally that of making a valve wrench. After spreading so that the iron forms a four-pointed star, the smith heats again to orange-red and bends each pair of diagonal points to 45-degree angles, each pair pointing in the direction opposite to the other. This forms the jack shape, and no matter how the caltrop is thrown it will rest on three points, leaving the remaining point heavenward, a menace to any man or beast that steps upon it. The same effect is achieved by double-pointing two ½-inch-square bars and cross-welding them in the middle. After welding, the points are bent as before. Still another method requires one bar 3½-inches long sharpened on both ends. Two additional bars 2-inches long, sharpened on one end and scarfed on the other, are lap-welded to the center of the long bar, and then the points are spread apart so that each is bent at a 45-degree angle to the other. The simplest form of caltrop may be cut with bench shears from red-hot ¼-inch sheet iron, and the points bent to the desired angle.

Another defensive weapon made by the smith was the stimuli. Examples of this ingenious, most powerful defense have been found in pre-Roman forts in France, described by Viollet le Duc. Actually it is no more than a barbed arrowhead with a tang from 3- to 6-inches long. After shaping the point on a ¼-inch rod, the tang is bent at right angles 1 ½ or 2 inches from the barbs, and again is bent at right angles in the opposite direction on the same axis about 2 inches from the first angle, leaving a portion of straight tang some 2- to 4-inches long. To use, the tang is stuck into the end of a 6-inch wooden stake as far as the first right-angle bend, and the stake is stuck into the earth so that the point will penetrate any unsuspecting foot that steps upon it.

Stimuli

Stimuli were the land mines of ancient times and when placed thickly enough, could kill a wounded man so unfortunate as to fall upon them.

In ancient times, certainly in the Middle Ages and Renaissance and even until modern times, the sword has been a status symbol. Over the ages it was developed in many forms from the short stabbing sword of ancient Greece and Rome to the ponderous two-handed sword of the medieval knight; from the heavy scimitars of India to the light rapiers carried by Elizabethan gallants and their continental contemporaries. Regardless of origin or period, most swords were of the same general form, a long blade and a short tang which was inserted into a wooden, a silver, or an ivory handle. During most of the period of man's social history, a sword was designated the weapon of a gentleman. This discrimination was so well-enforced that it was sometimes illegal for a man of low blood to carry a sword. His weapons were limited by law to plebeian articles such as butcher knives, billhooks, and quarterstaves.

The swords of gentlemen were often true works of art in which the sword itself, made by a specialist swordsmith from the Dark Ages onward, served merely as a *raison d'être* for the goldsmith, jeweler, etcher, and ironchiseler. The cutler, who made knives and scissors and such small items, usually ordered all the parts of a sword from the various craftsmen involved, assembled them, and acted as the selling agent.

Many sword blades, in times following the Renaissance, were made entirely of steel, either blister steel or the fine Wootz steel from India. Perhaps, in the periods when steel was a scarce and dear commodity, this explains why a sword enjoyed such exclusive social position. Many of the ancient Roman swords, however, as well as Merovingian, Indonesian, Indian, and Japanese swords, were made of iron and steel welded together. The remnant swordsmiths found in Toledo, Spain, today still follow this ancient method for making fine swords. The core is made of two or more iron rods, the number depending on the size of the rods. These are brought to a white heat and coiled together by fastening one end of the rods in the vise and twisting all rods tightly together with a pair of wide-lipped tongs.

One may suspect that many of the Roman swords were made from old horseshoes, which, straightened and drawn out by an apprentice, would have served admirably for twisting together into sword cores.

The twisted mass of iron is then welded together and drawn out into a sword shape with the edges drawn out, ready to be welded to the steel blades. Welding must be done with care. A shallow groove is cut with a hot set along the iron edge, as with the edge of an ax. Steel scarfed on one edge is inserted into this groove. When assembled, by hammering the lips of the groove tightly over the scarfed steel, the two metals are welded together in as many heats as necessary.

Welding twisted iron for sword core

One method of facilitating the joining together of such relatively long and awkward pieces is to tack-weld them together at a spot on one end. This is accomplished by clamping the two together with tongs held by a ring and bringing one end to welding heat; then they are joined at one small spot with a light hammer. After tack welding, the sword is put back into the fire immediately, both to save heat and to minimize scaling, and the rest of the blade is welded, perhaps in two or three heats for each.

After welding, the steel edge is dressed on the anvil face by drawing down to the final edge with glancing hammer-

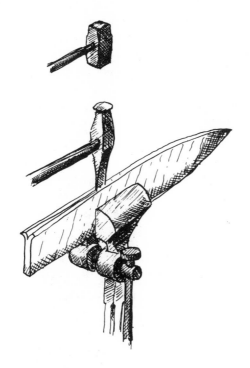

Splitting iron sword core for insertion of steel blade

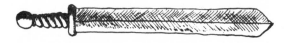

Roman-type sword

blows, which mold and pack the steel. They are finished with a flatter and polished with a file and emery. Often the twist of the core is apparent in the finished sword.

There is no extant record describing the methods of Roman swordsmiths. The techniques described above, therefore, are speculative, based on the methods suggested by modern smiths who were asked how they would make a Roman-type sword.

Based on very rare and sketchy accounts it is probable that the famed swords of Damascus were made in much the same manner, except that Damascus swords were made of twisted Wootz steel and that possibly the Romans learned their technique from Damascene smiths. Interestingly, the technique of twisting and welding iron and steel rods for sword cores anticipates by almost two thousand years the Damascus twist barrels of shotguns made in the eighteenth and nineteenth centuries. These modern weapons were often made from old horseshoe nails and cut-up carriage springs twisted and welded into bands which were then welded into a tube.

Because of the legendary quality of Damascus swords, many stories have been circulated over the centuries as to how these swords were made and tempered to the point that when sharpened and held edge-upward they would cut a silken cloth thrown into the air so that it landed across the sword's edge. Some stories state that the smiths of Damascus made their blades of iron and tempered them by cold forging, as copper and bronze are made harder. Iron, however, fibrous as it is, will not harden under cold forging without becoming brittle. Others state that the swords were made of iron and then brought to a white, almost a welding heat, and ruby and diamond dust was pounded into

352

the blade to carbonize the iron and transform it into steel. It's possible that diamond dust pounded in iron might make a sort of emery board, but the use of diamond dust to transform iron into steel is more appropriate to alchemy than to ironworking.

Cyril Stanley Smith, in his book *A History of Metallography*, states that the Damascus sword was made entirely of Wootz steel, which was composed of particles of steel embedded in soft iron. When an ingot of Wootz steel was drawn out and twisted, the relative incidence of steel and iron created the graceful texture apparent in a true Damascus blade, a texture emphasized by washing with acid. Some Damascene smiths were so skillful that they could create what was known as "Mohammed's ladder," areas of texture in which the design was perpendicular to the normal twisted texture, which followed the axis of the blade. Because steel and iron were integrated in Damascus blades, the blades could be used hardened without tempering, and would take and hold a finer edge than tempered blades of pure steel.

French and German swordsmiths of the eighteenth, nineteenth, and twentieth centuries, not having access to an understanding of Wootz steel, learned to make a simulated Damascus texture by welding iron and steel together. Usually the ratio was six parts iron to five parts steel. To follow this technique, several bars or rods of each are twisted tightly into a single rod. This is welded and flattened, then doubled over and welded again, as many times as is necessary to create the texture the smith has in mind. After forging to shape, the swords are polished and hardened. They are then rinsed in nitric-muriatic acid for seven to ten minutes. This dissolves the iron on the surface and leaves the steel portions slightly raised, to emphasize the twisted texture.

German smiths, who turned out fine Damascus blades through World War II, sometimes wrapped iron rods around a steel core, welded the two together, drew out, twisted,

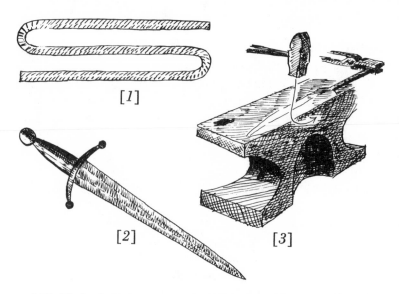

[1] *Method of faggot-welding twisted iron and steel to make imitation Damascus blade.* [2] *Dagger with Damascus blade.* [3] *Molding edge.*

doubled, and rewelded, and forged into blades. The pattern was etched with salt and vinegar mixed to a paste with finely ground charcoal, or with sal ammoniac, vitriol, and vinegar.

Indonesian swords and kris are made in much the same manner. Often, however, instead of twisting, the Indonesian smith welds thin layers of iron and steel together and forges the resulting bar into his blade. When taper-ground to an edge, the blade shows the various layers of steel and iron. The iron is etched out to a degree with lemon juice or acid to emphasize the inherent pattern.

Japan, since about the fourteenth century, has undoubtedly furnished the finest swords ever made. Japanese swordsmiths have signed their works over the centuries and, unlike European smiths, have left some records of the painstaking techniques employed in making fine, pattern-welded samurai swords. These techniques are described in some detail in *A History of Metallography*.

The base of a Japanese sword is soft iron. This is welded to steel in two different methods. Some smiths merely weld a steel plate to an iron plate to which a ¼-inch tang has already been welded. Others combine iron and steel by hardening a bar of steel, breaking it into many small particles under the hammer, piling the particles on the flat iron bar, bringing to welding heat, and welding the particles of steel to the iron. The ratio of iron and steel in both methods is about half-and-half.

After the first welding, the metal is drawn out to its original thickness and twice the original length. It is then doubled back over itself and faggot-welded, drawn out, doubled sideways, welded, drawn out, doubled lengthwise again, until the doubling and welding has been repeated from

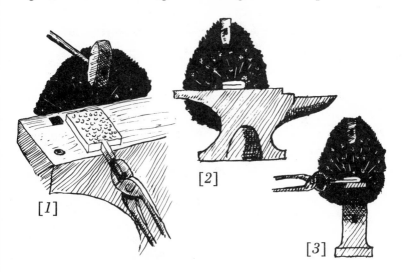

The making of a Japanese sword blade: [1] welding steel particles in iron, [2] doubling, [3] welding.

Another type of Japanese blade—cross section

twelve to twenty-eight times. Then the blade is forged into shape.

Other Japanese blades are made by forging a core of soft iron and encasing this, on either three or four sides, with thin strips of carbon steel. It was felt by ancient Japanese smiths and warriors that the iron core allowed the sword to swing for a longer time without tiring the arm.

To prevent scaling and oxidation in the many welding heats required to forge a sword, the Japanese smiths applied to the iron between each welding a flux paste made of fine clay, charcoal powder, and straw ashes.

During World War II it was demonstrated that a good samurai sword is capable of cutting through a machine-gun barrel, a feat requiring remarkable temper. Such swords are tempered by covering them with a thick coating of clay, charcoal powder, polishing-stone powder, and fusible salt, the coating being stripped off $\frac{1}{16}$ inch along the edge before putting in the fire. When the blade reaches cherry red it is quenched in oil. The coating is stripped off and the blade is found to have an edge harder than a cold chisel, with a body of diminishing hardness to its back.

Japanese sword guards were also pattern-welded in many cases. One of the more interesting techniques used to make a guard is to roll up thin bars of iron and steel, weld the roll together, and flatten by upsetting from one end. It may then be shaped with shears or chisel and etched to emphasize the coiled pattern.

While the medieval swordsmiths of Europe had little

356

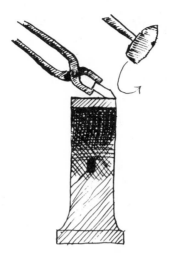

Chamfering sword blade

opportunity to acquire Wootz steel, they did turn out some fine swords, mostly large, heavy slashing swords. Many of these, from the forges of Scandinavia, as well as from the magnificent craftsmen of Spain and Italy, were as much as 4 feet in length. Some were forged to a diamond-shaped section, but others had wide blood gutters down the center of the blade. As with Roman swords and spearheads, the diamond-shaped sections were forged on the edge of the anvil face, or perhaps on a special block with a slanted face (such as that used in making chisels), and a hammer with a diagonal face. This special equipment used by modern tool dressers will make the job of forging an even chamfer much easier.

Forming blood gutters calls for a set of fullers, one top and one bottom, both of the same size. After bringing the partially formed blade to an orange-red heat, the blade is placed on a bottom fuller, perhaps a cheese fuller for larger swords. The top fuller is then placed on the blade so that its position carefully corresponds with the bottom fuller, and an apprentice pounds the top fuller with a 6- or 8-pound hammer. This same basic method may be followed in making cavalry sabers, court swords, and other special swords. The fine, long sabers of Cossack warriors often have several narrow blood gutters on both sides of the blade, and again the gutters are formed with a set of fullers of proper size.

After blood gutters are formed, a fine sword will have its edge packed, to mass the fibers of the steel and enable the weapon to hold its edge longer, even when used to cut through plate armor. Packing a sword follows exactly the technique of packing a chisel edge. The blade is heated until it barely turns red when viewed in a shadow, perhaps furnished by a barrel set on its side next to the forge. At this heat it is placed on the anvil face and quickly hammered with a 1- or 1½- pound hammer. Packing must be done with even blows, otherwise the blade may warp when quenched in brine during hardening. If this happens, there is only one way to eliminate the crookedness. The blade is brought to a bright orange-red and tapped smartly with a 4-pound hammer on the end of the tang. Such a blow will rearrange the molecules throughout the blade and allow it to be hardened without warping on the second trial. Of course, rearranging the molecules also destroys the packing, and this must be repeated before hardening and tempering.

Tempering is probably the most difficult aspect of sword making because of the length of the blade and the need to heat it evenly. The job is made easier with a long fire, but the blade may also be heated to the required cherry red by passing it over the fire until every section of the blade is an even color, and it is of utmost importance that the heat be even. Once heated the blade is quenched in brine or oil by inserting it in the fluid with the edge parallel to the surface of the fluid. After hardening, the surface is cleaned of scale and then tempered to a blue color for long thin blades, a purple or bronze color for heavy blades. To temper, the smith should heat a thick bar of iron as long as the blade to an orange-red. This red-hot bar may be placed on the anvil, and the sword blade is placed upon it until the desired color is reached on the edges, then it is quenched edge-down. When tempering two-edged swords, the hot iron bar is placed in contact with the center ridge or blood gutter of the blade. For single-edged swords, however, the blade is placed on the hot bar along its back. Thus when the edge has reached a bronze color, the back will be a blue, which gives the blade a hard edge supported by a tough, springy body.

Swords, being gentlemen's weapons, are always polished to reflect, hopefully, the manners and attitudes of their noble owners. Polishing is started with fine files, the finishing done with the file held crosswise on the blade and rubbed back and forth. Final polishing is done with grindstone and emery cloth. Diderot's *Encyclopedia* illustrates the strange prone position assumed by eighteenth-century French cutlers when grinding swords, scissors, and other cutting implements. In the old days, after polishing, the sword blade was sent to a jeweler for etching or engraving, and then to the cutler for final assembly of blade, quillon, pommel, and grips, and for sale to a customer.

In addition to making sword blades, the ironworker was also necessary to provide the cutler with pommels and quillons, the cross guard above the butt of the blade. During the sixteenth and seventeenth centuries, the heyday of the rapier, the simple cross hilts of the gentleman knight evolved into the progressively elaborate swept hilts, which included knuckle bows, *anneaux, pas d'âne,* and *ricasso* in addition to the basic grip, pommel, and simple quillon. This evolution reached its apogee with the development of the exceedingly ramified basket hilt, which is still seen on the officers' broadswords in certain Scottish regiments.

Swept hilts of all forms require special anvil or stake tools on which the various rods and small bars comprising the guard may be shaped and welded. Since there were hardly ever two swept hilts of identical design, only general principles of manufacture will be described here.

All elaboration develops from the quillon, and in making a basket hilt, for instance, the smith first welds the ends of the ¼-inch rods, or pretapered flat bars, to the quillon around the tang hole, shaping one end of the quillon to serve as one of the vertical bars. Next the vertical bars are shaped on a snarling tool, a stake or anvil tool which is either vertical with a semisphere upset on its end or bent into two right angles to provide both a flat anvil surface and a vertical portion which terminates in a semisphere. After shaping, the vertical bars are lap-welded horizontally or diagonally to the horizontal bars. In welding the horizontal bars, the smith will face the same question faced by smiths four thousand years ago: how can he position and weld small pieces before the welding

Basket hilt for sword

heat cools? There are two answers. He can tie the pieces together with small wire before welding. Also he can weave the crossbars in and out of the vertical bars to hold them in correct position. Quite likely, the welding of all interstices will require a separate heat for each. Welding should be done quickly, the hilt being returned to the fire immediately after two bars are properly joined, both to save heat and to minimize scaling.

Daggers of various forms and sizes over the centuries were also considered gentlemen's weapons, especially those with cross hilts, which distinguished them from butcher knives. In effect, daggers are but miniature swords, and the same techniques of forging and tempering were used for both.

Until the introduction of firearms, and for two or three centuries thereafter, foot soldiers of all nations, including those of the Orient, were equipped with a wide variety of polearms, so called because they were mounted on long poles up to 16 feet in length. This group of weapons is comprised generally of pikes, poleaxes, halberds, spontoons, bills, and voulges. Pikes and spontoons are actually no more than long spears which are held rather than thrown. Poleaxes and halberds are a combination of pikes and broadax-blades. Bills are chopping weapons, adapted from the ancient bill-hook used by European farmers for pruning fruit trees, modified for military slaughter with the addition of sharp points and rear hooks. Voulges are a combination of halberds and bills.

Halberds and poleaxes are more difficult to make, for they must be welded together from several preformed pieces.

Earlier halberds, made by the last of the medieval crafts-men in the fourteenth, fifteenth, and sixteenth centuries, were extremely well-made and strong enough to use with confidence against a'mailed knight on horseback. They consisted mainly of a socket from 3- to 8-inches long with a spike or spearhead welded into one end and two straps of iron welded to the bottom end. On one side of the socket a broadax-blade was welded, on the other a hooked blade.

To make a halberd, the smith takes two pieces of sheet iron each ¼-inch thick, 8-inches long, and 6-inches wide. He forms a semicylindrical depression, 1½ to 2 inches in diameter, down the middle of each, using a bottom round swage and a top fuller of the proper sizes. After the channel is formed he scarfs the edges of the iron that parallel the channel and welds the two pieces together so that the channels coincide to form a socket with wings on either side. Welding is accomplished by clamping the two pieces together with tongs held by a ring and by tack-welding the wings at one end. Once fastened together the two pieces may be easily handled and the wings welded from the socket to within ¼ inch of each wing's outside edge. Two thin 12-inch iron straps, already punched for rivets, which will extend down

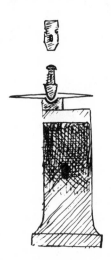

Using round-bottom swage and top fuller to form handle socket for halberd

the handle, are welded to the bottom of the socket. Each strap, of course, is scarfed at one end, and the socket is scarfed by forming a shallow depression with the end of a bar of the same thickness as the width of the strap, or with a fuller. When a fuller is used, the scarfing of the strap would be rounded to fit the rounded depression.

Next a bar of steel from 9- to 15-inches long and about 1-inch square must be tenoned for 1 inch on one end. This is then jambed while cold into the orange-red end of the socket, and the hot iron is hammered to hold the tenon tightly. Then the two pieces are brought to welding heat where the steel and iron meet, and they are welded with a light hammer. After welding, a button may be formed at the base of the steel bar, roughly, at first, with iron being worked between a top and bottom fuller, then perhaps swaged to final perfect form.

After welding, the spearhead, or spike, depending upon design, is formed. Then the blades are welded to the wings of

Iron core of halberd before welding blade

the socket exactly as in making an ax or tomahawk. The steel, 8-inches long, 4-inches wide, and ¼-inch thick, is scarfed on one edge and dented along the scarf with the pein of a cross-pein hammer to form a series of teeth. As with an ax, the cold steel is jambed into the unwelded ¼-inch scarf of one wing of the socket while the wing is orange-red or white hot. The scarf is then hammered tightly around the steel to hold it in place while joining the two.

Some halberds are shaped so that the bases of both blades are quite narrow, and the socket is extended several inches below the bases of the blades. This general design may be fulfilled by cutting the wings to shape after the socket is welded together, and dressing the cut with a light hammer after a drift has been inserted in the socket. If, by chance, the portion of the wing that is cut off is not immediately welded adjacent to the socket, then the cut edge of the socket must be welded again before the steel blade is joined. This may be done on an anvil bick.

Halberds are often highly decorated. Frequently the socket will be worked with ridges and fluting. This may be done with special fullers, made by the smith, or special swages. A drift must be inserted into the socket before such decorative molding can be applied. Most halberds, too, are punched with decorative punches of many shapes: crosses, diamonds, fleurs-de-lis. The finer ones are etched or engraved after tempering, and many are carved around the button and socket by the ironchiseling specialist before tempering.

Tempering is done in three phases. First the spearhead or spike is tempered to a blue. Then, in turn, each blade is tempered to a blue base and a bronze edge. Each section, after tempering, is wrapped in a wet cloth while another section is heated for hardening and tempering. This prevents the already tempered part from losing its temper.

Halberds were still used until about 1800 as badges of rank. After the seventeenth century, however, they were not used very often as weapons, and accordingly were made differently and with greater ease. Most, for instance, did not have a socket, but merely two straps welded to the spearhead, the straps extending from 12 to 18 inches down the shaft. Ax blades frequently were made as a separate piece, both blades being cut from a sheet of iron, inserted between the straps beneath the point, and held in place by the friction of the

Tanged halberd showing parts

straps. The blades, however, were frequently decorated with punched holes of various shapes. Some had a tang rather than straps. The smith who made this type would frequently brad the ax blades across the tang, and sometimes he would cross-weld the two pieces together. In still another form, the portion of iron between the ax blades is flattened to a plane perpendicular to that of the blades and punched so that the tang of the spearhead may be inserted through the hole and driven into the shaft. An iron hoop, sometimes decorated, is shrunk onto the end of the shaft before the tang is driven in.

Voulges, considered common men's weapons, are much more easily made than halberds. They consist merely of a steel blade, drawn to a point at one end, and welded on one edge to two separate straps which form sockets, the lower socket generally being longer than the upper. To make a voulge, the smith first makes his sockets, bending two flat pieces of iron around a drift to form eyes, and welding the extensions together, as in making a tomahawk. Welding, as with tomahawks, extends to ¼ inch of the scarfed ends into which the steel blade is welded. The blade is shaped into a blunt, flat point at one end, chamfered for the edge, and scarfed with a fuller at the points where the two sockets are welded. Sockets are clamped on by hammering while hot and are welded one at a time. Some voulges had a small steel spike welded perpendicularly to the back of the upper socket. With a spike present, the socket may be formed of two pieces, as with a halberd, with the extension on one side being welded and drawn to a point.

Another common foot soldier's weapon was the bill, or billhook. This, too, consists of an iron socket welded to a steel blade, with a steel hook welded to the back of the blade. To make a bill the smith requires a ⅛-inch-thick shield-shaped sheet of iron some 10-inches long and 5-inches wide at the base. This is scarfed on both long edges and doubled on the 10-inch axis, with a socket formed halfway into the length

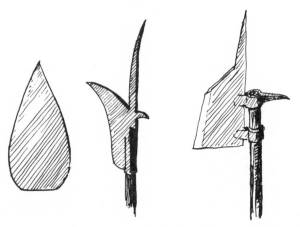

Left: Pattern for bill hook body. Center: Billhook. Right: Voulge.

by bending the iron around a pointed drift. Then the doubled iron is welded together, leaving the socket open, of course, and leaving ⅜-inch of the edge opposite the socket unwelded, to later receive the steel blade.

After welding the body is split downward from the point at a 30° angle, almost to the top of the socket. The wide side of the split is bent outward to from a shallow hook; the small side is left parallel to the socket to form a spike.

Forming a thin steel strip 1-inch wide to weld to the body to create a blade is done exactly as in forming an ax blade. The strip is scarfed on one edge, which will make the scarfed edge convex to fit the hook portion of the body. Small teeth are cut into the scarf. When cold, the edge is jambed into the slot of the cherry-red body and the edges of the slit hammered down upon the teeth. Blade and body are then welded.

The spike should also be given either a steel point or steel edges, a task accomplished by a simple lap weld of a piece of steel along the spike.

Lastly a smaller steel spike is either lap-welded or tongue-welded to the base of the spike above the socket, and given a sharp edge on its bottom to cut bridle reins. All steel is tempered to a blue.

Undoubtedly the finest ironworkers of history were the makers of defensive armor, the very specialized armorers of the Middle Ages and, especially, of the sixteenth and seventeenth centuries. The artistry of some of the armor of the Maximilian period, in the early sixteenth century, is quite unbelievable. Of all the ironworkers in history, the armorers, as a class, did not work in anonymity, but boldly signed their work, and they were known throughout Europe as true masters in their art. Augsburg, Milan, Florence, and London were the centers of armor making in its latter days. Some of the names which have come down from the seventeenth century are Helmschmid (literally, "helmet smith") of Augsburg, Hoden of London, Piccinino of Milan, and Holder, who was

imported from Augsburg to London by Henry VIII. Before
then, every lord went to great pains to acquire and maintain
a good armorer, whom he treated with the greatest respect.

Armor is ancient in concept. Bronze armor, some of it
delicately wrought, was common among warriors of the
ancient world long before the advent of ironworking. The
blacksmith, when first called upon to make armor, for the
most part adopted the methods and tools of the bronzeworker.
He formed small flat iron plates which were riveted or
bradded to leather vests, and he made leg guards of sheet
iron as well as iron caps. In some cases he made hundreds of
small iron rings, which were sewn to a leather shirt. It was
not until the third or the fourth century that the ironworker
developed a new type of armor, in the form of chain mail.
Mail was possibly invented in the Middle East, but it was so
relatively comfortable and so effective in stopping spears,
arrows, and swords that its use soon spread all over the world,
including the faraway barbaric lands of Scandinavia, before
the Christian era in that then remote region.

In its earliest form, chain mail was no more than a series
of small iron chains fastened together at alternate links to
create a metal fabric. As each circular link was only about
⅜ inch in diameter, chain mail would stop all but the finest
arrowhead or lancehead, and as the wire from which each

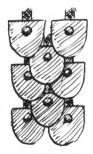 

Left: Scale armor. Right: Ring armor.

link was fashioned was ⅟₁₆ to ³⁄₃₂ inch in diameter, mail would also turn any but the heaviest sword edge and offered a considerable obstruction to a battleax.

Chain mail was usually manufactured by that branch of smiths known as wireworkers. It is not difficult to assemble, in principle, but awfully painstaking. Possibly the worst aspect of manufacturing such tiny chain in the beginning was to reduce iron by hand to wire of ⅟₁₆-inch diameter or slightly larger. This task was done by hand until wire-drawing machines were perfected in Germany during the thirteenth century.

Once wire is available, however, forming links is quite simple. The wire is coiled around a ⅜-inch rod and cut off with a chisel at each revolution. These round rings are then heated to cherry red, brought from the fire, and scarfed on the cut ends. A tiny hole is then either drilled or punched in each end; the link being heated to orange-red if it is to be punched. Drilling, however, is safer, as a punch may split the fiber of the small iron and weaken the link. Once drilled, the links are made into a series of chains, each link joined shut with a tiny brad. The best mail had the links of all vertical courses of chain welded, but this refinement is rare and

Left: Single-chain mail. Right: Bradded link in chain mail.

really not necessary, for a chain, quite literally, is no stronger than its weakest link. Once the small separate chains have been made, they are fastened together at alternate links with additional links which are also bradded shut.

When mail has been assembled in sheets large enough to form the front and back, sleeves and hoods of shirts, each piece is linked into shape, and then all pieces are linked together. Many shirts of mail are split up the back to facilitate donning them, the split being laced shut with leather thongs.

The technique of making chain mail never varied during the thousand years or more it was used by European and Oriental fighters. The style and weight, however, did change. As the weapons of the mounted knight grew heavier, so did mail. One method of increasing its protection is to make its chains of heavier wire. Another is to make each chain double —that is, have each link circle two links, and be circled itself by two links.

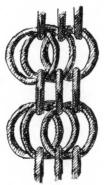

Double-chain mail

Suits of mail were almost always supplemented by iron or steel helmets. Then as the Middle Ages progressed, and weapons became heavier, and gunpowder was invented, the plate used for helmet making was extended to all parts of the body by the end of the sixteenth century. After that, the suits of armor began to grow smaller, until the eighteenth century, when the officers' gorget was worn as a mere vestigial symbol of the ancient knight's armor.

The use of plate armor was actually a renaissance of the bronze armor used in ancient Greece and Rome, and found in many styles in China, Japan, and India. It was artfully shaped to fit all parts of a man's body, and certain ceremonial suits made for the reigning queens of European countries were molded to fit the charms of a female figure. During the period of the Emperor Maximilian, plate armor reached its zenith of construction and decoration. Some suits almost exactly duplicated the current style of textile clothing, with puffed sleeves, flaring, fluted skirts, and pointed shoes. The armorer, at the high point of his art, was indeed a sculptor, but one who worked with iron and steel rather than with cold marble. He required tools and equipment beyond the ken of his ancient predecessor, the village blacksmith, but his imagination and intellect arose to the occasion. Also he borrowed and modified the tools of prehistoric bronze- and coppersmiths: special forming hammers, special anvils and swages and stake tools. But where the worker in soft metals could often form his products on wooden forms, the maker of steel armor required iron equipment.

Little has been written about the equipment or the material used by the armorer during centuries of his dominance of ironworking. Indeed, armorers in general kept every aspect of their work as a trade secret. Many experts describe helmets and other articles of plate armor as being made of steel, but until the fifteenth century, it all seems to have been made of soft iron. After 1400 a few armorers, but by no means all, case-hardened their suits by carburization, according to Mr. H. Russell Robinson, Assistant to the Master of the Armouries at the Tower of London.

Prior to the invention of rolling mills in the sixteenth century, the armorer worked with sheet which had been drawn out from great bars by water-operated trip-hammers into plates $\frac{1}{16}$-inch thick. Such crudely produced plate was uneven in its thickness, and one test of dating old armor is to measure its thickness in various spots with calipers. The old armor varies as much as $\frac{1}{32}$ inch from one point to another. One may assume, too, that in certain areas, where iron furnaces were small and ill-equipped, the armorer might have been satisfied with small plates that he could weld together to obtain adequate size for a breast plate or back plate. Some modern authorities indicate that welded plate is inferior to unwelded plate, but such a theory is not well-founded. A good smith can join two pieces of soft iron in a manner that cannot be detected and is fully as strong and malleable as unwelded plate.

Little has ever been written about armorer's equipment. About the only sources available are old woodcuts of the armorer at work in his shop with some of his special equipment. As a helmet is basically an inverted pot of steel, and a breast plate a peculiarly shaped platter, it is no surprise to find that the armorer shared certain tools with the coppersmith, the silversmith, and even the lowly tinker. In addition to the usual blacksmith's tools, the armorer had a special anvil with a large curved face for shaping breast plates and back plates. To shape helmets, greaves, sabbatons, vainbraces, kneecaps, and cuisses he used an anvil with a greatly extended horn or a stake bick. In addition he had a variety of straight stake anvils with upset rounded faces and several previously mentioned snarling irons.

Certain museums around the world, including the Metropolitan Museum in New York, have appropriately collected armorers' tools along with fine armor. The Metropolitan collection was found intact in the shop of a German castle, where

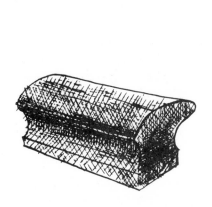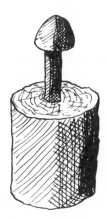

Left: Round-faced anvil. Right: Stake form for helmet.

it had lain unused since about the sixteenth century. Kept in the repair shop of the museum, this group of tools includes numbers of special stakes, hammers, bench shears, swages and others which demonstrate that making tools required almost the degree of skill needed to make armor.

We know that relatively modern blacksmiths used a semispherical depression in a cast-iron swage block to form the bowls of ladles. Probably the armorer, after ironfounding became professional in the fifteenth century, also used cast-iron forms to rough out the varying shapes of pieces of plate armor.

Again, as with the decorative ironworker and the coppersmith, it is probable that the armorer used a number of special hammers and fullers. The old woodcuts show the armorer using elongated hammers which appear very like the double-faced and leaf hammers used by the modern decorative smith. Also he must have had special sets of swages to provide the rope motif stamped so frequently on the edges of helmet brims and combs.

Most of the hammering of armor parts was done on the outside surface. Thus even though a cast-iron block with a depression might have been used to rough out the shape of a helmet or kneecap, the finishing was done on a stake or snarling iron, with the hammer smoothing the outside surface.

The making of a morion, that high-combed, wide-brimmed, gracefully shaped iron hat of the time of the Spanish conquistador and Sir Francis Drake, will adequately illustrate the techniques of forming all articles of armor. Harold L. Peterson, in his excellent definitive work *Arms and Armor in Colonial America*, states unequivocally that the finer quality helmets of the period, and earlier, were made from a solid billet of steel, while later and poorer specimens were made of two pieces welded together down the center. This is confirmed by Mr. Robinson at the Tower of London and Mr. Helmut Nickel at the Metropolitan Museum of Art in New York. Mr. Robinson adds that the practice of one piece construction was adhered to until 1580 when the French began making helmet skulls of two pieces which were clamped or riveted together.

Incidentally, the Romans made their helmets from one ingot of iron, according to Mr. Robinson, and the technique was rediscovered only in the late thirteenth century. The Romans even applied fine embossing to their one-piece parade helmets.

Armor, including intricately shaped helmets, was always forged cold according to the outstanding authorities in the field. No authority today, however, can be sure of how each medieval armorer did his work because of the deep secrecy which surrounded the techniques of each.

Raw material for helmets and armor begins as plate hammered, presumably by trip-hammer, from heavy bars of soft iron. This is then roughly cut into the proper size with bench shears and cold-forged into cuirass or helmet skull over specially shaped anvils and stake irons. As the iron is hammered into shape, its fibers are packed together, hardening the material and making it brittle. As a consequence the plate, during the early stages of shaping, must be frequently annealed in the forge to prevent, if possible, the splitting so commonly found in lower-grade helmets.

An excellent series of photographs from the Metropolitan Museum of Art, showing the steps of restoring a combed and visored helm by M. Tachaux in 1918, illustrates the technique of shaping such an intricately designed item.

First of all, the flat plate is roughly formed into a pan-shaped skull over a round stake iron. When half-formed, the face orifice is cut out with bench shears and the sides further drawn in by cold-hammering on the outside surface. The comb requires rather delicate shaping. To start it, the smith hammers a shallow groove down the middle of the skull, using a grooved stake iron and a double-faced hammer with a semi-cylindrical face. This technique may still be observed in the shops of Italian ironworkers who produce decorative leaves and blossoms for chandeliers and other lighting fixtures. Using a light hammer with a narrow cross pein, similar to the armorers' hammers illustrated in *De Wiesz Kuenig,* and a small grooved stake held in a post vise, the Italian smiths skillfully and quickly form the shallow veins of leaves.

The comb is further shaped from the outside over a narrow fan-shaped stake, with which the comb is formed as deeply as desired. A flat-faced hammer is used to form the sharp angle at the base of the comb over the edge of an anvil or a flat stake iron. The smith must not forget during the shaping process to return his metal to the forge for annealing when the iron becomes hard and brittle.

After the comb is shaped, the sides of the skull are drawn down over a snarling iron, or in the case of pot-shaped helmets, over the long, narrow horn of an armorer's anvil. When the sides are drawn down sufficiently, the edges are again shaped with bench shears and holes are punched for visor hinges and decorative studs.

There is a great deal of waste in trimming a helmet after

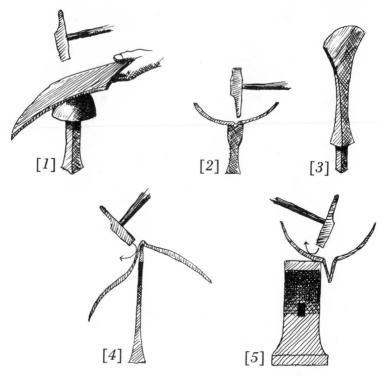

[1] *Molding plate on helmet stake.* [2] *Starting depression for comb.* [3] *Comb forming stake.* [4] *Forming comb.* [5] *Forming angle at base of comb.*

it has been formed, a fact particularly in evidence in the making of certain types of Roman helmets which fit around the ears of the wearer and are designed to cover his neck and shoulders with a lobster-tail-shaped back. Mr. Robinson states that much of this waste may be eliminated by using a narrow key-hole-shaped pattern for such helmets, the circular portion of the key hole intended for the lobster-tail back section. This elongated plate is formed into the skull, the sides being brought around to form the cavity for the ears.

Many Roman helmets of superior grade, as well as

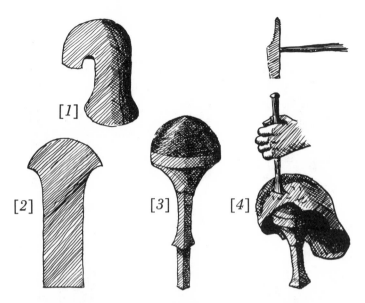

[1] *Roman helmet with lobster-tail.* [2] *Pattern for Roman helmet with lobster-tail.* [3] *Pitch ball for embossing.* [4] *Embossing on pitch ball.*

Renaissance armor, are elaborately embossed with figures of men and animals and mythical designs. Necessarily, embossing must be applied after the helmet is formed, and it must be done from the outside. It is accomplished by the use of blunt chisels and small hammers while the completed helmet rests on a large ball or semisphere of pitch. Pitch has a firm consistency which will yield under light hammering, but which supports the metal being formed. Designs are first outlined with small blunt chisels, or fullers, and finally shaped with a light double-faced hammer. Patience is as important as skill in perfecting the embossing process. When the pitch ball becomes too rough for good work its surface is heated over the forge or with a blowtorch and smoothed with a knife blade or flat bar.

Many Roman, and some later helmets, were decorated

with brass bosses and brass edging around the cheek pieces and the back. Bosses may be made individually, but this is a tedious task. Probably most were made, even in Roman times, and especially with later French armorers, with sets of dies, then riveted in place. Brass edging is formed from long strips of brass which are doubled across the width. The iron to be edged is then cut at ¼-inch intervals with a small chisel to form teeth, exactly as in preparing a steel-ax bit for welding into the iron blade of the ax. The brass edging is clamped over these teeth and shaped to the curves of the edges, then hammered tightly to the edge.

Polishing is the last step in making plate armor. First a series of files, of increasing fineness, are used. Next the surface is smoothed with a felt ball or pad and a paste of flour emery mixed with oil or water. Final polishing, which results in a mirror surface, is done with fiber balls and emery, or jewelers rouge or pumice, mixed with soft rainwater. Rainwater is the ingredient used by the armorers of all ages, and its lack of mineral content does make it more effective in a polishing paste.

The smoother the polish, the more effective the blueing or browning which decorates some helmets of the Renaissance period.

Examination of many old helmets shows that the olden armorers often ruined a portion of a helmet by allowing it to crack. Instead of discarding such a fiasco, however, they usually shaped a new piece to fit the ruined portion, brazed it into position with melted copper, and secured it with small brads set closely together. On helmets decorated with etching, such a patch is indistinguishable from the outside. A patch is practicable because it in no way weakens the strength of the helmet skull if properly applied.

Most helmets after 1580 were made of two pieces of sheet iron. Where a comb is part of the design, the comb on one half of the skull is rolled over the edge of the other comb section, and the two are crimped together. Where no comb occurs, a flange is left on each half and the two halves are riveted together.

Many cabassets are decorated with stamped brass bosses bradded 1 inch apart around the base of the crown.

Hammered plate of charcoal iron, the ideal material for making armor, is quite unobtainable for prospective armorers of the late twentieth century. A good substitute, however, is the mild plate steel developed for cold-forming electrical switchboxes and steel containers of various sorts. Indeed, the new types of steel are not so likely to crack as the old plate of charcoal iron, nor will they, on the other hand, form quite so easily. When using the new plate, the modern armorer must be careful to order it of proper thickness so that his shaping under the hammer will leave the metal thicker on top and in front of the skull, as was the custom in olden days.

Other articles of armor used the same type of equipment for forming as was used for making helmets. Since the off-set of the surface of a breast plate, however, is far less than that of a helmet, thinner plate may be used for body armor. The main difficulty in forming large items of body armor is in the size of plate the smith must handle. A large forge, which will heat a large flat surface, is needed. While more than one heat is required for larger articles, the smith must still take as few heats as possible, to minimize scaling. Also, he must be careful not to heat one portion of the plate more than another, or else scaling will weaken the part that has been heated the most. As shown in old books, armor was generally shaped by cold forging and heat used only for softening.

Examination of old plate armor often indicates that the plate was laminated from two very thin pieces of iron, but appearances are sometimes deceiving. Some old armor had additional thickness riveted to a certain part for extra strength. What appears to be lamination in thin sheets, however, is merely the result of cold-forging soft iron.

Charcoal iron, the type used until the nineteenth century, may be thinned by cold forging from ⅜-inch to ¹⁄₁₆-inch thickness without splitting. Personal experiment has shown that iron drawn out while cold separates into two distinct layers, giving the appearance of lamination. Pure iron made with coal or gas or electric fuel does not separate into two layers as readily as the charcoal iron, perhaps because of a lower ratio of slag.

Much armor, especially that made in the fifteenth and sixteenth centuries, was highly decorated with etching, gold inlays, and blueing or browning in patterns. Usually this was done outside the armorer's shop, but some armories employed jewelers and artists for this work.

One fact sometimes forgotten in the appreciation of fine armor is that it was extremely expensive, and consequently the master armorer was quite well-to-do. This means that he could afford to hire adequate, well-trained help, which made a great difference in the productive capacity of his shop. A helmet may be made entirely by one craftsman, but the handling of the large sheets needed for body armor and horse armor required several men who knew precisely what they were doing.

Firearms replaced armor after a thousand years of hand-to-hand combat, and, appropriately, the gunsmith took over the position of prominence vacated by the armorer in the field of ironworking. There was, of course, a great deal more to gunsmithing than forming gun parts with hammer and anvil and all the assorted tools at the blacksmith's command. But shaping and welding barrels, lock plates, tumblers, triggers, barrel bands, and other parts were a basic part of the gunsmith's trade. He has always been called a smith because he smote metal to form it. Had not forge and anvil been part of the gunsmith's equipment he might have been called a "gunwright."

From the earliest days of firearms until the 1870s, the barrels of handguns and shoulderguns were made of wrought iron. Most manufacturing gunsmiths during this long period made every part of a gun in their own shops. In addition, countless blacksmiths over the world employed their regular equipment to make gun and rifle barrels at their own forge, mounted, especially in America and in Canada, on stocks made in their wagon shop and fitted with locks made in the gunshops of Europe and Asia. The locally produced arms included pistols, shotguns, and rifles. The barrels of all of these types were made by welding wrought iron, often the scrap left from tiring a wagon, into tubes which are finished by reaming and rifling. A plug is threaded in the breech; drum and nipple inserted in percussion guns.

There are several methods of welding rifle and pistol barrels, the most common being to bend a ½-inch wrought iron bar around a ¼- to ½-inch rod, or mandrel, and butt-weld the edges of the bar together. It is important to use hard-to-find wrought iron for a gun barrel rather than mild steel, for one cannot always trust the strength of a weld in mild steel.

The width of the bar is such that it can be wrapped tightly around the mandrel with a gap between the edges equal to the thickness of the iron. Welding rifle barrels follows exactly the same principle as welding bolt heads except that the barrel is welded around a cold mandrel.

Welding should start in the middle of the barrel to facilitate withdrawing the mandrel after each heat. The wrapping process is started by bending the iron at yellow heat across its width, usually done with a large round bottom swage and a top fuller. When the section is "U" shape the

Welding flat bar around rod to make rifle barrel

mandrel is laid in the groove and the iron hammered tightly around it. Then the mandrel is withdrawn, the iron brought to sparkling welding heat, the mandrel is reinserted, and the butt weld is made, usually not more than 6 inches per heat. This process is continued until the barrel is welded along its length. The outside can be rough-forged into an octagon after each heat.

Some barrels were scarfed on the edges and lap-welded. This technique, however, is considered inferior because it often made the bore off-center.

Another method of welding a barrel is to coil the flat bar around the rod and weld about half a coil at a time. Some feel that, because of the fibers in wrought iron, this method makes a stronger barrel. Actually, with a barrel in which black powder is fired it makes little difference. Black powder burns down the full length of the barrel instead of at one point, as with modern smokeless powder, and the chamber compression of black powder is very low. Most of the old barrels are welded longitudinally. It's easier than coiling a heavy bar

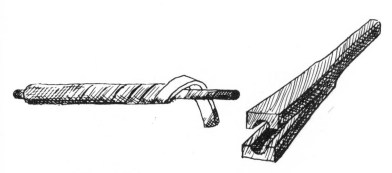

Left: Coiling flat bar around rod to form barrel. Right: Two bars welded together to form barrel.

of iron, and with a good weld its strength is just as solid as with the coiled barrel.

Easiest of all methods for welding rifle barrels was that used by John Whitley, of Vinings, Georgia. Whitley, as described by his son, Jim, used two flat pieces of iron for his barrels. Each was as wide as the outside diameter of the barrel and half as thick. To follow the Whitley method the smith first fullers a ¼-inch semicylindrical depression down the center of each bar. Then the two bars are welded together on either side of the depression and shaped to the usual octagon section on the outside. This method eliminates all the awkwardness and problems of having to curve a flat piece of iron down its long axis, of having to insert a cold rod quickly into a partial cavity while the iron is at welding heat, and of having to remove the rod by hammering after the iron has cooled.

Dressing the outside of a rifle barrel to the usual octagon shape is done with hammer, flatter, or swage when welding is completed. When this is done the barrel is drilled with a horizontal mechanical drill or with a long bit held in a hand brace. Then the barrel is straightened with a lead or copper hammer. Rifling, applied with a rifling machine, and described in a number of books on gunsmithing, is the next operation, followed by boring the touch hole, for a flintlock, or boring and threading a hole for the drum of a cap-and-ball rifle. The last step is to thread the last ½ inch of the breech for screwing in the breech plug.

Musket barrels are made in the same manner, except that they are drawn out thinner at the muzzle and are shaped to a round section on the outside.

Shotgun barrels of the old type also consist of welded tubes of soft iron. Common shotgun barrels may be made of much thinner stock than rifle barrels, but with heavy iron around the breech, either by drawing out the original bar before forming so that it is thin at the muzzle end, or by welding an extra thickness of iron around the breech. Many country blacksmiths, however, made what is known as "Damascus steel" barrels, with implied tribute to the ancient swordsmiths of the Middle East. Damascus barrels may be made of nail rod, iron wire, drawn-out horseshoes or discarded horseshoe nails, and sections of old carriage springs. The ratio is two parts of iron to one of steel. Small sections of iron and steel must first be welded together into a wire. Two wires are then twisted tightly together and flat-

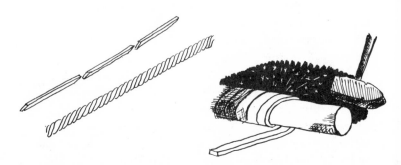

Welding nails and steel, twisting together and coiling around rod to make shotgun barrel

tened into a small bar. The bar is then coiled around a rod the size of the intended shotgun base and welded, which fuses the original twist together even as it joins the edges of the coils. Heavier wire is used for the breech of the barrel. A larger portion may be welded each heat if the mandrel rod is heated orange-red, to help maintain heat on the thin twisted wire while it is being joined.

After welding, the bore is reamed and polished with emery paste, then straightened, and fitted with a breech plug.

Breech plugs for rifle, shotgun, and pistol barrels may be made in several ways. One method is to forge a rectangular section on the end of a rod of proper size to thread and fit into the breech. The rectangular portion should start ½ inch from the end of the rod and extend about 1½ inches. Shoulders must be squared with the set hammer and by swaging in a rectangular cavity in the swage block. After the rectangular section is formed it is split down its center on the wide dimension to within about ⁵⁄₁₆ inch from the round section, and the legs of the split are spread to a right angle from the original axis. The inside of the split is smoothed with the hammer, working at an orange-red heat, until the surface is smooth and the end of the split has disappeared. One of the legs is then cut off with a chisel at a point where it extends beyond the round section a distance equal to the thickness of the barrel between its outside surface and the bore. The other leg is bent at a right angle in the direction of its original axis, the inside corner of the bend being rounded and the outside corner then being upset so that it is square. One way to form a square corner at this point is to use the set hammer or anvil corner, to form a shoulder on the side of the leg adjacent to the round section before bending. After the shoulder has been formed, the leg is then bent away from this shoulder. The outside corner should be at a point equal to the length of the other leg of the split. When the corner has been bent and properly

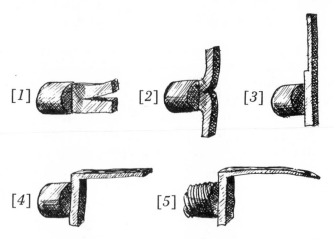

Steps in making a breech plug

squared, the tang is drawn out to its desired length and thickness and is drilled for screws.

Breech plugs may be made by following one of several techniques, depending on the taste and skill of the smith. One method is to fuller a rod, of the size to fit the breech, to form a tenon 2 inches long and ½-inch wide. This tenon is split down its center to within ½ inch of the round section, the split opened and hammered flat, so that the legs are perpendicular to the original axis, and one leg cut off the thickness of the barrel below the round section. The other leg is then offset at the thickness of the barrel and bent to a right angle to form the tang. Finishing is done by filing.

Trigger guards and butt plates of muzzle-loading rifles are usually made of cast brass, with a few being made of iron. Musket stock fittings, however, are almost always forged from iron. Butt plates, generally with a broad tang which is curved to fit on top of the butt, are formed to a convex shape where they meet the shoulder. They may be made from sheet iron ¹⁄₁₆-inch thick. A piece long enough for plate and tang is cut with shears to a pattern. The sheet is then bent to a right angle where tang and shoulder plate conjoin. Convexity,

386

or concavity, depending on the view, is formed with cheese fuller and large bottom swage, the swage being one of the depressions in a cast-iron block or one placed in the hardie hole. Shops that made muskets in the days of hand-manufacturing undoubtedly had special anvil tools which facilitated the shaping of butt plates. Making a butt plate is much like making a miniature breast plate for armor.

Trigger guards may be made of one piece of strap iron faggot-welded at a couple of places, or of three pieces welded together. A strap 9-inches long is rounded on one side for about 3 ½ inches in the center, the rounding process upsetting the width slightly. Rounding may be done with a small hammer or, preferably, by pounding in a 1-inch bottom swage.

When this is done the bar is heated to orange-red and the rounded portion is curved over the horn, flat surface inside.

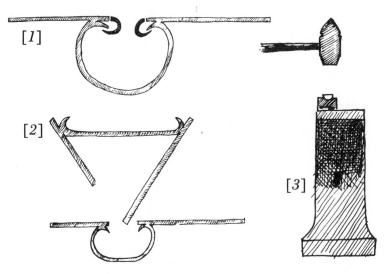

Trigger guards: [1] *welding from one piece and cutting off loops,* [2] *welding and bending three pieces,* [3] *forming guard in swage.*

At the points where the rounded portion stops the bar is bent back double. The doubled portion on each end of the curve is then faggot-welded for ¼ inch. After welding, the curved part is formed into an incomplete oval with the ends of its partial circumference 1½ inches apart, and the straight bars, or tangs, extending from the oval on the same axis. Tangs are then drilled for screw holes, the hole to be placed beneath the barrel tang being threaded for the tang bolt.

The trigger guard on early muskets was screwed on the bottom of the stock over a flat bar in which the trigger was mounted. Eli Whitney, at the time of the War of 1812, simplified the traditional trigger-trigger guard assembly in the interest of production efficiency. He designed his trigger guard separately from the tangs, and combined tangs and trigger plate into one, drilling holes in the strap on both sides of the rectangular slit in which the trigger was mounted. The guard was then formed separately with round tangs which fitted into the two holes. The guard tangs were either bradded through the tang plate, or they were threaded and fastened to the plate with nuts.

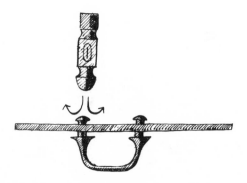

Eli Whitney trigger guard design showing how guard is bradded to bar

Barrel bands, used on muskets and pistols to bind barrel and stock together, are lap-welded, as with common chain links, then formed with a special drift or mandrel. The half-round section of the band is first formed in a bottom round swage of suitable diameter. Scarfing in preparation for welding requires a special swage for the end on which the flat side is scarfed. This swage is formed on the edge of a block that fits into the hardie hole. The block has a half-round depression fullered in at the angle of the intended scarf so that the depression is half-round at the edge of the block and runs out on top of the block. The orange-red end of the intended band is placed in the swage rounded-side-down and hammered so that the scarf is level with the top of the swage block. Of course, the opposite scarf is made with the hammer on the anvil face.

Forming musket band with drift

Bands on many early model muskets were made of flat thin iron, ½- to ¾-inch wide. Such flat bands are scarfed and welded exactly as hub bands and wagon tires, no special equipment being needed. Flat bands are, however, formed with special drifts after welding.

Gunlocks have always been the prerogative of gunsmiths rather than blacksmiths. The making of a lock, whether doglock, flintlock, or percussion, requires a number of special swages and other tools not normally found in a village smithy, though a few country smiths, especially in the Southern Appalachians, made whole rifles and made them well. Some examination of the tools and techniques of making flintlocks will cover all types of locks made before Eli Whitney took gun making out of the category of hand-manufacturing.

Flintlock plates are no more than small, shaped plates of iron from ¹⁄₁₆- to ⅛-inch thick, with a number of reinforcing bosses at several interior points where screw holes are to be bored and threaded. A plate usually starts from a ⅛-inch or thicker flat piece of iron and is drawn down with the hammer, except where bosses occur. The bosses are refined and shouldered with a small set hammer or small fuller.

Pans, which project on the outside of a flintlock plate, require careful forming of pan depression, flash shield on the hammer side, and bridle for the frizzen screw on the front side. Some pans are welded into the plate; others are attached

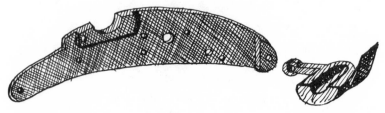

Left: Inside of flintlock plate showing bosses. Right: Flintlock pan.

by screws to the inside of the plate. Both types are formed in the same manner.

For a normal musket pan, a flat piece of iron ¼-inch thick, ¾-inch wide, and 1-inch long is needed. If a number of pans are to be made the smith will indulge himself with the convenience of forming them one after the other on the end of a long bar that can be held without the use of tongs. As always, the depression, or inside of the powder pan, is formed first. This is done with ⅜-inch fuller with one end of its edge rounded, the depression being pounded ⅜-inch deep with its edge ⅜ inch from the edge intended for the shield, with the rounded end ⅛ inch from the side edge, while the open end penetrates the inside edge. Next the shield is formed. The partially formed pan is again brought to orange red and placed on the anvil face with the depression down. A set hammer is used to make a shoulder ⅛-inch deep, ³⁄₁₆ inch from the edge. The portion extending from the

Forming pan shield with set hammer

shoulder is then drawn down to a flat tapered edge that later will be bent upward to form the shield. To form the bridle, the iron, at orange-red heat, is placed on its edge on the anvil face and a fuller is used to roughly form a stud, ⅜-inch long, ¼-inch thick, and ³⁄₁₆-inch wide, which projects from the center of the pan opposite the shield. If the pan is being formed on the end of a bar, it is now cut off at the end of the stud. Stud and shoulders are now dressed smooth with a set hammer. Next the bottom surface of the pan is rounded with set hammer and light hammer. The last step before jump welding to the top edge of the pan is to bend the shield upward at about a 70-degree angle.

Frizzens, or batteries, also require considerable care in forging to a rather intricate shape. Essentially a frizzen is no more than a flat piece of iron bent almost to a right angle

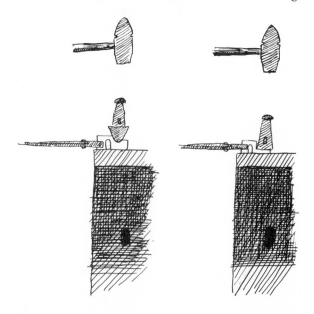

Forming pan brindle with fuller and set hammer

Flintlock frizzen

in the middle, with thin steel welded on its face and formed
so that it may be screwed to pan-bridle and lock plate in a
manner that will allow it to fit snugly over the pan and pivot
around the screw. The first doglock frizzens, as differentiated
from the curiously shaped batteries of snaphances, were flat
on all surfaces. Later frizzens of the seventeenth and eighteenth centuries, however, were chamfered and ridged on
the surfaces opposite the face and pan cover.

One begins with a flat bar of iron $\frac{3}{16}$-inch thick, $\frac{1}{2}$-inch
wide, and $2\frac{1}{2}$-inches long, though, as usual, it is much easier
to work on the end of a bar of handle length. First the end
of the bar is drawn out to form a $\frac{3}{4}$-inch-long stud in its
center, the stud being $\frac{3}{16}$-inch thick and $\frac{1}{4}$-inch wide at the
base. About $\frac{1}{4}$ inch from the base enough iron is left to form
a rounded boss, later to be drilled for the frizzen screw.
Beyond the boss the stud is drawn out for $\frac{1}{2}$ inch and tapered
to a chisel edge. Shoulders at the bases of stud and boss are
dressed square with a set hammer. Next the steel face is
welded on. A thin piece of steel, only $\frac{1}{16}$-inch thick, $1\frac{1}{2}$-
inches long, and slightly less than $\frac{1}{2}$-inch wide, is cut off.
Bench shears are used to cut the long edges of the steel with
two acutely angled cuts extending $\frac{1}{8}$ inch into each side.
The sharp points thus formed are then bent at a right angle
to the steel. Then the iron bar is brought to a white or yellow

heat, bordering on welding heat, and the cold steel, its points downward, is hammered into the iron so that the end of the steel is ½ inch from the screw stud. Flux is sprinkled around the edges. Before the iron cools it is put back into the fire and brought to welding heat. Because steel welds at a lower heat than iron, the pieces are heated with the iron down and the steel on top, in order to protect the thin steel. When welding heat is reached, the two pieces are joined with a light hammer.

Now the iron is cut off where the steel ends, and the end is forged or cut to a blunt elliptical curve.

Next the frizzen is bent to a 95-degree angle, 1 ¾ inches from its end, the bend being opposite the screw boss on the stud. When bent it is brought to white heat, the curved end is quenched in the slack tub for ½ inch, and the outside corner of the angle is upset to provide extra metal for a sharp corner. Then the corner is dressed square on the outside.

Chamfering of the surfaces opposite the face and pan cover may be done with a light double-faced hammer. The ridge between the chamfered faces may be emphasized with the veiner used by decorative ironworkers, and the inside of the corner, which is a mitered chamfer, is dressed with a special small top swage designed to provide a clean inside angle. Frizzens are finished by giving a slight concave curve to the battery face. The screw hole is drilled while the frizzen is in position, the pan bridle hole serving as a guide for the drill. The face is then hardened at a cherry-red heat. It does not require tempering because its iron backing will prevent any breakage of the thin steel face.

Hammers of flintlocks are also rather complicated mechanisms in themselves, consisting of three separate parts which must fit precisely. Shaping them uses some of the techniques of the decorative ironworker. This is appropriate, as the graceful goosenecks which characterize early- and middle-eighteenth-century locks are inherently decorative.

Early doglock and flintlock hammers were basically made in the same manner as early snaphance cocks—that is, with the horizontal shank forged as an integral part of the cock. Later this shank was transferred to the tumbler and the hammer fitted over it where it projected through the lock plate. Both types present some problems in forging.

Probably the easiest way to forge a hammer with attached shank is to follow the technique by which hinge pins are made. A strap of iron is welded tightly around an iron rod of ¼- or ⁵⁄₁₆-inch diameter. The joined pieces are then brought to orange-red and the rod is inserted in a hole in a plate, or in the swage block and upset, as with forming a nailhead, until the shank has been flattened perpendicularly to its original plane. After this the hammer is formed into its serpentine shape and dressed with a double-faced leaf hammer.

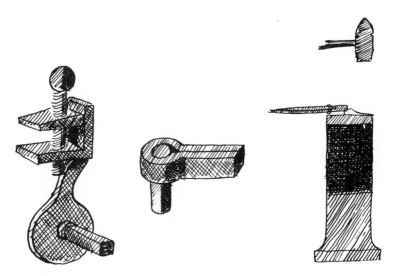

Left: Flintlock hammer with shank. Center: Forming shank. Right: Upsetting flat.

The type of lower jaw of early doglock and flintlock hammers can be formed by splitting the portion of the original strap to the point where the lower jaw and its perpendicular guide stud for the upper jaw occur. After splitting, the two legs of the split are bent so that they are at right angles to each other, and the bottom of the lower jaw is carefully shouldered with a set hammer where it projects from the stem of the hammer. On later hammers the guide stud is drawn out to the same thickness as the flat stem, and the shoulder where stud and jaw meet is dressed with a set hammer.

Top jaws are no more than flat pieces of iron the same dimensions as the lower jaws with the front edge tapered. Where a thin guide stud is used, the top jaw has a square notch punched on its back edge that fits the stud. Where a flat stud is used, no notch is needed.

The clamp screw for the hammer is generally upset into a spherical- or egg-shaped form on one end to serve as a head. Some have a notch cut into the top of the head with a chisel, others have a ⅛-inch hole drilled through the head. Finishing the hammer consists merely of drilling a hole in both jaws, the one in the top jaw being slightly larger than the other, and the hole in the lower jaw being threaded to receive the clamp screw.

Any competent smith can probably visualize a number of ways to form small objects of iron, such as an eighteenth-century flintlock hammer. The easiest, however, is to apply the basic techniques of fullering, offsetting and forging, with careful filing to develop final shape.

A hammer for a Kentucky or Pennsylvania rifle can be made on the end of a ½-inch by ¾-inch bar. When at a cherry-red heat the bar is fullered three-quarters of its width to rough-form the guide stud and the top of the lower jaw. The fuller is then moved ½ inch down the bar and the fullering repeated to rough-form the bottom of the lower jaw and

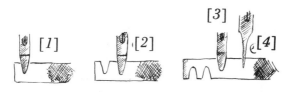

Steps in making later flintlock hammer

the top portion of the gooseneck. After this the bar is turned over and fullered on its opposite edge to form the remainder of the gooseneck and the base through which a square hole will be formed. A bottom fuller or a short length of rod may be used for fullering. Finished forging follows regular techniques.

The only other part of the outside mechanism of a flintlock is the frizzen spring, a V-shaped spring that holds the frizzen cover tight against the pan and also holds the cover up after firing. This may be made from a bar or rod of good cast steel of .75-percent carbon, ¼ inch in diameter and 2-inches long. First the rod is drawn out to a flat taper. Then the thick end is offset so that the set hammer may be used to flatten a small square portion perpendicular to the plane of the taper. This is drilled for a screw hole. Halfway down the spring, immediately adjacent to where the bend will occur, a small flat stud, projecting no more than ¹⁄₁₆ inch, is formed. The spring is heated to cherry red and bent approximately in its middle to form a V-shape. It is then tempered to a blue color. There are three methods of tempering, however, other than by color. One is to harden by bringing to a cherry red and quenching in an oil bath. The spring is then put on the fire and as soon as the oil adhering to it blazes it is again quenched. After three quenchings the spring is properly tempered. Another is to harden, wipe off all oil, and cover the spring thoroughly with a coating of soot created by a burning pine splinter. Then the spring is placed on a plate heated to orange-red. The moment the soot burns off the spring is again quenched in oil, which gives it proper temper. Still another method is, after hardening, to place the spring

397

Frizzen spring

on a hot plate and sprinkle it with sawdust. When the sawdust on the spring turns to tiny coals, the spring is quenched.

But the classic and most dependable method of tempering all the springs of a gunlock is by flashing. First the spring is let down by a wire into a pot of molten lead on the forge and left until the iron becomes cherry red. It is then quenched in oil to harden (or, in eighteenth-century terminology, to temper). Any residue of lead is picked or filed off and the spring is put into a container of oil which is placed on the fire. When the oil flashes, or catches flame, the container is taken from the fire and the flames smothered with a board placed over its top. When cool the spring is properly tempered (or drawn in eighteenth-century terms). This method was learned from Gary Brumfield, gunsmith at Williamsburg.

Frizzen springs are attached to the lock plate with a screw and are held in a solid position by the small stud at the bend, which is inserted into a tiny slot cut into the outside of the lock plate with a chisel corner.

The inside mechanism of a later-model flintlock consists of only five items, excepting screws. These are tumbler, mainspring, sear, searspring, and a bridle, which reinforces the pivot of both tumbler and sear. Percussion locks, and later the factory-made locks of hammer breech-loading shotguns, are identical in mechanism. All of these parts are rather easily formed except for the tumbler.

The sear is no more than a flat bar of iron, drawn out to a sharp edge on one end and bent to a right angle on the wide plane at the other end, with an upset portion in the middle to receive a screw. The searspring is of the same shape and is made in the same manner as the frizzen spring.

The bridle is made from a piece of flat iron $\frac{5}{16}$-inch

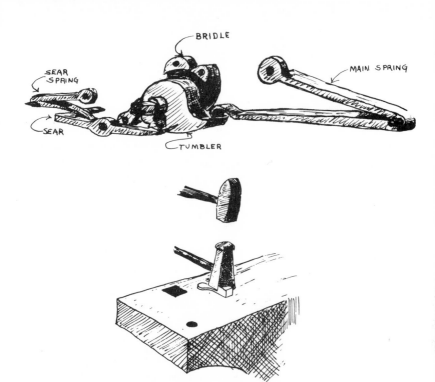

Top: Inside parts of a gun lock. Bottom: Forming brindle with round set hammer.

thick and ½-inch wide. It is shaped roughly into a modified isosceles-triangle form, the distance between the base and apex being long enough to reach from the front of the tumbler to the sear. After rough shaping, a boss ⅛-inch wide is formed at the base by drawing out the remainder of the piece to ¹⁄₁₆-inch thickness. In dressing the shoulder of the boss, a set hammer with a round, instead of the usual square, face is used, so that the shoulder will fit the curve of the tumbler as it is pivoted. After this a screw hole is drilled in each corner of the base, through which screws will be inserted into threaded holes in the lock plate. Two other holes are then drilled, one for the sear screw, which also screws into the lock plate, and one small hole that supports the inside pivot stud of the tumbler.

Tumblers are shaped like irregular elipses, the front portion having an arc, the bottom portion being notched in two places for the nose of the sear. A round shank ¼ inch in diameter with a square end which fits into the hammer is forged on the outside surface of the tumbler. The inside surface has a small ⅛-inch-diameter stud that protrudes ¹⁄₁₆ inch. This stud has precisely the same center axis as the shank.

Much the same technique is used in fashioning tumblers as in making bolts. A rod ½ inch in diameter is drawn out on one end, but offset to one side of the original center to a ¼-inch diameter and ½-inch length. Now this shank is given good square shoulders by heating it to orange-red, inserting it in a ¼-inch hole in the swage block or a heavy punch plate and hammering until the tumbler is ⁵⁄₁₆-inch thick.

Forming the pivot stud on the inside presents a little more of a problem. First the exact center of the pivot must be determined. This is done by lining up the center of the shank

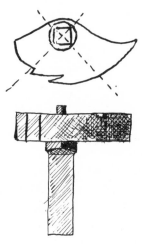

Lining up pivot stud

on two quarters, marking these points on the inside face of the tumbler with two lines drawn with soapstone. Where these lines cross marks the center of shank and stud. This point is then marked with a center punch. The tumbler is brought to orange-red and the intended stud is shouldered down with a small fuller. Then the surface is drawn out to the edge with a set hammer. The stud is rounded with a file and the tumbler is dressed to a proper shape with a file.

The mainspring is no more than a larger, more powerful version of frizzen and searspring, fastened to the lock plate with a screw and held in position with a small stud on the inside adjacent to the V bend. It has only one notable difference, a hook on the free end that fits into a notch on the tumbler. Later and finer locks had this hook split to fit a pin in a small hinge which was pinned to another slot in the tumbler.

Gun screws, which are made by the gunsmith, are formed with a small header. From the last quarter of the eighteenth century they were finished in a milling cutter held in the vise.

All sorts of guns, especially rifles and muskets, required a number of accoutrements, some of which were made by the blacksmith or gunsmith. One, essential for the rifle, was a bullet mold. This is easily made.

It resembles a pair of pliers with box-shaped jaws. First the blank is forged from a bar ⅜-inch square, or larger if intended for a musket or trade fusil. The bar is drawn down from its original dimensions to a long tapered flat tang, which will be the handle, with a square boss on its end. At times the boss may be made cylindrical or octagonal. Shoulders are squared with the set hammer. Two such pieces are needed to make the complete mold. The center of each boss is marked carefully with a center punch. Then the bosses are brought to orange-red and a shallow depression formed at the mark with the rounded end of a rod slightly smaller than the caliber of the bullet to be molded.

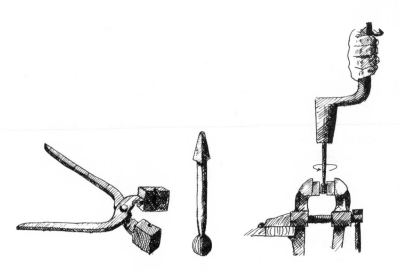

Left: Bullet mold. Center: Cherry. Right: Cherry rotating to dress depression in bullet mold.

After forging into shape the tangs are bent across their widths so that they will cross when the bosses are held together, as in forming the joint for a pair of tongs. A hole is drilled through both tangs where they cross and the two are bradded together.

A device called a "cherry" is now needed to cut accurately a spherical cavity in the mold. This, too, may be made by the smith. For a .30-caliber rifle ball, a rod of carbon tool steel 3-inches long and $\frac{1}{4}$ inch in diameter is needed. This is upset on one end to form a rough sphere nearly $\frac{5}{8}$ inch in diameter. The upset portion is dressed with the leaf hammer, and the rod is drawn out to $\frac{3}{16}$ inch in diameter where it meets the sphere, the drawn-out part tapering into the spherical part. Both sphere and taper are then smoothed with a file.

To insure that the sphere is round and that the taper enters it in the center tangent, the unfinished cherry should be put in either a lathe or a post drill and rotated slowly while a fine triangular file is held against it. It may be trued by the eye, but a sure way to determine its sphericity is to cut a small pattern from thin sheet metal. This may be held against the sphere and stem as it is filed, to show exactly where more filing is needed.

When as nearly perfect as eye can make it, the unfinished cherry is laid on a lead block, and vertical teeth are cut into sphere and stem with a small chisel, exactly as with cutting file teeth. Teeth should extend up the shank ⅜ inch above the sphere.

To temper, the cherry is covered with a mixture of one part flour and one part salt, mixed with water to the consistency of mud. It is then heated cherry red and quenched in brine to harden. Temper is drawn to a straw color on the sphere and purple on the stem.

Now the cherry is placed in the post-drill chuck, and the unfinished mold is clamped lightly around it so that the cherry fits into the rough depressions already formed in the mold blank. Then the drill is rotated slowly to dress the rough depressions in the blank and to cut the sprue channel. The sprue, incidentally, is the small projection formed on the rifle ball when lead is poured into the mold.

Dressing the mold can also be done in a hand brace, the mold block being held in the vise, which is tightened as the depression is cut out. Of course, the smith forges a square shank on the end of the cherry when he anticipates using a hand brace.

Many bullet molds have the handles filed to a sharp edge just behind the brad. This portion is used as a convenient clipper, or sprue cutter.

The smith also may make other small tools for the rifleman. For instance, most riflemen kept a small combination wrench–screwdriver in the bullet pouch, the spanner wrench fashioned on one end of a flat steel bar, the screwdriver on the other, both tempered to a blue color. The wrench is for removing the breech plug. Also, for percussion rifles, a wrench is needed to remove and replace nipples. Most flintlocks were also equipped with a pick, no more than a short piece of steel wire, sharpened on one end and formed into a ring on the other, and tempered to a blue. The pick is used to clear the touchhole on the side of the breech.

The worm, which fitted on the end of the ramrod, is also a necessary adjunct to a muzzle-loading firearm. It is used to pull out a charge already loaded into the barrel. To make one type of worm, the smith requires a small piece of spring steel ½-inch wide and 1-inch long. This is split to within ⅜ inch from one end, and the legs of the split are drawn out to thin wires. The unsplit section is then scarfed on its edges and welded into a socket over the tip of an anvil bick heated to cherry red. After welding, the two wires are loosely spiraled clockwise around a rod. The worm is tempered like a spring. A small 1/16-inch hole is drilled through both sides of the upper end of the socket so that when it is placed on the end of a wooden ramrod it may be pinned securely to the ramrod.

Left: Combination screwdriver-wrench. Right: Socketed worm.

Some ramrods are equipped with a threaded socket into which the worm screws. For this design the worm is formed by splitting a steel rod and drawing out the legs of the split as before. They are then spiraled around another rod, the butt is threaded, and the worm is tempered.

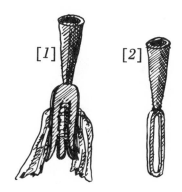

Cleaning tips: [1] flat, [2] oval.

Another rifle and shotgun accouterment is the cleaning tip. Early cleaning tips were made from flat steel, one end being welded into a socket, as with the worm, the remainder being split to form three projections. Each projection is tapered slightly, with file or by forging, and tempered like a spring. The cleaning rag is woven between the three projections. Cleaning tips can also be made on the end of a rod which is threaded to screw into the socket on the ramrod.

On later cleaning tips, the lower part is split once and the ends of the legs are drawn out and welded together as with a chain link, thus forming a long steel oval into which the cleaning rag is inserted.

Many cannon parts, particularly the trunnion hinges and key bolts, are quite difficult to forge accurately.

The front key bolts on both naval and field cannons must have a head that is slotted vertically, so that the hinge key may be inserted to lock the hinge in place. Also, it has a collar below the slot which acts as a regular bolthead. On some naval carriages the bolthead and key slot are forged at about a 10-degree angle from the axis of the bolt.

Making the slot is fairly easy. The end of the rod is drawn out to a tang two and one half times as long as the width of the key. If the outside of the slot is to be round, it is

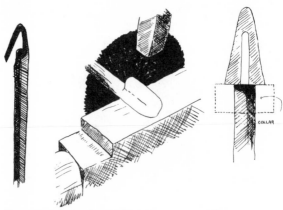

Left: Drawing out key slot showing welding position. Center: Doubling stock by welding. Right: Finished slot before collar is welded on.

drawn out while placed in a lower round swage of the same diameter as the rod. The set hammer is used to form a square shoulder at the beginning of the drawn-out portion. Then the end of the drawn-out portion and the edge of the rod adjacent to the shoulder are scarfed. The drawn-out portion is then formed around a drift the size of the key, so that the scarfed sections meet.

For a heavy cannon it may be necessary to have the walls of the slot heavier than is possible with drawing out. In such a case the end of the rod is doubled, if of wrought iron for a distance slightly longer than the width of the key, and faggot-welded. The welded portion is then forged square and offset on the side opposite the doubled end, to form shoulders on each side of the rod. Mild steel may be upset to acquire the desired thickness. After welding or upsetting, the square portion is punched with a rectangular punch and drifted to fit the key.

The collar below the slot is formed usually from a square bar which is wrapped around the rod, exactly as in making regular bolt heads, and butt-welded at the same time that it is welded to the rod.

When wrapped prior to welding one must be sure that there is a gap between the ends of the collar iron equal to its thickness. The exact length of the collar bar may be determined by wrapping a piece of lead around the bar, then straightening to see its length. Another method is to wrap a square bar around the rod spirally so that the end is overlapped. This may then be removed and cut while hot to provide the necessary gap. The collar thus cut may then be hammered flat, the rod inserted in it and the two welded together.

Collars may be dressed with a hammer around the edges, or swaged in a regular boltheader. A set hammer is used to dress the joint between slot wall and collar. Some key bolts are bent at an obtuse angle at the point where bolt and head join. To form this accurately the smith requires a special boltheader, which he may make himself, consisting of a plate with a hole drilled in it, forged so that its top surface is slanted to the proper degree to form the desired angle in the bolt.

Left: Method of measuring and cutting collar.
Right: Angled plate for crooking hinge bolt.

In addition to the key bolts, cannon carriages, naval and field, also require hinge bolts with heads through which the hinges rotate. The heads of naval hinge bolts are no more than rings, usually unwelded and with no collar. There are special heads on the hinge bolts of field-artillery carriages, however. These are rectangular in one dimension and roughly triangular in the side section. This part is forged at the end of the rod with a depression half the width of bolt and the collar formed at its base. Then the collar is welded on and the extension bent over perpendicular to the rod and fitting over the collar. A second welding heat is then taken, the rod dropped into a boltheader, and the extension welded to the collar. The depression that fits over the hinge pin is formed with a fuller and dressed by hammering on a rod the same diameter as the pin section of the hinge.

Trunnion hinges are a little more difficult to shape than

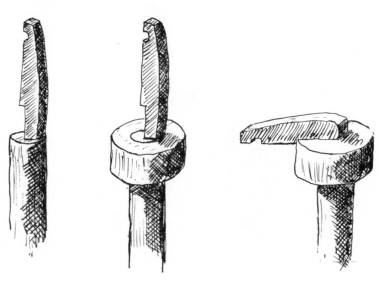

Steps in forming a hinge bolt.

may be imagined at first glance. The complications rest on the fact that cannon cheeks are not parallel, and the trunnions, therefore, are not quite perpendicular to the axis of the cheeks. Therefore the curved portion of the hinges must be formed at a slight angle to the edges.

Trunnion hinges are normally forged from flat iron from ⅜ - to ½-inch thick and of a width that matches the thickness of the cheeks, usually about 2½ to 3 inches. The exact length, however, should be determined by shaping a heavy wire or a lead bar over the trunnion and the top surface of the cheeks as the trunnions rest in the half-pound depression in the cheeks. When this pattern has been made, it is accurately marked where the corner of the flat and curved portions of the hinge occur, and then it is straightened.

The flat iron is then heated to a white heat where the corners are to be formed and upset at these points, then forged so that the upsets protrude from only one surface of the iron.

Next the curve is formed in a large round swage, cast from a wooden pattern made by the smith or a patternmaker. This swage differs from the swage block in that the corners where half-round depression and top surface meet are rounded off. The heavy flat iron is heated to white heat, placed on the swage so that the angle is correct, and formed roughly into the depression with a large top fuller. It is dressed by laying

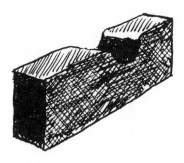

Special angled swage for forming trunnion hinge

a rod of the same diameter as the trunnion across the iron and beating it down with an 8-pound sledge. While the large rod is still in place, the corners on the bottom of the hinge, coincident with the previously upset portions, are dressed by further upsetting against the rod and by using the flatter or set hammer to make the bottom surface of the hinge parallel to the top of the swage.

There are two alternative methods of forming corners. One is to weld on a triangular section of iron where corners occur. The other is to make two perpendicular cuts halfway through the iron. After the curve has been formed a square section of iron is welded into the cuts to form a sharp corner.

Trunnion hinges have rounded ends, upset so that the section is circular. Upsetting should be done at a light red heat, and in the same heat the ends may be dressed by holding them upside down and hammering into a bottom round swage of proper diameter.

Trunnion hinges are finished by punching a hole immediately adjacent to each rounded end. On naval carriages

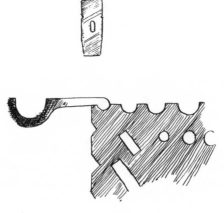

Forming cylindrical end of hinge with a swage block

both holes may be round, one to fit the circular head of the key bolt, the other to fit the hinge bolt. On field-artillery pieces, holes for the key bolt and hinge bolt are round, but a rectangular hole must be punched between the hinge-bolt hole and the rounded end of the pin to accommodate the right-angle extension above the head of the hinge bolt.

A number of other special bolts, hooks, eyes, and rings are found on both naval and field guns. There are no particular problems to forging any of these pieces, except, perhaps, in the ring nuts needed for horizontal bolts in certain field carriages. These may be made by welding a straight rod

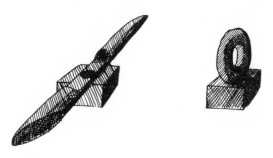

How a ring nut is made

across a square nut blank. Then the rod is flattened across the weld and a hole of proper diameter is punched through rod and nut blank. The rod is now scarfed on both ends, formed into a ring, and welded as with a chain link. Lastly the hole is reamed true and threaded to fit the bolt end. For ringed boltheads the ring is made on the end of the rod then the collar welded. The square collar is formed in a boltheader.

Field cannons and some naval and garrison cannons have an elevating screw, which raises or lowers the breach of the tube. These are equipped with four handles exactly in the form of a four-handled valve wrench, and they are made exactly the same way, from a heavy bar formed with a boss in the middle and with the ends split, spread, and shaped to form the handles.

The unfortunate need for more and more powerful weapons in a more and more populous world probably has had as much to do with the disappearance of the blacksmith as any other one factor. Eli Whitney's concept of mass production for muskets began the substitution of milling machines for forge and hammer and anvil as a means for shaping gun parts. The development of steampower brought on the increasing use of swage and die under great mechanical hammers and eliminated the need for a skilled and highly trained craftsman working with double-ended hammers.

Even by the time of the Civil War, when many communities over the world were still utterly dependent on the blacksmith for utensils, weapons, and tools, the manufacturing of musket barrels was done by methods impossible in the village smithy. Most American muskets of the time had barrels formed from a large round billet of iron, about a foot long and 4 inches in diameter and pierced through the center. After inserting a rod in the center hole, these billets were repeatedly heated and run through a series of reducing rollers until drawn out to the proper diameter of musket barrels. Not a hammer touched them from beginning to end.

In contrast, as reported in *The Armourer and His Craft*, by Charles ffoulkes (published in 1912), in the early years of the twentieth century there were smiths in Syria who were still making chain mail by hand. Syria, however, had fallen far behind and was still living in an older time. The industrial armorers of the modern West had by then replaced the skill and improvisation of hand and brain for engineering efficiency. They thereby sounded the tocsin for Hephaestus and his unique breed in the actual making of weapons. The smith, though, is still important in making the tools that keep modern, mechanized weapons in operation.

11.

THE MODERN BLACKSMITH

One time, about the time this book was first published, most people considered the art of blacksmithing "dead," relegated to the lost arts, having outlived its usefulness in an age of machinery and electronic devices. Those people were wrong. To paraphrase Samuel Butler, they reached sufficient conclusions based on insufficient premises.

The epilogue of the first edition of this book talked sadly of the demise of a noble activity. It described the curfew, the covering of the fire in the ancient, once indispensable smithy and sadly described the nostalgic excitement, the color and action, the inexplicable mystique of the glowing forge, the flying sparks, the ringing anvil that gave the smith a distinction that had been denied his fellow craftsmen and had been lost in the rush of impersonal progress.

But the mystique, the basic fascination of blacksmithing cannot be lost, it seems, so long as the human heart responds to its basic nature. The old forges, described as forever cold, had an unnoticed phoenix slumbering in the ashes, stirring sleepily in the shell of the hearth, waiting until the breath of interest once more fanned the fire and made it burn again. Now the fire is once more glowing brightly and the phoenix is rising. One can easily enumerate the events and happenings which fanned the flame to life once more. It is rather more difficult to explain why these things happened.

Of course, a most important factor is the rapid growth and revitalization of the craft movement in America, starting slowly in the 1920s and expanding greatly since World War II. During that period, especially after 1945, the crafts earned status as arts and began to be taught in formal courses in the schools of art in many universities. Crafts taught in the university level consisted mainly of pottery, weaving, silversmithing, and, in a few cases, glassblowing. At the same time established craft schools such as Penland in North Carolina, Haystack in Maine, John C. Campbell in North Carolina, and a few others in Kentucky and the Northeast, began to grow. People suddenly wanted to learn crafts as a means of livelihood. Many succeeded in making a good living from their craftsmanship. This success both exposed the crafts to the public, expanding the market, and stimulated even more young people to learn a craft.

Blacksmithing was largely overlooked in the early years of the craft movement, but probably for good reasons. The equipment needed for a good smithy is far more complicated and much more expensive generally than that needed for pottery and weaving. Besides, there were no instructors. Most of the smiths extant at the time were old-time general smiths or farm smiths, most of them oriented to the mechanics of blacksmithing instead of to its artistic potential. Also the style of houses and office buildings, churches and schools being built did not call for elaboration of design with wrought iron. And, there were few places indeed in America where truly good design in wrought iron could be produced. Of course, the forced economics of the Great Depression discouraged the use of an enduring but relatively expensive art form. But there were a few people, who having been exposed somewhere to the fascination of ironworking had become enthusiastic about its potential and enthralled by its mystique. Among others there was L. Brent Kington, a professor in metalwork in the art department of Southern Illinois University. During the 1960s he began to produce wrought iron sculpture, formed of red-hot iron between hammer and anvil. As he got into the craft his enthusiasm grew as did the frustration born of ignorance and the lack of a source for learning techniques.

Mr. Kington organized and executed the first workshop on blacksmithing, held on the SIU campus in the spring of 1970. Participants consisted of art students from ten university art departments located from Colorado to Georgia. For three days, under the tutelage of one of the few known people at the time who had some knowledge of all aspects of the field, about sixty students observed basic techniques at a battery of forges and anvils set up on an outlying section of the beautiful campus. On the first day the forges were still lit and the anvils still ringing until after dark, and on succeeding days the forges were lit at the crack of dawn and continued until after dark again. Most of the students and instructors involved had never seen a blacksmith in action before. A few had worked in iron peripherally, but lacked knowledge and experience. All responded with fervor and dedication. Blacksmithing as an art earned recognition in academic circles because of this workshop. Several of the students who attended have since become full-time artist-blacksmiths.

In 1973 a second event occurred which was to have a most important effect on the renaissance of blacksmithing as an art, this time as an event tied with history. Westville, a fine restoration village of the 1850s located near Lumpkin, Georgia, held a two-day Blacksmith's Convention in March and sent invitations to some 150 people all over the country who had indicated past interest in blacksmithing. The response was amazing. Fifty participants came, several from California and more from the Northeast and the Midwest as well as the Southeast. Some were older men who practiced the trade in small rural communities. Others were young smiths who operated their own shops in various parts of the country. Amazingly, the rest was composed of doctors, advertising executives, industrialists, airline pilots, salesmen, and a goodly number of students and college instructors. This convention, as with the SIU workshop, again demonstrated the power of enthusiasm for working iron as a means of getting people of diverse backgrounds together as friends and dedicated students. Before the affair was over the assembled smiths formed the Artist-Blacksmith Association of North America (ABANA) with twenty dues-paid members and promise of the first annual conference the following year. Also established at this time was *The Anvil's Ring*, a quarterly newsletter distributed to members.

Jud Nelson, the venerable and expert smith from Sugar Valley, Georgia, was delighted. He remembered that as a young man he took every opportunity to visit smiths and smithies, to observe techniques, ask questions, and discuss problems. But, he said, in the last twenty years the smithies and smiths had disappeared. Now ABANA and its conferences could replace his visits, for he could talk to fifty or more smiths at the same time in one place, with gratifying results.

Undoubtedly ABANA has had a startling influence on the art of blacksmithing just because it does offer a means of communication. By this writing its rolls have grown from the original twenty to almost four hundred, with members located in all parts of the United States, as well as a number in Canada and at least two in Europe. Since its formation the group has held two additional conferences, the first at Westville again, the other in Greenville, South Carolina. The next is planned for 1976 on the campus of SIU with an exhibition representing two hundred years of the art of blacksmithing in America, a fitting recognition of the basic importance of the smith in American history.

But while the academic art community may be given credit for first exposing blacksmithing to the craft movement, certainly ABANA has done more to stimulate interest in the art than any other force, mainly because it has fulfilled the function that Jud Nelson finds so essential—that of providing communication among smiths of all degrees. It has brought together a most interesting and devoted group composed of professionals, amateurs, students, and instructors, all of whom contribute as much as they draw out of the groups.

Also ABANA has encouraged the formation of local blacksmithing groups which meet more frequently than the national organization and which expose the beauty of wrought iron art as well as the fascination of its techniques to local communities.

There are undoubtedly many blacksmiths in the country who have not yet heard of ABANA and are not members of that new organization. What induced them to become smiths no one, not even themselves, can always say. Most of them have had only a fleeting exposure to forge and anvil before succumbing to the lure of blacksmithing. Some became artistic blacksmiths after becoming farriers, where they learned the basic tools and techniques of blacksmithing as a part of shoeing horses. A few, and the number is growing, have observed blacksmithing workshops while preparing for art degrees at various schools and universities and have made the decision, while students, to become blacksmiths instead of smithing in other metals such as silver and gold. In some cases professors of metalworking, such as Brent Kington and Al Paley, have switched the emphasis of their creative urge from other metals to iron and by so doing have inspired their students to investigate the potential of iron as an art medium.

A few years ago students and instructors leaned heavily toward iron sculpture, but that is changing as the art grows. In the late 1970s many of the students are planning to open their own shops to produce some sculpture, but mostly to provide sculptural beauty to such utilitarian items as hearth tools and screens, cooking utensils, gates, lighting fixtures, and hardware, some of these items being forged in traditional style, others reflecting outstanding contemporary design.

Most of these young smiths find that blacksmithing can provide a comfortable living if they attend to the business aspects of the shop as required in a modern, sophisticated society. They must find a source of essential capital, for instance. They must track down and learn to use some modern equipment such as power hammers, electric grinders, and acetylene and electric welding devices. They must find, and often the search is difficult, such things as anvils and anvil tools, basic tongs and basic set tools. Also they must find a reliable source for good coal, a factor which seems to become more and more difficult as the steel mills of the world buy trainloads and shiploads of coal for their own massive production.

Fortunately, the list of suppliers which offer blacksmithing equipment is growing slowly and there are still reliable sources for such equipment in America, Europe, and Japan, although the cost is high.

Of course, the blacksmith can make most of his own tools. But without the tools the starting blacksmith must spend his productive time making what he can, substituting his valuable time for capital, retaining enough capital only to provide himself and his family with the necessities of life. Even by this approach, however, he cannot make his basic anvil, or power hammer or modern welding equipment, without which he will be forever enslaved to making small items by hand, and might therefore chance a risky livelihood.

Another problem of the blacksmith is that the items he makes are sturdy and enduring. They do not wear out quickly if properly designed and made; they do not need replacing; they seldom break.

Regardless of the lack of a replacement market for expendable merchandise, however, so important to the cosmetic affluence of the modern-western world, the blacksmith has a marvelous potential market for all types of production. For, cosmetic or not, the relative affluence we now enjoy has swelled the middle economic class of homeowners and given them to a large degree an opportunity to purchase elegant, artistic items for their homes. These include the blacksmith's production of small things such as durable kitchen utensils and large things such as garden gates and house railings of contemporary or traditional design. As the number of smiths grows and the exposure of their art increases, so does the market for what they make.

Architects are once more getting interested in artistic but functional ironwork as are their colleagues, the interior designers. Office buildings, schools, churches, apartments, hotels, restaurants all may be enhanced by wrought-iron banisters and lamps and chandeliers, and iron adapts very well under the attentions of an artist to the contemporary design frequently chosen and sometimes dictated to modern architects by circumstances of cost and technology.

Iron has been important to architecture for centuries. It never really lost its importance in this exciting field; it merely lost its source of supply. But as the number of blacksmiths grows the interest of architects and designers is once more being focused on the beauty of wrought iron. After all, at one time, all of the hardware of any building, all hinges, door knobs, locks, knockers, grilles and screens, was provided by the smith, each item carrying with it to posterity the indefinable contribution of the artist, the exclusive beauty of a unique piece of art. The civilizing presence of artistic, handwrought iron has an excellent chance of once more adding to the overall effect of architectural design in any sort of building.

Artistic ironworking is undoubtedly at the forefront of the revival of blacksmithing as a part of modern life. Yet, the mechanical skills and understanding of the ubiquitous nineteenth-century blacksmith are also regaining importance, again based on the changing economy and society found in the last twenty-five years of the millennium. Once, before energy shortages, inflation, and lack of capital, many industries bought tools, used them, wore them out, and replaced them with brand new pickaxes, probes, air hammer bits, and other tools. Now, suddenly, as an economic measure, there is a demand for blacksmiths capable of resharpening such tools, or in some cases making, by hand, new specialized tools in quantities insufficient to justify mass production. The smiths who have a knowledge of steel and tempering are few indeed at this time, but the demand for such knowledge will undoubtedly entice many young mechanically minded smiths into this specialized field.

In smaller towns and rural areas the smith who is mechanically inclined should be able to build a most lucrative trade repairing and altering, and perhaps creating, hand and mechanical farm equipment. He will, of course, use modern welding and grinding equipment on many jobs, but the availability of forge and anvil and ancient blacksmithing techniques offers great advantages and much wider creative latitude than can be found in a regular welder's shop.

David Wall, of Atlanta, Georgia, comfortably supports his family by forging artistic items and using the modern equipment of his shop, along with his forge, to fabricate exciting special projects for industrial and recreational markets.

Perhaps the greatest problem that hampers the growth of

blacksmithing's revival is a lack of training facilities and a lack of instructors in using the specialized equipment of the smithy. Certainly this situation has improved greatly in the last six years. Good training is available at Southern Illinois University under the tutelage of Brent Kington, and the same may be said for the instruction of Al Paley at New York University, and at a few other universities. Frank Turley, of Santa Fe, offers an eight-week course in basic, and some advanced, techniques of blacksmithing. His enrollment is limited, however, and his courses are usually filled a year or two in advance. Alexander Weygers, blacksmith, sculptor, and author, offers some training at his school of sculpture located at Carmel Valley, California, but as with Turley, his enrollment is limited.

Ivan Bailey, a professional smith of Savannah, offers a maximum of three apprenticeships a year, all that he can handle in addition to producing commissions which keep him constantly busy. Other practicing smiths offer openings for apprentices but, alas, not all of them are qualified by experience and knowledge to properly teach the art. Several of the younger practicing smiths with successful operations have learned the basic techniques and use of tools from older, sometimes semiretired smiths. Smiths of the old school, however, are becoming scarcer and scarcer. And the young men who learn from the few left should certainly supplement training with art education.

Another limited source of instruction may be found in workshop programs sponsored by various historical foundations, folk art schools and craft organizations. Cooperstown, New York, occasionally offers a three- or four-day workshop for eight or ten people. The John C. Campbell Folk School, Brasstown, North Carolina, offers several two- to three-week courses in blacksmithing every year as does the Naples Valley Craft School at Naples, New York, and the Peter Valley operation in Layton, New Jersey. The American Crafts Council, in conjunction with regional and state councils, is including blacksmithing in more and more of its very well organized two- or three-day craft workshops which are conducted several times a year. A few art schools such as the Philadelphia School of Art and the Atlanta College of Art offer special courses or one- to three-day workshops in blacksmithing once or twice a year.

One dedicated to becoming a smith who can find no place to obtain formal instruction should search his area for the growing number of amateur/professional blacksmith's clubs or guilds which are springing up all over the country. These can introduce the neophyte to basic equipment and techniques. Furthermore, the people in such groups, men and women of all ages and occupations, can be of great help in suggesting training schools and where to purchase equipment and material.

Of course, the best teacher is still experience. Aspiring blacksmiths must have all possible exposure to established smiths, but the art can only be learned eventually with forge aglow and hammer in hand. Those who wish to become smiths should set up a shop in the basement or back yard, purchase the basic tools, buy or build a forge, find a source for good shop coal, acquire some iron, and start smithing. The aspirant should enroll in a painting or drawing course, read all available literature on smithing and art, find workshops to attend, and seek diligently any smith in his area who will talk and demonstrate. Most established or retired smiths are generous with their help to those who want to learn. There are many more smiths around the country now than would have been imagined in the 1960s. ABANA, for instance, has members, amateur and professional, in most areas, and the gaps are being filled as smiths learn of the existence of ABANA.

It seems that more and more historical restorations are springing up in all regions, most with plans to establish a working smithy as part of the restoration. These restorations offer potential employment to many who wish to make a career of ironworking, but there are pitfalls of which both smith and restoration should be aware. This time of rebirth for blacksmithing is not in the same world economically as the halcyon days portrayed by restorations. A smith simply cannot produce enough to guarantee a good livelihood with the hand equipment proper for an historical-type shop. Either he must be paid a salary by the restoration or he must have a well-capitalized modern shop somewhere to produce items for sale at an acceptable price, in quantity enough to make a decent living.

And while he may find and make enough equipment for a back yard shop in which to learn, he must find $10,000–$20,000 capital to equip a production shop which he can operate profitably by himself or with one or two helpers. Fortunately, some banks are beginning today to recognize a smithy as a good business risk, as are the managements of some historical projects.

The risk will not pay off, however, if the smith does not charge enough for his work. A retired Texas blacksmith once said that there are two reasons for a blacksmith's going to Hell: one is hitting blue iron, the other is not charging enough. Young smiths starting out simply must charge $12–$15 an hour or they will not make a living. Modern equipment will allow them to produce an item more quickly, without compromising the unique quality of a hand-wrought piece, but skill and a sense of design are of equal importance. Attractive items must be designed to be made relatively quickly and sold at a proportionately lower, and more attractive price.

The new blacksmiths are beginning to gain more exposure to the public through newspapers, television, magazines, and craft fairs. As a consequence their skills are becoming more familiar to the public and the market for their production of things large and small is growing. Numbers of professional artist-blacksmiths shops are being established in every part of the country. One- to ten-man shows devoted solely to ironwork are being organized more and more frequently from places as far away as Chattanooga, Tennessee, and Worchester, Massachusetts, giving the art status and recognition of the sort long enjoyed by other arts and crafts. The resulting competition, still not intense in the 1970s, is raising the standards of craftsmanship and design.

Blacksmithing, it seems, is the last of the basic crafts to enjoy a revival, possibly because its art function was necessarily abandoned to a large degree in the waning days of handcraftsmanship in the later nineteenth century. Of course, there are outstanding exceptions to this premise such as the late Samuel Yellin, Julius Schramm, Fritz Kuhn, and Fritz Ulrich, and the living Francis Whitaker, Jess Hawley, Jud Nelson, and others, who have maintained high standards of excellence and intellect until today.

Blacksmithing as an art is now being reborn with a vengeance. It has proved in the last few years that its mystique, its character is as sound and compelling as in the legendary days of Hephaestus. Its place in modern life is far from being filled, leaving ample opportunity for young men and women who will apply themselves to the work and to the critical design criteria required by the blacksmith.

The art will grow in its contributions to the quality of modern life; it is growing. Its attraction seems as immortal as the race of man.

LIST OF SOURCES FOR
EQUIPMENT AND SUPPLIES

COAL

Good blacksmith's coal is difficult to find but still available in a limited number of local coalyards in the United States. In other areas the smith must find a mine in his region which produces metallurgical coal and make arrangements directly with the mine for buying coal by the truckload. Metallurgical coal mines are found in Alabama, Alberta, Arkansas, Georgia, Montana, Oklahoma, Pennsylvania, Tennessee, Virginia, West Virgina, and Wyoming. A letter to the Department of Geology or its equivalent in any of these states will usually yield a list of mines producing metallurgical coal with addresses.

It is suggested that several smiths in an area cooperate in obtaining coal by together ordering a 10- to 20-ton (or larger) truckload. Most full-time shops require from 3 to 10 tons of coal a year.

In areas where industrial charcoal (not briquets) for chemical and other type filters and for making briquets is produced, charcoal may sometimes be bought at the kiln. It makes a very good fuel.

METAL

Rods, bars and sheets of 10-20 hot rolled mild steel may be purchased at almost any local steel supply house.

Frequently tool steel, spring steel, and scrap mild steel can be found at local junkyards at a good price. Junkyards also might yield scrap wrought iron, which was used for pipes and bridge members until the 1960s.

Hand-puddled wrought iron may also be found at Creative Metal Crafts, 1616 9th Street, Santa Monica, California, 90404.

Tool steel and specialty steel, such as stainless, may sometimes be found at local steel supply houses or ordered direct from the companies listed below. Inquiry should be made before ordering, however, regarding minimum orders and local supply houses which may stock the type steel desired.

Colt Industries, Crucible Specialty Metals Division

St. Mark Street, Auburn, Mass. 01501	(617) 832-5353
321 West 32nd Street (P.O. Box 21128), Charlotte, N.C. 28206	(704) 372-3073
4501–4531 W. Cortand Street, Chicago, Ill. 60639	(312) 722-0300
10555 Taconic Terrace, Cincinnati, Oh. 45215	(513) 771-1310
31400 Aurora Road (P.O. Box 39099) Solon, Ohio 44139	(216) 248-9400
6999 Huntly Rd, Columbus, Oh. 43299	(614) 885-2751
P.O. Box 5248, Arlington, Tex. 76011	(817) 261-7721
4920 E. Nevada Avenue, Detroit, Mich. 48234	(313) 366-4400
105 South Keystone Ave. (P.O. Box 11138), Indianapolis, Ind. 46201	(317) 638-4501

22400 S. Lucerne St., Carson, Calif. 90749	(213)	775-7344
9125 Cote de Liesse Dorval 760, P.Q., Canada	(514)	636-1250
P.O. Box 556, West Caldwell, N.J. 07007	(201)	226-9300
Buffalo Area		Ent. 9389
New York City Area	(212)	461-6500
Rochester Area		Ent. 9389
Syracuse: State Fair Blvd. (P. O. Box 1391) Syracuse, N.Y. 13201	(315)	487-4114
1730 S.W. Skyline Blvd., Portland, Oregon 97221	(503)	292-0144
Sorel, Quebec, Canada	(514)	743-7931
2 Blair Drive, Bramalea, Ontario, Canada	Brampton:	(416)	457-2501
	Malton:	(416)	454-1211
2911 Como Avenue, S.E., Minneapolis, Minn. 55414	(612)	331-6320

Uddeholm Steel Corporation

721 Union Blvd., Totowa, N.J. 07511		
	N.J.	(201) 256-8000
	N.Y.	(212) 594-6872
4540 E. 71st Street, Cleveland, Oh. 44105	(216)	271-2223
30712 Industrial Rd., Livonia, Mi. 48150	(313)	522-0030
1400 Nicholas Blvd., Elk Grove, Il. 60007	(312)	437-2710
Box 2428, Santa Fe Springs, Cal. 90670	(213)	945-1551
797 Industrial Rd., San Carlos, Cal. 94070	(415)	591-7358

38 Edwin R., South Windsor, Ct.   (203) 289-7955
06074

16140 S.W. 72nd Ave., Portland, Or.   (503) 620-1032
97223

500 Lee Industrial Boulevard, Austell,   (404) 944-3200
Ga. 30001   .

7901 Sovereign Row, Dallas, Tex.
75247

110 Florida St., Farmingdale, L.I.,   (516) 694-4367
N.Y. 11735

5711 Cunningham Road, Houston,   (713) 466-1500
Tex. 77040

U.S. Steel Supply

P.O. Box 81107, Atlanta, Ga. 30341   (404) 451-4204

1600 Bush Street, Baltimore, Md.
21230   (301) 837-4900

P.O. Box 8252, Birmingham, Ala.   (205) 783-4364
35218

P.O. Box 276, Brighton, Mass. 02135   (617) 782-9400
Boston, Mass.

P.O. Box 222, Buffalo, N.Y. 14240   (716) 891-7500

P.O. Box 7310, Chicago, Ill. 60680   (312) 646-3211

4524 West Mitchell Avenue,   (513) 541-4285
Cincinnati, Oh. 45232

P.O. Box 6808, Cleveland, Oh. 44101   (216) 441-3434

2920 East Randol Mill Road, Arling-   (817) 261-3881
ton, Tex. 76011, Dallas, Tex.

4305 East 60th Avenue, Commerce   (303) 288-0781
City, Col. 80022, Denver, Col.

P.O. Box 368, Taylor, Mich. 48180,
Detroit, Mich.   (313) 292-8000

EQUIPMENT

Brodhead-Garrett Company
4560 East 71st Street
Cleveland, Oh. 44105
(Warehouses all over the U.S.)

Buffalo Forge Company
Buffalo, N.Y. 14203

The Centaur Company
117 North Spring Street
Burlington, Wis. 53105

Champion Blower Company
Pottsville, Penn. 17901

The Forge & Anvil
P.O. Box 179
Helen, Ga. 30345

Little Giant, Inc.
Mankato, Minn. 56001

T & H Pettinghaus
261 First Street
Palisades Park, N.J. 07650

Other sources of equipment include secondhand industrial supply houses in larger cities, junkyards, antique dealers specializing in tools, and the farm publications published by some states which include classified advertising. Smiths desiring equipment may advertise for what is wanted in farm publications and antique periodicals.

BIBLIOGRAPHY

American Indian Tomahawks, Harold L. Peterson (New York: Museum of the American Indian, 1965).

Armourer and His Craft, The, Charles M. ffoulkes (New York: B. Blom, 1967, based on copyright of 1912).

Arms and Armor in Colonial America, Harold L. Peterson (New York: Bramhall House, 1956).

Art in Iron (Chicago: *The American Ironsmith*, 1932–1934).

Blacksmith, The (London: Rural Industries Bureau, 1959).

Blacksmith's and Farrier's Tools at Shelburne Museum, H. R. Bradley Smith (Shelburne, Vt.: The Shelburne Museum, Inc., 1966).

Blacksmith and the Welder, The (TM10–440), United States Army (Washington: War Department, 1941).

Blacksmithing, R. W. Selvidge and J. M. Allton (Peoria, Ill.: Manual Arts Press, 1925).

Daggers and Edged Weapons of Hitler's Germany, The, Maj. James P. Atwood (Berlin: Privately printed, 1965).

Decorative Antique Ironwork, Henry René D'Allemagne (New York: Dover Publications, Inc., 1968, from the 1924 French catalogue of the Le Secq des Tournelles Museum of Rouen).

Decorative Iron Work (London: Rural Industries Bureau, 1964).

De Re Metallica, Georgius Agricola, trans. by Herbert Clark Hoover and Lou Henry Hoover from the first Latin edition of 1556 (New York: Dover Publications, Inc., 1950, based on copyright of 1912).

Elemental Wrought Iron, Thomas Walter Bollinger (Milwaukee, Wisc.: The Bruce Publishing Co., 1930).

Encyclopaedia Britannica, "Forging" and "Iron and Steel" (1910).

Encyclopedia of Iron Work (New York: Weyhe, 1927).

Encyclopedia of Trades and Industries, Denis Diderot, ed. by Charles Coulston Gillespie (Paris: Briasson, David, Le Breton et Durand, 1767; New York: Dover Press, 1959).

Examples of Metal Work (Boston: Boston Architectural Club, 1930).

Forge, The, Thomas Sigismund Stribling (Garden City, N.Y.: Sun Dial Press, 1938).

Forge Practice, John Lord Bacon (Brooklyn, N.Y.: Braunworth and Co., 1919).

431

Forging Handbook, Waldemar Naujohs (New York: The American Society for Metals, 1939).

Forging and Heat Treatment of Steel, Thomas P. Hughes (Minneapolis, Minn.: Burgess-Roseberry Co., 1930).

Forging and Smithing, Lynn C. Jones (New York and London: The Century Co., 1924).

Furniture Treasury, Wallace Nutting (New York: The Macmillan Co., 1963).

History of Metallography, A, Cyril Stanley Smith (Chicago: University of Chicago Press, 1960).

Iron and Brass Implements of the English and American House, J. Seymour Lindsay (London: Alec Tiranti, 1964).

Iron Making and Iron Working in Ancient Russia, U.S. Department of Commerce (Alexandria, Virginia 22151).

Järnsmidet i vasatideus decorativa Konst, by Brynolf Hellner (Stockholm: Nordiska Museet, 1948).

Making of Tools, The, Alexander G. Weygers (New York: Van Nostrand Rheinhold Company, 1973).

Mechanick Exercises, Joseph Moxon (London: Printed for *Dan. Midwinter* and *Tho. Leigh,* at the *Rose and Crown* in St. Paul's Church-yard, 1703). (Reprint: New York, Praeger Publishers, 1970.)

Modern Blacksmith, The, Alexander G. Weygers (New York: Van Nostrand Rheinhold Company, 1974).

Modern Blacksmithing, J. G. Holmstrom (Chicago: Fred J. Drake and Co., 1904).

Plain and Ornamental Forging, Ernest Schwarzkopf (New York: John Wiley & Sons, 1916; London: Chapman & Hall, 1930).

Spon's Mechanics Own Book (London: E & F. N. Spon, Ltd., 1904).

Steel Working and Tool Dressing, Warren S. Casterlin (New York: M. T. Richardson Co., 1919).

Successful Craftsman, The, Alex W. Bealer (New York: Barre Publishing Company, 1975).

Traditional Country Craftsmen, J. Geraint Jenkins (New York and Washington: Frederick A. Praeger, 1966).

Wrought Iron, James Aston and Edward B. Story (Pittsburgh, Pa.: A. M. Byers Co., 1959).

Wrought Iron Railings, Doors and Gates (London: Iliffe, 1966).

Wrought Iron Work (London: Rural Industries Bureau, 1961).

Wrought Iron, Fritz Kühn (New York: Architectural Book Publishing Company, 1969).

INDEX